Unusually Cruel

UNUSUALLY CRUEL

Prisons, Punishment, and the Real American Exceptionalism

—◆—

MARC MORJÉ HOWARD

OXFORD
UNIVERSITY PRESS

OXFORD
UNIVERSITY PRESS

Oxford University Press is a department of the University of Oxford. It furthers
the University's objective of excellence in research, scholarship, and education
by publishing worldwide. Oxford is a registered trade mark of Oxford University
Press in the UK and certain other countries.

Published in the United States of America by Oxford University Press
198 Madison Avenue, New York, NY 10016, United States of America.

CIP data is on file at the Library of Congress
ISBN 978-0-19-065934-9 (pbk)
ISBN 978-0-19-065933-2 (hbk)

For my friend and inspiration,
Marty Tankleff

Contents

List of Figures and Table

Figures

Table

Preface

LITTLE DID I KNOW at the time, but this book originated in the summer of 1985, when I was an adolescent sitting in a jail cell in London. On the last day of a week-long trip to England with my traveling soccer team from Long Island, our group of soon-to-be ninth-graders was let loose in the streets of London. For some reason, with all the logic and wisdom of our teenage brains, along with some mutual peer pressure to strengthen our backbones, a teammate and I sauntered into an HMV music store and decided to shoplift cassette tapes. It seemed particularly appropriate to swipe a copy of the Clash's *London Calling*, which I intended to give to my father as a birthday present. We got away with it, which was such a thrill that we wanted to do it again. So we went to another HMV and stuffed some more cassettes into the various pockets of our baggy painter's pants. This time we got caught.

We were interrogated for almost an hour by HMV security personnel, and it did not go well. When they found the tapes from the other HMV store in our backpacks, the lead interrogator referred to us as "bloody Americans who come over here to nick our things." He called the police, who came and took us away in a police van to the station, where they placed us in a holding cell for several hours.

The British police were by no means lenient, and they were neither impressed nor amused by our youthful adventurism. They filed an arrest report, explained that we now had a criminal record that would be expunged when we turned 17, and told us that we were banned from HMV stores (the time period of the ban was unclear—but I have never entered one since that day). Although at first they insisted that we could not be released until a responsible adult picked us up, they eventually relented when we explained that we had no phone number to call (this was long before cell phones), and that the only way to contact our coaches was to show up at the prearranged meeting point in downtown London later that afternoon. They drove us there, leading to a humiliating exit from the police vehicle in front of our bewildered teammates and furious coaches.

I have rarely shared this story about an embarrassing stage in my life, when this was just one of many stupid choices. Although I made a decisive change about a year later, I have often reflected back to a time when my life trajectory could have gone in a different direction. I've realized that I did not embody my foolish actions, and I was extremely fortunate that they did not come to define me. I got a "second chance," and I made the most of it.

Not everybody is so lucky—especially in the United States. Indeed, over the course of researching and writing this book, I've come to realize that countless Americans—and particularly those who don't receive the "benefit of the doubt" and "privilege" of being white—were not afforded viable second chances. Far too many have been condemned to a life defined by a criminal record that started with stupid acts of adolescence and peer pressure like my own. I know, of course, that my actions—primarily shoplifting and sometimes drinking hard liquor before school—may be considered relatively tame and innocuous compared to more serious criminal acts. But for many other kids, that first arrest and the subsequent "record" it creates is the beginning of the end.

The U.S. arrests, prosecutes, and locks up far more people—both juveniles and adults—than any democratic country in the world. This occurs despite evidence showing that a person's incarceration often leads to more—and bigger—criminality afterward, thus making society even less safe. Overall, as this book will show, when compared to the United Kingdom and to other democratic countries in the world, the U.S. is particularly harsh—or, in a slight twist on the words of the Eighth Amendment, "unusually cruel"—in terms of how severely it punishes crime and how ruthlessly and unforgivingly it treats those who are (or have been) incarcerated.

My journey from that London jail cell to this project was by no means straightforward or direct. On the contrary, after taking advantage of my post-London opportunity for a fresh start, and then devoting my time more constructively to both academic and athletic pursuits, I moved on through various stages of education and life—from high school to college to graduate school to becoming a political science professor to receiving tenure at Georgetown University. Along the way, I conducted research and wrote a book about civil society and democracy in post-communist Europe, and then another one about immigration and citizenship in the countries of the European Union, along with various academic articles dealing with democracy and authoritarianism. I became well established in my field, and the logical path would have been to continue working and publishing in my areas of strength.

But during a time that should have been characterized by personal and professional satisfaction, I became plagued by a nagging issue that gradually grew into what some called my "obsession." The starting point had occurred well over a decade earlier, on the first day of my senior year of high school, when a childhood friend and classmate, Marty Tankleff, was arrested for the murder of his parents. Despite the shocking accusations and headlines, the evidence suggested to me that Marty was likely innocent. Notwithstanding my naïve attempt to defend the presumption of innocence on the editorial page of our high school newspaper, *The Purple Parrot*, Marty stood little chance in the face of a corrupt homicide detective, overzealous prosecutors, and shameful coverage by the mainstream media. He was convicted and sentenced to 50 years to life, to be served in an upstate New York maximum-security prison.

Over the ensuing decade, although I occasionally mentioned to friends that I knew a convicted murderer whom I believed was innocent, I have to admit that the case—and Marty's plight—became more and more distant. Our paths had diverged at age 18, as Marty went to jail and I went to Yale. But we reconnected in 2004, and what started with occasional letters grew to become an extraordinary collaboration and friendship that reshaped my life. I began to visit Marty in prison regularly, conducted research for him, sent him documents and materials, met with his legal team and public supporters, published an op-ed on his case and plight in the *New York Times*, wrote an amicus brief on behalf of our high school classmates that became part of his final appeal, and promised him that I would never give up fighting for his freedom or helping him after he would attain it. And I flew back from Paris to be present when Marty was finally exonerated and released on December 27, 2007—after over 17 years of wrongful incarceration—and joyfully celebrated with him, his family, and the rest of his "team."

Although one might have thought such a "happy ending" would put to rest my obsession with criminal justice, Marty's experience was just the beginning for me. In fact, what originated as my individual quest to support justice for my friend transformed into a much broader goal and a much bigger challenge. Simply put, what happened to Marty opened my eyes to the major and fundamental problems with the American criminal justice system. My personal and intellectual trajectory went through three stages: (1) it started with my concern for Marty as an individual and my friend; (2) my interests then expanded to the larger issue of wrongful convictions, as I met numerous other "Marties" who had served countless years and decades before being exonerated—while also learning about hundreds of others, and understanding that there are likely tens of thousands more that we will never even hear about; (3) finally, my journey led me to realize that the problems with the American criminal justice system go far beyond the innocent people it has trapped and mistreated, and that at core it is astoundingly and unacceptably punitive, vindictive, and unforgiving, while also based on underlying racial discrimination. I didn't arrive at this conclusion overnight, as it was a long and difficult learning process that required me to question—and ultimately reject—the facile platitudes that American children learn about having a justice system that "guarantees and protects the rights of the innocent," is "the best in the world," and treats people in a way that is "colorblind."

While Marty was still incarcerated, and as the 18th of his 19 appeals was denied, my desire to correct the injustice of his situation—and perhaps to influence the plight of many others—led me to decide to enroll in law school. This was certainly considered an unusual step, given that the academic lifestyle of a tenured professor is often viewed as a life of leisure, and there is nothing leisurely about being a law student. But thanks to the inspiring courses by some of my teachers/colleagues at the Georgetown University Law Center— especially Stephen Bright, Rosa Brooks, Sharon Dolovich, Peter Edelman, Gregory Klass, John Mikhail, and Robin West—the seven semesters it took me to finish my J.D. went by surprisingly quickly. And I even took and passed the New York bar examination to officially mark the completion of my journey to becoming an attorney—albeit one who has not practiced law (yet?).

This book represents the next step in the development of my interest in and passion for criminal justice and prison reform. It brings together my background and training in the political science subfield of comparative politics with my study of prisons and punishment in the U.S. I came to this project over the course of my law studies, when I realized that even though there are numerous excellent works that focus on the problems of American criminal justice and prisons, very little of it is explicitly comparative. And my prior work has taught me that there is tremendous value to comparison—that one can better understand the features of a particular country by contrasting it to others that are different. I therefore wrote early drafts of several of the chapters in this book as seminar papers for my law classes.

The best research and writing are often combined with teaching, and indeed this project came together on both sides of the lectern. At Georgetown, where I have now taught six cohorts of my "Prisons and Punishment" class, I have been fortunate to have the opportunity to broaden my knowledge while also refining my ideas in the company of some of the brightest and most passionate students imaginable. For a long time, my experiences inside prisons had been restricted to visiting rooms, tours of several facilities provided by wardens and administrative staff, and a memorable three hours of playing tennis and interacting with the San Quentin "Inside Tennis Team" (which I wrote about for *Sports Illustrated*).[1] But starting in the Fall of 2014, my engagement has become much deeper, as I have had the opportunity to teach a weekly class to a dedicated group of students within the confines of the Jessup Correctional Institution, a maximum-security prison in Maryland. I have taught a version of my "Fascism and Extremist Movements" class (which the Jessup officials asked me to rename "World History"), a comparative criminal justice class, and several semesters of an ongoing "World Politics" colloquium, where I have brought in guest speakers who have lectured and led discussions on their topics of expertise, while always leaving the prison feeling amazed and inspired by the intellectual curiosity and engagement they encountered—and many have referred to it as "the best teaching experience I've ever had." In the Spring 2016 semester, I also taught an "inside-outside" class called "Prison Reform Project," which brought together 15 of my best Georgetown students with 16 of my top Jessup students, and they all worked side by side on informative and engaging multimedia criminal justice and prison reform proposals that were presented to several hundred people (including family members of the incarcerated students) at a very emotional public event at Georgetown.[2]

My students have been a tremendous source of inspiration to my research and life. The Georgetown students have given me hope that the next generation of leaders will have a radically different approach to the punishment of crime. The Jessup students have helped to convince me that formal education and intelligence are not necessarily correlated, while inspiring me to appreciate the human potential that lies within all people when they are given a genuine opportunity to perform and to shine. And the occasions when I was able to combine Georgetown and Jessup students together in the same classroom have without question provided the most extraordinary and gratifying teaching moments of my career.

This book would not have been possible without the help of many people. I am grateful to my agent Will Lippincott, who saw the value in this project, and to my editor David McBride and his outstanding colleagues at Oxford University Press, for supporting it and bringing it to fruition. Moreover, I was fortunate to receive excellent research assistance with different aspects of this project from Jeremy Dang, Christina Dibartolo, Jolene Hansell, Julia Kerbs, Thijs Kleinpaste, Jenna Lefler, Michael Malinics, Lisa Rudolph, and

Nicholas Zaremba. Thanks to support from a "book incubator" grant from Georgetown, I was able to host an event that provided me with extremely helpful feedback from Sharon Dolovich, Jennifer Hochschild, Mary Katzenstein, Marc Mauer, and Michael Tonry—all distinguished scholars and experts whose work has informed this project since its very inception. And by teaching a course at Jessup that was based on earlier versions of the chapters in this book, I was able to receive a different—but just as valuable— kind of "expert" feedback from a group of men who know American criminal justice and prisons from the "inside." Although it was bittersweet for many of them to learn about the more humane, forgiving, and supportive practices that exist in other countries, the insights of my Jessup students—including Eddie Adamson, Thomas Anderson, Kenneth Bond, Thomas Davis, Ronald Epps, Clifton Fitzgerald, Darren Glenn, James Gorham, Hakim Gurley-Bey, William Horton, Leslie Humphrey, Warren Hynson, William Johnson, Arlando Jones, Denatian Kent, Delonte Kingsberry, Donald Knight, Marcus Lilly, Lewis Lucas, Zakaria Oweiss, Robert Pittman, Avion Rose, Harlow Sails, Virian Simms, DeWalt Stewart, Marcus Tunstall, D'Quinta Uzzle, Derrick Webb, and Michael White—helped advance this project immensely. My friend Vincent Greco, who served time with these men inside and helped to create and run the education programs at Jessup, has been an invaluable source of insight in the several years since his release. And I am very grateful to Joshua Miller and the Prison Scholars Program for giving me the opportunity to teach—and learn—about prisons from within prisons.

I am also very appreciative of the understanding and encouragement I've received from many of my Georgetown colleagues, who for years put up with my endless rants about Marty's wrongful conviction, and who then withheld judgment (at least in my presence) when they learned that my indignation was leading me to go "back to school." My department chairs—George Shambaugh, Michael Bailey, and now Charles King—have provided unwavering personal and institutional support and flexibility as I followed my passion and this new path. Over 45 colleagues—most from Georgetown, but many from other institutions as well—have come to give inspirational guest lectures at Jessup for my "World Politics" speaker series. And by supporting my proposal to launch the Prisons and Justice Initiative in the Spring of 2016, President John D. DeGioia and his university administration have demonstrated their genuine commitment to the Jesuit educational pursuit of *cura personalis* (care of the whole person). This core Georgetown mission encourages students to make connections to the world outside the classroom, to embrace ethnic, cultural, and religious diversity, and to maintain a commitment to social action. In just a very short time, the Prisons and Justice Initiative has already generated a tremendous amount of attention to, and enthusiasm for, this bipartisan cause—on the Georgetown campus and beyond.

Other friends, near and far, have also contributed to what became much more than a "research project," as it turned into a "life project" that is really only just beginning. Many friends, too numerous to name individually—but they know who they are—have provided spurts of motivation and energy at times of self-doubt. Thank you all for encouraging, supporting, and pushing me to follow my passion, and to do what I feel is morally important and politically necessary.

Finally, I want to acknowledge the unwavering support of my family. My parents, Brigitte and Dick Howard, continue to provide me with intellectual nourishment and encouragement throughout my sometimes unpredictable twists and turns—even if they are not thrilled that I've chosen to recount my youthful indiscretions above. My wife, Lise Morjé Howard, not only tolerated but actually encouraged my "unusually cruel" plan of getting a J.D., and she has endured countless conversations about a topic that was far removed—though perhaps not as different as it might initially appear—from her own research and writing on civil wars, ethnic conflict, and peacekeeping. And our children, Zoe and Julien, know much more about prisons than just about any two teenagers could—and probably should. I've learned more from my conversations with them about this topic than they will ever realize.

I've chosen to dedicate this book to Martin Tankleff. Marty has been and continues to be an inspiration to me, as well as a close friend. His fortitude in the face of such extreme injustice and unusual cruelty, along with his boundless optimism and positive energy, have motivated my new calling and vocation. I can only hope that some of this passion will be felt by readers in the pages ahead.

I

Introduction

ALEXIS DE TOCQUEVILLE has been rightly considered one of the most astute and prescient analysts of American democracy and culture. Indeed, his many predictions included the distinctive and lasting strength of American civil society, the looming civil war over slavery, and the future conflict with Russia. Yet even he could not have predicted the dramatic turn that has occurred in the very realm—criminal justice and prisons—that initially brought him to the United States in the early 1830s. After observing prisons in several parts of the country, Tocqueville concluded, "In no country is criminal justice administered with more mildness than in the United States."[1] Yet today, over 180 years later, it would be utterly inconceivable to refer to the "unusual mildness" of American punishment. On the contrary, the American criminal justice and prison systems have become—borrowing from the language of the Eighth Amendment—"unusually cruel."

This assessment of contemporary American punitiveness is hardly original. In fact, in recent years, it has become commonplace for journalists, political commentators, and scholars to acknowledge that the American criminal justice system is among the most punitive in the world—and certainly the harshest among Western democracies. In order to provide empirical substantiation for this claim of "American exceptionalism," newspaper articles often mention that although the U.S. is home to only 5 percent of the world's population, it contains almost 25 percent of the world's prisoners.[2] In addition, many excellent works of scholarship have described, explained, and bemoaned the morass of criminal justice and prisons in America.[3] Most of them present data showing that the U.S. incarcerates about 700 people per 100,000 in the population, a rate that is 7–10 times higher than incarceration levels in Europe or Canada.[4]

The overall disparity in incarceration rates between the U.S. and other advanced democracies—as made clear by such basic statistics on incarceration levels—is so dramatic and clear that there seems to be little need to describe it more closely. As a result, while many scholars from disciplines as diverse as law, criminology, sociology, or political science have been examining and decrying various aspects of mass incarceration in the U.S., the discussion has largely eschewed broader comparative analysis. Although there are some important exceptions,[5] most scholars provide rudimentary statistics on cross-national per capita incarceration rates as prima facie evidence of the comparatively high level of American punitiveness, before focusing almost exclusively on the U.S. Some also mention that until the mid-1970s, the incarceration rates in the U.S. were quite similar to those of other industrialized democracies. Yet very few attempt to specify how, to what extent, and why criminal justice has become so much harsher in the U.S. than in other countries. Without such a comparative perspective, it is difficult to grasp just how much the U.S. has changed over the past several decades, and to realize how egregiously far the American criminal justice system lies outside the norm of established democracies. Moreover, the lack of cross-national comparisons prevents an important and constructive consideration of what models or options work elsewhere—and might potentially be available for adoption in the U.S. one day.

This book pushes much further in that comparative direction. It seeks to provide a careful and systematic analysis of the criminal justice and prison systems in the U.S. by placing them in direct comparison with a set of countries that are otherwise similar—whether in terms of democracy, economic well-being, cultural heritage, or strategic alliances. By crafting explicit comparisons to these other countries, we can better explore the distinctive features of American punitiveness. Such a comparative perspective provides a much more informed assessment of the American system than an analysis based solely on the U.S. or one that refers to an abstract and universal moral or normative standard. Furthermore, the discussion of alternative models and practices in other countries suggests possible solutions and reforms to the current situation, which so many scholars and commentators—from all political persuasions—have criticized.

The analysis and findings of this book provide a new perspective on American exceptionalism—a topic with a long and sometimes contradictory intellectual tradition.[6] The concept has been applied—for the most part very positively—with reference to many different American features, ranging from Tocqueville's characterization of American freedom and democracy,[7] to Werner Sombart's explanation for why there is no socialism in the U.S.,[8] to Louis Hartz's account of the American liberal consensus,[9] to Presidents Wilson, Roosevelt, Kennedy, Reagan, Clinton, and Bush's appeals for patriotism and sacrifice during wartime,[10] to the larger religiously-inspired historical mission to "promote liberty or liberal democracy in the world."[11] American public opinion seems to support this largely positive approach to American exceptionalism, as 80 percent of respondents to a Gallup survey agreed that "Because of the United States' history and its Constitution [. . .] the U.S. has a unique character that makes it the greatest country in the world."[12]

The subtitle of this book, however, refers to the "real" American exceptionalism because—as subsequent chapters will show—the criminal justice and prison systems in the U.S. lie so far outside the mainstream of other comparable countries that the size of the difference dwarfs most other respects in which the U.S. has been cast as being exceptional. And the negative interpretation of this American exceptionalism in the context of criminal justice and prisons should prompt some soul-searching about how this can fit within a wider American history and tradition that is supposed to be more enlightened and superior.

The rest of this introductory chapter synthesizes the field of comparative criminal law that focuses on American punishment in comparative perspective. I start by discussing the methodological challenges in developing a refined indicator of punitiveness across countries, which explains why most analysts apply the standard "incarceration rate" measure. I then apply this indicator to the U.S., showing both the tremendous increase in American imprisonment since the mid-1970s and the massive differences between the U.S. and other advanced democracies today. Next, I lay out the research design and justify the methodological approach I use in the book. After a brief discussion of cross-national variation in both crime rates and police practices, I introduce and justify my use of a qualitative, comparative perspective while addressing the key stages of the "life cycle" of criminal justice. Finally, I provide a roadmap of the chapters that follow, before reiterating the overarching purpose and contribution of the book.

Measuring Punitiveness

Most analysts of comparative punishment have—often reluctantly—applied a common indicator to distinguish between levels of punitiveness across countries. The measure, derived from national-level data provided by each country's national prison administration, captures the number of prisoners (including pretrial detainees and those serving short jail sentences) at a given point in time per 100,000 people of the national population. The Institute for Criminal Policy Research (ICPR) calculates and distributes its "World Prison Brief,"[13] showing the prison population total, the relevant date associated with the figures, the estimated national population, and the "prison population rate (per 100,000 of national population)," which is the measure that then gets widely used.

In an ideal statistical world, we would have much more precise cross-national data that would allow for a disaggregated picture of how countries compare on very specific criteria and indicators. Indeed, one might expect to find common quantitative measures of the average sentence length and time served for certain crimes, which would allow for a different perspective on cross-national punitiveness. But the field has not yet reached that point.[14]

One reason has to do with the multiplicity of laws, policies, and applications in a diverse federal country such as the U.S.[15] In fact, there are few solid measures of punitiveness across U.S. *states*, much less national-level indicators that can be applied across countries. Within prisons themselves, there is a lack of access to hard data, as prisons largely operate "behind closed doors," and they are not particularly forthcoming about what happens inside.[16]

On the international level, there are tremendous research obstacles to collecting good, comparable data. Aside from linguistic differences, there are also definitional problems in terms of how key crimes and concepts are incorporated into statistics. William Selke points out that "robbery is classified as a violent crime in some nations and as a property crime in others."[17] The same goes for numerous other crimes. This type of problem plagues all aspects of crime statistics, from tabulating arrests to establishing conviction rates. Moreover, each national (much less subnational—which complicates things further) distinction is one element of a larger criminal justice system, and it can be methodologically dangerous to "cherry-pick" certain figures separate from their broader context. For example, high conviction rates may be a result of ruthless prosecutors, but perhaps they are actually caused by a police system that is very careful about determining which cases to pursue.[18] To compare conviction rates blindly would thus be foolhardy.

Over the past few decades there have been several attempts to create more unified data collection on criminal justice issues. Two of the most prominent have been INTERPOL (created by the International Criminal Police Organization) and the United Nations surveys on "World Crime."[19] These

and other studies have attempted to come up with standardized categories that can accommodate countries that have different legal definitions of
crimes. The problem, according to Michael Tonry and David Farrington, is
that the reports consist of "undigested police data," which are "subject to all
the standard noncomparability problems and the additional ones that no one
knows how accurate and complete the national reports are, or how consistently the data are reported and recorded over time."[20] A related problem is
the underreporting of crimes, which can occur for many reasons and may vary
significantly across countries, thus undermining the comparability of national
statistics.[21]

In other words, as Michael Cavadino and James Dignan argue, "Alternative
measures—such as numbers in prison as a proportion of crimes officially
recorded, or prison population per number of criminal convictions—might
in theory seem preferable, but suffer from their own drawbacks."[22] This type
of data has questionable reliability—both in terms of the different ways in
which convictions are reached across jurisdictions and the reporting of crimes
to the police. As a result, "It becomes difficult to generate even a very basic
data set that is comparable from country to country."[23]

In short, we are still a long way off from having excellent cross-national
quantitative measures of punitiveness. As Tonry and Farrington put it, "The
best way [. . .] would be to conduct a longitudinal study that tracked offenders through the criminal justice system, using a unique identification number
for each offender at each stage."[24] But this is not in the realm of the possible—
especially not cross-nationally. Cavadino and Dignan add that "Other, better, measures might include the probability of imprisonment and average
days of imprisonment served, in the aggregate or disaggregated by types of
offense, relative to victimization, recorded crimes, arrests, prosecution, convictions, or (for sentence length) prison sentences."[25] Again, this is simply not
feasible. In the end, for better or worse, the numerous methodological problems with cross-national data usually leave us with the standard measure of
incarceration rates.

Incarceration Rates in the U.S. and the World: The Empirical Results

There are several ways to analyze American incarceration rates in comparative perspective. Although this book focuses on the cross-national dimension,
one can also fruitfully consider the number of prisoners over time, as well as
explore the differences across gender and racial groups.

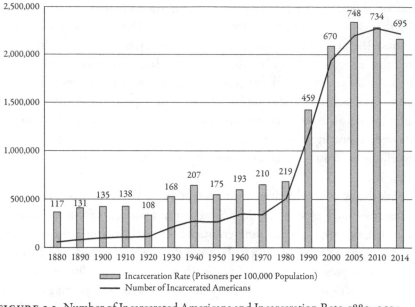

FIGURE 1.1 Number of Incarcerated Americans and Incarceration Rate, 1880–2014
Sources: Bureau of Justice Statistics (BJS); U.S. Census Bureau
Note: 1900 BJS data not available (scores are the average of 1890 and 1910)

Figure 1.1 presents the changes in levels of American incarceration in two ways: the line shows the raw number of prisoners from 1880 to 2014, whereas the bars adjust for population size by indicating the number of people incarcerated per 100,000 in the population (which is the standard measure for "incarceration rates"). While the early years indicate only modest prison growth rates, the figure shows that the numbers and rates spiked up starting in the mid-1970s, exploding from about 503,000 in 1980 to over 2.2 million by 2014 (and actually surpassing 2.3 million in 2008), a roughly 500 percent increase in just three decades.

In addition to the 2.2 million incarcerated, numerous other Americans who are not currently in prison are still under some type of correctional supervision, namely probation (i.e., as sentenced by a judge, usually instead of jail time) or parole (i.e., the conditional release of a prisoner who has served part or all of his or her sentence). Figure 1.2 shows the evolution of those numbers from 1980 to 2014. The increase has been steep in each category, as the number of people on probation has increased from about 1.12 million to 3.86 million, and those on parole from approximately 220,000 to almost 860,000.[26] By 2014, the grand total of people in the U.S. who are under one of

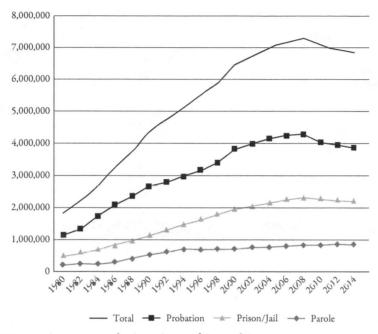

FIGURE 1.2 Americans under Some Form of Carceral Supervision, 1980–2014
Source: Bureau of Justice Statistics (BJS)

these forms of supervision is now just under 7 million (up from about 1.8 million in 1980, and having reached a high of 7.3 million in 2008), corresponding to well over 3 percent of the adult population. Moreover, in many states, *former* convicted felons—even those who may have accepted a plea bargain and served little or no jail time, as well as those who are out on parole or have completed their "debt to society"—are prohibited from voting for many years or even in some cases the rest of their lives, in addition to facing other long-term economic and social consequences and stigmas.[27] In other words, the effect of incarceration often lives well beyond a given person's continuing correctional supervision.

Figure 1.3 presents the American prison population rate, based on 2014 data, showing the gender and racial/ethnic disparities of imprisonment. When adjusted for each group's respective 100,000 population, it shows a tremendous gender gap between men and women in all three of the measured racial/ethnic groups—a finding that is not surprising given that men commit crimes at much higher rates than women in all societies. What is particularly striking is the overwhelming racial and ethnic disparity, with over 2,700 black men per 100,000 locked up in 2014, well over double the proportional

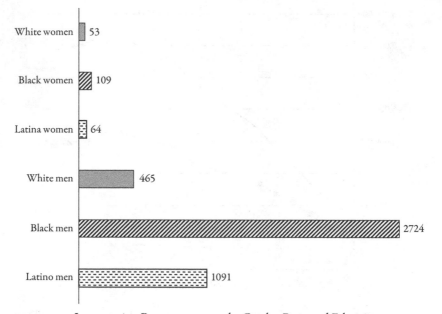

FIGURE 1.3 Incarceration Rate per 100,000, by Gender, Race, and Ethnicity, 2014
Source: Sentencing Project 2015a

amount of Latino men, which is itself more than twice the level of white men. The proportion of incarcerated black men is almost six times higher than that of white men. Although a sustained discussion of gender and race in American criminal punishment goes beyond the bounds of this chapter, it is worth stressing the staggering differences shown in this figure.

If we look at these data somewhat differently, Figure 1.4 shows the likelihood of a person within each respective gender and racial/ethnic group of being imprisoned at some point in his or her life. Again, the gender disparities are obvious—though it should be mentioned that women represent the fastest-growing population in American jails and prisons[28]—and the distinctions across racial/ethnic groups (within both genders) are tremendous. Most strikingly, the figure shows that one in three African American men will spend some time in prison in his lifetime.

The next set of figures turn to the cross-national perspective, which is the central focus of this book. Figure 1.5 presents the prison population rates per 100,000 people in 2015 for 21 selected countries, all of which are advanced industrialized societies, liberal democracies, and Organisation for Economic Co-operation and Development (OECD) members. The figure speaks for itself, showing that most of the countries have rates below 100 (i.e., under 0.1 percent of the population is in prison), whereas several are above 100, with

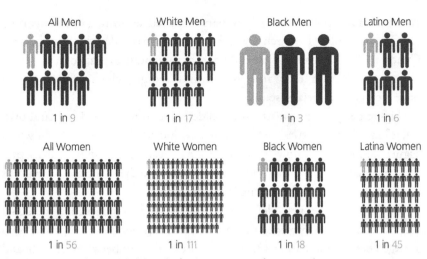

| All Men | White Men | Black Men | Latino Men |
| 1 in 9 | 1 in 17 | 1 in 3 | 1 in 6 |

| All Women | White Women | Black Women | Latina Women |
| 1 in 56 | 1 in 111 | 1 in 18 | 1 in 45 |

FIGURE 1.4 Lifetime Likelihood of Imprisonment of U.S. Residents Born in 2001
Note: Figure reproduced from Sentencing Project 2015a (based on BJS data from 2001)

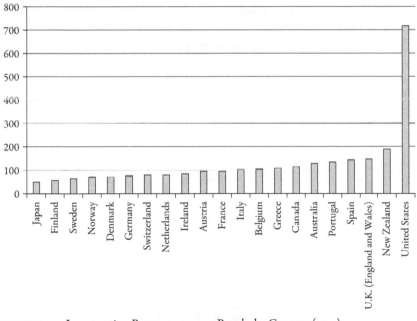

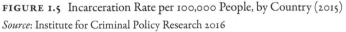

FIGURE 1.5 Incarceration Rate per 100,000 People, by Country (2015)
Source: Institute for Criminal Policy Research 2016

New Zealand at 194. But the U.S. is clearly on a different level altogether, with a rate of nearly 700. At the high-water mark of 2008, its incarceration rate had reached 756, corresponding to roughly 0.75 percent of the total population—including women, children, and the elderly—with more than 1 percent of the

American adult population behind bars.[29] Indeed, according to the Institute for Criminal Policy Research—which until 2014 was called the International Centre for Prison Studies—the only significant countries that come remotely close to the U.S. rate are Rwanda, Russia, and Georgia, which certainly do not have exemplary judicial systems.

Figure 1.6 separates out the pretrial detainees (often called "remand prisoners" in other countries), which were also included in the totals shown in Figure 1.5. Figure 1.6 shows that the U.S. has nearly four times as many pretrial detainees as the next closest country, and more than six times as many as the average across all other countries.

Figure 1.7 isolates juvenile prisoners for selected countries for which data are available, and it provides the rate of prisoners per 100,000 people who are aged between 10 and 17. Once again, the difference between the U.S. and the other countries is overwhelming, with 336 juvenile prisoners per 100,000 juveniles in the population, which is almost five times higher than the next closest country, and over 14 times higher than France or Germany.

Finally, if we turn to gender, Figure 1.8 shows that the U.S. incarcerates nearly 65 women per 100,000, corresponding to a rate over 5 times greater than the next-highest country (New Zealand), and more than 10 times the

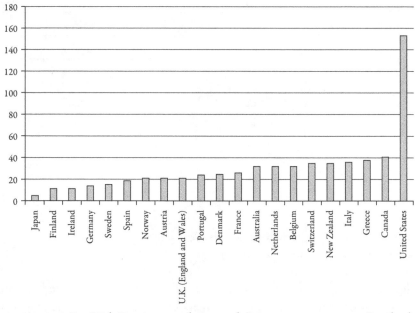

FIGURE 1.6 Pre-Trial Detainees and Remand Prisoners per 100,000 People, by Country (2014)

Source: International Centre for Prison Studies 2014

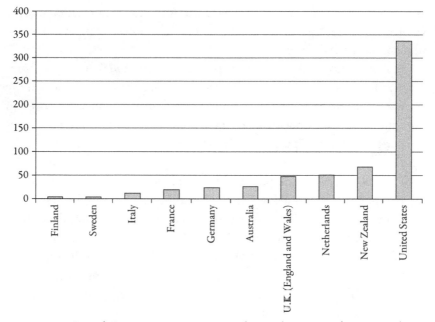

FIGURE 1.7 Juvenile Prisoners per 100,000 Aged 10–17, by Country (2003–2004)

Source: Cavadino and Dignan 2006, p. 301

Note: Figures based on the authors' estimates from national statistics obtained around 2003–2004

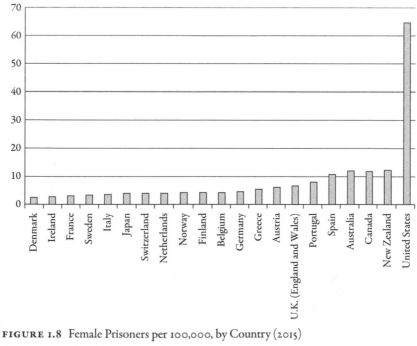

FIGURE 1.8 Female Prisoners per 100,000, by Country (2015)

Source: Institute for Criminal Policy Research 2015

average of the other 20 countries. In fact, the American incarceration rate for women is actually higher than the *overall* incarceration rates in several otherwise comparable countries.

As illuminating as these recent snapshots are, a *dynamic* approach to comparative incarceration rates over time best captures the extent to which the current American exceptionalism represents a dramatic change compared to just four decades ago. Indeed, looking at the changes over time provides a crucial perspective that helps to highlight both the level and timing of American punitiveness.

The most revealing and powerful figure of all is Figure 1.9, which shows the prison population rates at 5 different points in time—1971, 1985, 1995, 2005, and 2015—in the 10 countries for which there are available data, along with the European average. The 1971 starting point represents the earliest date for which there are comparable European data. The results show that the U.S. was actually quite similar to the nine European countries in the early 1970s, with incarceration rates that were slightly higher, yet not far outside of the range of other European countries. But the gap increased substantially

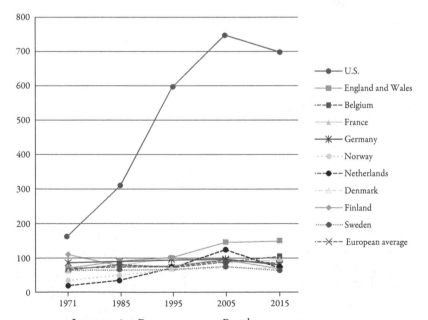

FIGURE 1.9 Incarceration Rate per 100,000 People, 1971–2015

Sources: All U.S. figures from Bureau of Justice Statistics (BJS) and U.S. Census Bureau; 1971 European figures from Lappi-Seppälä 2001, p. 106; 1985 and 1995 European figures from Tak 2001, p. 152; 2005 and 2015 figures from International Centre for Prison Studies 2005 and Institute for Criminal Policy Research 2016

from 1971 to 1985, when the U.S. rates rose to become over three times higher than any other European country. And that high rate of increase continued over the ensuing decades. Looking at the nine European countries collectively, we find that the average European imprisonment rates increased from 63.2 in 1971 to 66.1 in 1985 to 73.9 in 1995 to 91.2 in 2005—thus representing a 44 percent increase over a 34-year period—and then dropped slightly to 82.1 in 2015. In contrast, the American rates increased by 468 percent over that same time period (1971–2005), before dropping slightly over the subsequent decade.[30] Even after the latest drop, the 2015 figures show that U.S. rates are still over 8.5 times higher than the European average.

In short, although the basic "incarceration rate" measure is a rather blunt instrument that leaves out nuance and detail, it produces a clear and striking finding of American punitiveness that is beyond question or dispute. [31] Moreover, the comparative empirical evidence yields three important conclusions: first, if we look back historically, the levels of imprisonment and correctional supervision in the U.S. used to be roughly comparable to those in European countries; second, the differences today between the U.S. and other liberal democracies are massive and unprecedented; and third, putting the first two together, the contemporary gap is a relatively recent phenomenon. In other words, the United States was not always exceptional in terms of prisons and punishment, but over the past four decades it has become unusually cruel.

Research Design

Fortunately, the limitations on quantitative cross-national data identified above do not preclude rigorous examination of the U.S. in comparative perspective. This book therefore employs a qualitative, case-based analysis to explore exactly how and why the U.S. is more punitive than other comparable democracies. The research design of the book brings together two overlapping dimensions: the first explores what I call the "life cycle" of criminal justice, with chapters covering the topics of plea bargaining, sentencing, prison conditions, rehabilitation, parole, and societal reentry; the second dimension carries out sustained comparisons to three countries—France, Germany, and the United Kingdom. Within each chapter that addresses a different step in the criminal justice life cycle, I lay out the history, law, policies, and practices in the U.S. and in the three comparison cases. The result is a sustained comparative analysis of American punitiveness that covers the key stages of criminal justice.

The Very First Steps in the Life Cycle of Criminal Justice:
Crime and Policing

Although the next chapter begins the life cycle with the plea bargaining process, two prior steps deserve mention here. The first is the initial starting point of crime itself, which of course varies across both time and space. The second is the official state reaction to crime, namely policing.

Crime

The logical, even instinctual, response to the question about what explains variation in criminal punishment is that it is a direct reaction to crime itself. In other words, according to this view, state punitiveness is simply a function of the level of crime in a given community or society. And if American incarceration rates are higher than those in other countries, it must be because Americans commit more crimes. Although this argument is intuitive and tempting, the reality is more complex and multifaceted.[32] On the one hand, it is undeniable that a genuine rise in crime in the 1960s, 1970s, and 1980s did contribute to the "punitive turn" in the U.S., but on the other hand, the punitiveness continued to increase over the course of the subsequent and sustained *decline* in crime that has occurred since the early 1990s. And in comparative perspective, studies of crime and incarceration point to a disconnect between these two phenomena, thus putting into question the direct relationship that so many people assume is naturally the case.

For the first half of the twentieth century, American crime rates were not particularly unusual or frightening. Yet, as Henry Ruth and Kevin Reitz write, "With alarming suddenness in the 1950s and 1960s, U.S. crime rates, especially those for serious violent offenses, broke from their long-established slide as if they had acquired a perverse will of their own."[33] By the early 1990s, "By all measures, the United States was the most dangerous of first-world countries." This outlier status applied especially to homicides, but also to "other categories of grave violence, such as armed robbery, rape, and assaults with life-threatening injuries"—but not to "less serious offenses [. . .], such as property crimes, or violent crimes without serious injury."[34]

Both the actual spike in violent crime and the fear it engendered were real and politically influential. They also took place within a climate of economic crisis and societal angst that led to what David Garland calls a new "culture of control," which emphasized a host of new punitive measures, including mass incarceration, private policing, surveillance measures, and gated communities.[35] The "competition" that emerged between candidates and parties to propose and support ever-tougher crime control policies led to what Jonathan Simon terms a "culture of fear," whereby crime—and especially media-driven fear of crime—became an American obsession that distorted and threatened the very fabric of American freedom and democracy.[36] And this fear led to what Peter Enns has shown to be a well-articulated public opinion pressure for politicians to propose and pursue increasingly punitive measures.[37] Moreover, as Michael Javen Fortner has argued, these fears were not only within white society, but the push for punitive reforms in response to high crime rates also came from many black political leaders, as well as the "black silent majority."[38]

Although one should not overlook or downplay the importance of the rise in crime—both real and perceived—for sparking the punitive response in the U.S., crime rates cannot explain the persistence and even further expansion of punitive policies, as those rates have declined precipitously and continuously since the early 1990s, while incarceration rates continued to soar. As Ruth and Weitz explain, "In every year after 1993, homicide rates dropped until, at the turn of the new century, they had fallen back to the death tolls of the mid-1960s. Other categories of grave violent offenses declined in the same time period, and the United States enjoyed drop-offs even among many less serious offenses."[39] More recently, Inimai Chettiar added that "Crime is about half of what it was at its peak in 1991. Violent crime plummeted 51 percent. Property crime fell 43 percent. Homicides are down 54 percent."[40]

Could the rising incarceration rates *explain* the declining crime rates? In other words, could the fact that more criminals are locked up—incapacitated, in the language of conservative criminologists following the tradition of James Q. Wilson[41]—be the reason why fewer crimes are being committed? At first glance this seems plausible and perhaps even logical. Yet on closer examination, numerous scholars have found that incapacitation can only account for a small fraction of the crime decline.[42] Chettiar's analysis shows that "Increased incarceration accounted for about 6 percent of the property crime decline in the 1990s, and 1 percent of that drop in the 2000s. The growth of incarceration had no observable effect on violent crime in the 1990s or 2000s." She adds that "This last finding may initially seem surprising. But given that we are sending more and more low-level and non-violent offenders to prison (who may never have been prone to violent crime), the finding makes sense. Sending a non-violent offender to prison will not necessarily have an effect on violent crime."[43] In short, even if there is an initial—albeit still small—effect of incapacitation on crime rates, the massive expansion of incarceration clearly reached "diminishing returns" on crime reduction.

A more detailed analysis of the connection between crime and incarceration rates—from several different comparative perspectives, both domestic and international—is especially instructive. Within the U.S., a cross-state analysis of crime and incarceration rates in the 50 U.S. states shows that there is little systematic relationship between the two factors.[44] States with higher crime rates do not necessarily have higher incarceration rates. Moreover, states that have recently cut their incarceration rates (primarily New York, New Jersey, and California) have not seen a subsequent rise in crime rates.[45] In other words, variation in crime levels has little to no connection to variation in incarceration rates across the American states.

If we look at the relationship over time, Figure 1.10 provides a revealing picture of the dissociation between crime and incarceration rates. Whereas from 1960 to 1980 the levels of both property crime and violent crime fluctuated somewhat in line with both incarceration rates and the total population in the U.S., a stark divergence began in 1980. From that point onward, even though the crime rates remained close to level—albeit with some occasional spikes and dips, most notably in the late 1980s and early 1990s, when violent

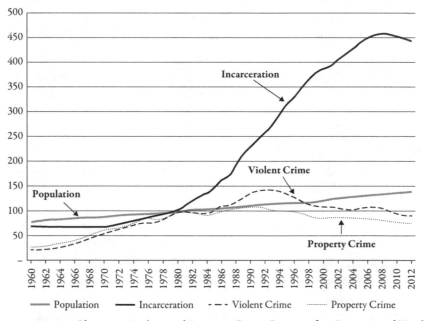

FIGURE 1.10 Change in Violent and Property Crime Compared to Prisoner and Total Population, 1960–2012

Source: Bureau of Justice Statistics (BJS) and Federal Bureau of Investigation (FBI)

Note: Figure adapted from Schmitt, Warner, and Gupta 2010, p. 8 (with updated data)

crime rose, before dropping consistently ever since—incarceration rates shot upward. The disparity shows clearly that the rise in incarceration cannot be explained by a rise in crime.

When we turn to a comparative perspective on crime, even though levels of violent crime—particularly murder, given the prevalence of guns—are indeed higher in the U.S. than in comparable countries,[46] victimization studies show that the risk of being a victim of crime is *not* considerably higher in the U.S.[47] And other measures show that throughout the Western world, after long-standing historical declines in crime rates over centuries, levels increased somewhat from the 1960s to the 1990s, before once again continuing to decline since then—leading Michael Tonry to conclude, "There is only one story: crime rates are falling throughout the developed Western world."[48] This perspective alone is an important contribution to a debate that often focuses on the U.S. in complete isolation from other countries, not taking into account that crime trends in the U.S. are not in fact uniquely American.

Moreover, in terms of the supposed crime-prison nexus, Tonry and many other scholars have demonstrated that although crime rates in the U.S. have fluctuated according to the same general pattern as other Western countries, only American imprisonment rates have soared. In a 2005 article, Tonry and Farrington show that even though the crime rates in the U.S. and Canada have remained parallel for decades, there is "no resemblance between American and Canadian imprisonment trends."[49] And in his 2014 contribution, Tonry shows that North American homicide rates "moved almost in lockstep" and robberies "were also closely similar," whereas incarceration rates in Canada remained essentially flat over the entire period of American mass incarceration.[50]

In short, putting these three comparative perspectives—cross-state, cross-time, and cross-national—together, there is little evidence to support the otherwise enticing argument that American crime rates explain American levels of incarceration. Although certainly the initial spike in crime had a strong effect on crime control policies and the general culture of hysteria about crime and a desire for harsh punishment, crime and incarceration rates have not moved together. Subsequent chapters will demonstrate that it was specific policy changes that directly led to today's mass incarceration reality.

Policing

Another prior step to the criminal justice life cycle involves the role of policing. Here there are not only very few comparative analyses available, but even within the U.S. recent events have shed light on the problem of inconsistent or nonexistent data on a crucial and explosive issue.[51] It is difficult to generalize based on unsystematic information, but a cursory comparison indicates that American police tend to be more aggressive, violent, and militarized than their European counterparts.[52] Moreover, Jacqueline Ross's research on undercover policing and covert operations shows a much greater official tolerance and support for deceptive tactics in the U.S., whereas her three comparative cases of France, Italy, and Germany maintain significant legal and practical protections for targets of police investigations.[53] Within the ordinary context of a criminal investigation, this means quite simply that American police can (and routinely do) lie to suspects in an attempt to trick them, whereas this practice is not allowed in European countries.

One of the main roles of the police in investigating crime involves stopping potential suspects. Although comparable statistics on "stop and frisk" practices do not exist, studies show that minorities are also distinctly targeted for such searches in European countries, just as in the U.S.[54] The European studies are based on percentages—derived from surveys or samples of specific observations of police practices at certain locations—because the police do not tabulate the number of interventions or the race of the people being stopped or frisked. For example, one 2008 survey found that in France, 42 percent of North Africans and 38 percent of Sub-Saharan Africans had been stopped by the police in the previous 12 months, compared to 22 percent of whites.[55] Other European countries had slightly lower totals, but all had clear differences between minority and majority populations. That said, despite the racial imbalance, it is unlikely that the European cases reach the same quantity of police stops as in many American cities—and probably not the same level of racial targeting. For example, in New York City, the police made a total of 3,919,977 stops between the years 2006 and 2012—averaging over 500,000 stops per year. Of that total, 54 percent of the people stopped were black, 32 percent Latino, and only 11 percent white—and, incidentally, roughly 88 percent of the total were actually innocent.[56] Although direct cross-national comparisons are unfortunately not possible, existing research shows that in both the U.S. and Europe, "stop and frisk" practices decrease police legitimacy and increase hostility toward police on the part of the minority groups that are being targeted.[57]

In terms of violence committed by the police, it would be inaccurate to suggest that police in European countries are docile and unbiased. On the contrary, Cathy Schneider's comparative work on race riots in New York in the 1960s and Paris in 2005 highlights the similarities between the racialized police responses.[58] Yet there is one major and overwhelming difference: the extent of deaths at the hands—or, rather, guns—of the police.

Little public attention was placed on this issue until 2014, when a series of shooting deaths of unarmed black men began to receive broader coverage in the media—especially social media—largely thanks to video recordings showing (parts of) these incidents and the public attention given to Black Lives Matter and other organizations. The killings of Michael Brown (Ferguson, MO), Eric Garner (Staten Island, NY), Tamir Rice (Cleveland, OH), Akai Gurley (Brooklyn, NY), Walter Scott (Charleston, SC), Freddie Gray (Baltimore, MD), Samuel Dubose (Cincinnati, OH), Laquan McDonald (Chicago, IL), Alton Sterling (Baton Rouge, LA), Philando Castile (Falcon Heights, MN), Terrence Crutcher (Tulsa, OK), and others have launched a broader debate about police violence that shows no sign of going away or being resolved. Aggregate statistics of policing killings in the U.S. are either imprecise or absent until 2015, when careful tracking began. According to data from the *Washington Post*, the number of fatal shootings by police reached 991 in 2015, before dropping slightly to 963 in 2016.[59] This recent perspective on police violence echoes earlier analyses of American police forces, showing that over the past several decades they have become increasingly aggressive, invasive, and militarized.[60]

In comparative terms, it is striking to note that in England and Wales, police have only fired their weapons an average of five times per year—*in total*, meaning for the entire police force—over the past decade, and there have been only two people killed at the hands of British police officers in the past three years.[61] The 55 people killed by the police in the U.K. over the past 24 years was already surpassed by the 59 Americans killed in that manner in just the first 24 days of 2015 (and there were 60 more killed in the first 24 days of 2016).[62] In Germany, the police killed seven people in 2014, with similar numbers for other recent years.[63] In Iceland, a small country with a population comparable to Stockton, California, only one person has been killed by the police in the country's 71 years of existence—whereas Stockton had three fatal police shootings within the first five months of 2015.[64] Even in neighboring Canada, there are only an average of 25 deaths from police shootings per year.[65] These massive disparities result from a vastly different tradition of gun control in Europe (and Canada), extensive police training in defusing conflict, and the European Convention on Human Rights' "absolute necessity" standard for the use of deadly force (which is much stricter than the American standard, which requires only that police officers "reasonably perceive imminent and grave harm").[66] In short, despite the absence of pre-2015 statistics in the U.S., the difference in levels of deadly police violence is clear and striking.

As the chapter has now addressed the two "prior" steps to the stages of the criminal justice life cycle that will be explored in depth in the ensuing chapters, the next subsection provides an overview of the book's incorporation of other countries in order to highlight the extent to which the United States is, indeed, unusually cruel.

Case Selection

The second dimension of this book's research design involves the comparative reference to the cases of France, Germany, and the United Kingdom. I selected these three particular cases for deliberate methodological reasons. In addition to being fellow members of the larger "family" of advanced industrialized democracies, they display considerable variation within that group of countries. They vary not only in terms of their criminal justice and prison systems but also according to other features of their society and political economy. France is often treated as having an antiquated and decrepit prison system, postwar Germany's criminal justice system has typically been viewed as relatively lenient or humane (although perhaps not quite as much so as the Scandinavian countries), and the U.K. is the country whose legal system most closely matches the U.S., and which has supposedly been moving in a harsher "Anglo-American" direction in recent times.[67] In terms of their societies, Germany has a traditionally homogenous society that has faced recent challenges with immigration; France and the U.K. have long histories of immigration and diversity, resulting from their earlier periods as colonial powers along with early democratization.[68] France is a traditionally Catholic country, the U.K. is historically Protestant, and Germany is mixed. And Germany has a corporatist political economy model, whereas France is more state interventionist, and the U.K. economically liberal. Overall, these three distinct cases provide a great deal of variation that helps to analyze the U.S. in comparative perspective.

The next six chapters attempt to place the U.S. in this broader comparative perspective. Perfectly balanced comparisons are not always possible, however, due to limitations in data and information on certain issues. All of the chapters focus on the U.S., and most of them include mini-case studies of France, Germany, and the U.K. as reference points. The chapter on sentencing policy—the one issue for which other sources have actually provided broader cross-national data—also explores numerous additional countries beyond these three. It is important to stress that the purpose of the comparative cases is not to provide a comprehensive picture or account of each issue in France, Germany, or the U.K. Rather, the objective is for these brief comparative analyses to form enough of a baseline to allow for a meaningful and informative assessment of the extent of American exceptionalism—much more so than would be possible by looking at the U.S. in isolation. In other words, although the comparative perspective is crucial to this book, the core of the analysis—and any potential recommendations for reform that could derive from it—remains focused on the U.S.

Roadmap

The book serves two main purposes: Chapters 2–7 *evaluate* American punitiveness, looking at six different issues connected to the criminal justice and prison systems, whereas Chapter 8 attempts to *explain* the overall pattern that clearly emerges. In other words, the next six chapters chart the ways in which the U.S. compares to other similar countries—primarily France, Germany, and the U.K.—and they highlight the political forces behind these quite different national trajectories. The sequence of six chapters brings the reader through the life cycle of the punishment of crime. Each chapter explores a different stage, including plea bargaining (Chapter 2), sentencing (Chapter 3), prison conditions (Chapter 4), rehabilitation (Chapter 5), parole (Chapter 6), and societal reentry (Chapter 7). All of the chapters show the distinctively high levels of punitiveness in the U.S.—not just on balance, but on *each and every individual indicator*. The advantage of this step-by-step approach—especially when viewed in this comparative perspective—is that it allows for analysis of the distinctive features of American policies and practices in each of these important domains. Moreover, by putting them all together we can see an overwhelmingly clear picture of the tremendous American exceptionalism in punitiveness.

The comparative findings show that the disparities between the U.S. and the set of advanced democracies are even greater than the incarceration rates would suggest. Indeed, the cumulative body of evidence from Chapters 2–7 shows just how far the U.S. stands apart from other Western democracies, based on its extraordinarily and consistently harsh treatment of criminals and prisoners—whether before, during, or after their incarceration. At every level of the criminal justice system, people are treated more cruelly—despite the Eighth Amendment's supposed prohibition of "cruel and unusual punishment"—in the U.S. than elsewhere.

What can explain this harsh reality of American punitiveness? Chapter 8 develops an argument based on four main factors—each of which receives its own section—that are both distinctively American and that have changed in important ways since the 1970s: race, religion, politics, and business. First, it is impossible to deny or understate the importance of race in the context of criminal justice and prisons throughout American history, from slavery to convict leasing to Jim Crow laws to contemporary mass incarceration. Second, the recently-politicized Christian fundamentalist fervor of many Americans (among both ordinary citizens and politicians) has emphasized a retributive interpretation of religion—rather than one favoring forgiveness, rehabilitation, and redemption—to justify severe punishment. Third, the particularly American version of democratic judicial politics—whereby most politicians, prosecutors, and even judges raise funds and campaign for office—has further exacerbated the "tough on crime" climate. Fourth, the prison industry has created tremendous economic interests and revenue to actors who have treated prisons as opportunities for business and profiteering, thus further entrenching the massive carceral state in the U.S. Combined, the four factors of race, religion, politics, and business—each of which has undergone significant changes since the 1970s, at the same time as the explosion of mass incarceration—help to explain why American criminal justice and prisons are unusually cruel.

Finally, the Conclusion evaluates the extent to which a new "window" has opened—or at least was temporarily ajar before perhaps being shut again by the 2016 election of President Donald Trump—raising the possibility of genuine reform to the criminal justice and prison systems. Drawing on the comparative perspective and lessons learned from the European cases, it suggests potential avenues for reducing and improving the American mass incarceration crisis.

On the one hand, the findings presented in this book provide a clear picture of the indisputable reality of American punitiveness, along with compelling arguments for the factors that may explain it. On the other hand, however, the field of comparative criminal law is still in its relative infancy. As James Whitman, one of the leading scholars in this area, writes, "The study of comparative criminology remains too isolated from the study of comparative criminal law. There is plenty of work to do."[69]

This book attempts to carry out some of that work. It shows just how punitive the American system of criminal punishment has become, by putting it into a broader comparative perspective. While numerous scholars have addressed and criticized American punitiveness, these analyses usually focus on the U.S. in isolation. Although many do start with the comparative figures on imprisonment rates, they move quickly to a domestic analysis of the American situation, without much sustained comparison to other liberal democracies. Yet, as this book demonstrates, it is precisely through this comparative lens that American punitiveness becomes striking and shocking. Moreover, by contrasting the American approach to crime and punishment with those of comparable countries, analysts may perhaps be able to identify solutions that are less harsh and more productive—which could eventually be considered for implementation in the U.S.

Overall, this book seeks to update Tocqueville by understanding, evaluating, and explaining the relatively recent punitive turn in American criminal justice within a broader comparative context. For even if his assessment of the "mildness" of American criminal justice has not held up as well as his evaluation of American democracy and civil society, Tocqueville clearly recognized that the way in which a country treats its criminals is an indicator of its "civility." The overarching goal of the book is therefore to show how, when, and why the U.S. has lost its way. And its comparative perspective will suggest a path for restoring American civility to the lofty heights once attributed to it by Tocqueville.

2

Plea Bargaining

PEOPLE WHOSE ONLY exposure to the American criminal justice system is through the courtroom drama portrayed in movies and television shows might assume that trials are the standard mechanism for evaluating the guilt and punishment of criminal defendants. This certainly makes sense, given that defendants do have an explicit constitutional right to a trial by jury. Yet in reality, trials have become relatively rare occurrences. Approximately 95 percent of criminal cases in the United States are settled through the process of plea bargaining, and this percentage has been rising over the past several decades, as the increasingly overburdened courts have welcomed solutions that spare them much-needed time and resources, while still leading to convictions and (at least the perception of) "justice."[1] It is no exaggeration to say that plea bargaining is the overwhelming norm in American criminal justice, and trials—even if much-heralded in American popular culture—are the exception.

Given that plea bargaining has become "business as usual" in the U.S., some might assume that this is the case internationally as well. In fact, an expert who only focuses on the U.S. might think plea bargaining is simply the "natural" or ubiquitous state of affairs, even in other national systems. Yet a closer look at the practices of other countries points to an American exceptionalism—even if, at first glance, it would appear to be an Anglo-American distinctiveness—both in terms of the prevalence of plea bargaining and the extensive power granted to prosecutors to control the process.

This chapter focuses on the theory and practice of American plea bargaining in comparative perspective. The first section provides a detailed examination of plea bargaining in the U.S. It starts by laying out the abstract theory of plea bargaining and its supposed benefits to the parties and to the court system, all of which are based on the central assumption that a plea agreement is voluntary. It then contrasts this theory with the harsh reality of the practice of plea bargaining in the U.S. The latter shows a vast imbalance of power between prosecution and defense, putting into question the assumption of voluntariness.

The second and third sections develop comparisons to our three European cases, all of which have their own versions of plea bargaining. The second section focuses on the comparison to France and Germany, where plea bargaining is a recent innovation that is still applied quite rarely and in very restricted ways, thus providing a stark counterpoint to the American model. After describing the status of plea bargaining in the French and German criminal justice systems, the section delves into the reasons for the "continental divide" that distinguishes the (Anglo-)American model from the continental European version—namely the crucial distinction between adversarial and inquisitorial systems.

The third section turns to the U.K., which provides an instructive comparative example. On the one hand, the British system does included widespread plea bargaining, which therefore seems to indicate an affinity with the American practice that contradicts the "American exceptionalism" argument. On the other hand, upon closer inspection, an analysis of the specifics of plea bargaining in the U.K. reveals clear and crucial procedural and substantive distinctions between these two "Anglo" systems.

Overall, this comparative perspective helps to shed light on the exceptionalism of the U.S., especially in terms of the role and power of American prosecutors in comparison to their European counterparts.

Plea Bargaining in the United States

This section discusses the logic and reality of American plea bargaining, highlighting the lack of congruence between the two, which puts into question this increasingly ubiquitous practice.

Plea Bargaining in Theory

In theory, plea bargaining represents a mutually agreeable arrangement between two opposing sides (prosecution and defense) in criminal cases. Black's Law Dictionary defines it as the "process whereby the accused and the prosecutor in a criminal case work out a mutually satisfactory disposition of the case subject to court approval. It usually involves the defendant pleading guilty to a lesser offense or to only one or some of the counts of a multi-count indictment in return for a lighter sentence than would occur with the more serious charge."[2] The principle behind plea bargaining is that both sides can be spared the time and expense of a trial when they are in agreement as to the acts committed and the appropriate punishment. As Stephanos Bibas puts it, "the classical model [of plea bargaining] supposes that trials set normatively desirable benchmarks and cast strong shadows. These shadows ensure that plea bargains allocate punishment fairly, both in the aggregate and in particular cases."[3] Most importantly, plea bargaining is based on the core assumption that the defendant has knowingly waived his or her right to a trial, that the waiver was entirely voluntary (i.e., not made under threats or even subtle coercion), and that there is an accurate factual basis to the charges and terms of the plea bargain agreement.[4]

All defendants in the U.S. are guaranteed the right to jury trials, based on Article II, Section 2 of the U.S. Constitution, which states that "The Trial of all Crimes, except in Cases of Impeachment, shall be by Jury,"[5] and by the Sixth Amendment, which specifies that "In all criminal prosecutions, the accused shall enjoy the right to a speedy and public trial, by an impartial jury of the state and district wherein the crime shall have been committed."[6] Yet plea bargaining has a long-standing and revered tradition in American criminal law, dating back to the "second half of the nineteenth century," and it was largely unquestioned and uncontested for decades.[7] Long after it had become an established practice, the Supreme Court addressed the issue of plea bargaining in several cases, moving from reluctance in 1968 to acceptance in 1970 to outright support in 1971. In *United States v. Jackson*, the Court was worried that defendants would accept plea bargains as a means of avoiding the death penalty.[8] The problem for the Court was not so much a fear of coercion, but of excessive encouragement for defendants facing possible capital charges to accept a plea bargain. In *Brady v. United States*, just two years later, the Court clarified its opinion in *Jackson* by specifying that the plea must be entirely voluntary, but adding that such arrangements were beneficial to both sides.[9] A year after that, in *Santobello v. New York*, the Court fully endorsed plea bargaining, stating that it was "an essential component of the administration of justice," and that when "properly administered," it should "be encouraged."[10]

The apparent rationale for the Court's position was based on "the separation of powers, the faith in prosecutors to discharge their duties properly, and the concern that vigorous judicial supervision over prosecutors may produce a chilling effect on law enforcement."[11] Moreover, the Federal Rules of Criminal Procedure also support plea bargains within Rule 11.[12] Although the practice was already widespread, this official seal of approval by the

Supreme Court gave greater legitimacy and impetus for the continuation and even expansion of plea bargaining. In 1978, in *Bordenkircher v. Hayes*, the Court further facilitated the task for prosecutors to pressure defendants into accepting plea bargains when a narrow majority affirmed a life sentence for a Kentucky man with two prior felony convictions who rejected a five-year plea offer for his third crime (forging a check for $88.30), and who then went on to be charged under the state's Habitual Crime Act.[13] In short, despite the fact that the text of the Constitution emphasizes jury trials, plea bargaining has a long history in the U.S., and it is firmly established within modern criminal law—with clear support from the Supreme Court.

Plea bargains can occur in three different varieties: charge bargaining, sentence bargaining, and fact bargaining. The first two are by far the most common. Charge bargaining occurs when the two sides negotiate the actual charges that will be brought against the defendant. The idea is that the defendant will plead guilty to a lesser charge (e.g., manslaughter), thus guaranteeing that the prosecutor will win a conviction for a crime that might otherwise be difficult, costly, and risky to pursue at trial with a higher charge (e.g., murder). For the defendant, the plea takes away the risk of a trial conviction that could bring about a much more severe sentence than the agreed-upon charge will likely carry. In contrast, sentence bargaining takes place at the same charge level, but with an assurance for the defendant of a more reduced sentence than would be the case if he or she lost at trial. Once again, there are perceived advantages for both sides in pursuing such an agreement. Finally, fact bargaining, which is much more rare, involves an agreement by the defendant to admit to specific facts (thus obviating the need for the prosecutor to prove them), in exchange for the prosecutor's agreement not to raise others (perhaps embarrassing to the defendant). All three types of plea bargaining are built on the assumption of voluntariness, and they serve the goal of justice in a way that suits both parties (and the court) by expediting the process and reaching a fair outcome.

In terms of actors, there are either three or four parties to a plea bargain agreement—depending on one's perspective of the defense side—the prosecutor, the judge, the defense lawyer, and the defendant. For prosecutors, plea bargaining is the lifeline of their otherwise impossible caseloads. By being able to gain convictions without needing lengthy and costly trials, by avoiding the risk of possibly losing at trial (which could be embarrassing or politically costly to elected prosecutors), and by reaching agreements that satisfy their objective of punishing crime—even if to a lesser extent than might otherwise be the case if successful at trial on a higher charge—plea bargaining presents a "win-win-win" proposition for prosecutors.[14] Similarly, plea bargains allow judges to clear some of the backlog from their schedules and dockets, while simply ratifying agreements that seem to suit both sides. It is certainly difficult to imagine how the legal system could function if individual trials were held for all of the cases that routinely reach plea bargains.

On the side of the defense, plea bargains give guilty defendants a chance to get a better deal than they would if charged with, and convicted of, a higher-level crime, and it thereby serves to reduce uncertainty and risk. For the defense lawyers, the objectives are a bit more ambiguous, and perhaps contradictory, depending on how they are being paid. If they are simply receiving a flat fee or a regular salary (as would typically be the case with indigent clients), it is in their self-interest to resolve cases as quickly as possible. Pushing to bring numerous cases to trial would only increase their already substantial work overload and case backlog, without necessarily paying them more. But this incentive structure leaves open the question of whether defense lawyers are actually serving their clients' best interests by pursuing and pushing for plea agreements in cases where they might achieve better results by going to trial (or at least waiting for more discovery to see how strong the prosecution's case actually is). In any event, the role of defense lawyers should probably be distinguished from that of their clients, the defendants. Both may be well-served by the process and outcome of plea bargaining, but not necessarily for the same reasons.

Overall, plea bargaining—at least in theory—presents numerous advantages to all parties in a criminal case, and to the system overall. If all sides can agree on an appropriate charge, sentence, and/or set of facts, the system should be more efficient. And if the opposing sides reach a general consensus that they can genuinely accept and support, fairness and justice should ensue as well.

American Plea Bargaining in Practice

Having presented fairly abstract arguments about plea bargaining in theory, this section now turns to a more critical evaluation of it in practice. As with many legal concepts and doctrines, there can often be a gap between how a system is "supposed to" work and how it actually *does* function in practice. Many scholars and practitioners have objected to the de facto coercive nature of plea bargaining, whereby defendants are heavily pressured to accept deals that are not genuinely voluntary. In other words, when the core assumption of voluntariness is not met (or even if it is put into question), agreements that derive from threats and/or rewards can be erroneous and unjust. And in extreme cases, not only is the plea bargaining process highly coercive, but it can resemble a form of legal extortion.[15]

Plea bargaining can also lead to wrongful convictions based on false guilty pleas. This might sound surprising, but according to the National Registry of Exonerations, over 300 of the 1,900 people who have been exonerated since 1989 had pled guilty—including 68 of the 157 exonerations that occurred in 2015.[16] According to Josh Bowers, it is actually "rational" for innocent defendants to "swallow principle and utter false words" by promoting "judicial efficiency" with a guilty plea that results in mild penalties, without having to take the risk of severe consequence if they go to trial and lose.[17] Martin Yant views this type of outcome much more critically:

> Even when the charges are more serious, prosecutors often can still bluff defense attorneys and their clients into pleading guilty to a lesser offense. As a result, people who might have been acquitted because of lack of evidence, but also who are in fact truly innocent, will often plead guilty to the charge. Why? In a word, fear. And the more numerous and serious the charges, studies have shown, the greater the fear. That explains why prosecutors sometimes seem to file every charge imaginable against defendants.[18]

As another critic, Timothy Lynch, puts it, "The truth is that the government officials have deliberately engineered the system to assure that the jury trial system established by the Constitution is seldom used. And plea bargaining is the primary technique used by the government to bypass the institutional safeguards in trials."[19] Lynch adds that this system "rests on the constitutional fiction that our government does not retaliate against individuals who wish to exercise their right to trial by jury."[20] He therefore concludes that plea bargaining—as it is currently practiced, at least—is unconstitutional and should be revisited by the Supreme Court.[21]

Similarly, Bibas shows how the practice of plea bargaining deviates from the classical "shadow of the trial" model mentioned above, in two crucial respects.[22] First, various "structural impediments" distort the pure bargaining model. When defendants are held for lengthy periods in pretrial detention or unable to post bail, they face extraordinary pressure to accept any agreement that will return them to liberty (and thereby perhaps allow them to keep a job, or to maintain custody of their children). For example, in cases when a defendant has been detained for a considerable period of time, he or she may be offered a plea bargain for "time served," rather than to await trial. This puts a potentially innocent person—or at least someone who might be found "not guilty" at trial—in a very difficult position, with tremendous pressure to accept the deal and be released, rather than remain in detention. In such situations, Bibas states that plea bargaining "often happens in the shadow not of trial but of bail decisions."[23] Moreover, inadequate defense counsel—whether the attorneys are overworked, incompetent, or driven by self-serving reasons that are very different from the interests of their clients—may also pressure defendants to accept a "bad" deal instead of pressing for a trial.[24] This often occurs despite the fact that trials—which are rarely counseled by the legal representatives of indigent defendants—could essentially call the prosecution's bluff, and/or force it to show what may be a much weaker case than originally stated in the context of a plea offer.

Second, Bibas argues that the reality of plea bargaining contradicts the assumption that actors are rational, and that in actuality "overconfidence, self-serving biases, framing, denial mechanisms, anchoring, discount rates, and risk preferences all skew bargains."[25] Although the basic theory of plea bargaining assumes that both sides calculate their expected chance of winning, their likely outcome if they do win, and their probable costs if they go to trial—which collectively allows them to construct and negotiate a "zone of possible agreement" that is acceptable for each of them—the practice is much more vague and uncertain, filled with irrational decisions, misinformation, and bravado. And all of these features serve to undermine the purity of the logic of plea bargaining theory.

Another problem with plea bargaining in practice involves the flip side of the positive argument about how the efficiency of plea bargains spares the court and all parties much-needed time and resources. The near-ubiquity of plea bargaining in criminal cases has become standard practice within a system that already suffers from massive caseloads. This "caseload pressure" puts a tremendous burden on both sides of the adversarial system, and on the courts as well, to reach a speedy resolution that eliminates the large majority of cases from the docket.[26] Furthermore, the regular professional cooperation between members of what Schulhofer calls "the courtroom 'work group'" creates a strong incentive structure to reach a plea agreement regardless of the position of the defendant.[27] Again, these features challenge the classic model of plea bargaining.

Finally, a crucial distinction between the theory and practice of plea bargaining involves the role and power of prosecutors. As Michael O'Hear writes, "it is easy to overstate the extent to which plea bargaining really is bargaining."

He then adds that "there tends to be massive power imbalances between prosecutors and defendants."[28] Indeed, the following description of plea bargaining in action, by Milton Heumann, hardly suggests a sustained negotiation or even discussion about facts, trial outcomes, or sentence estimates:

> Typically [. . .] a line forms outside the prosecutor's office the morning before court is convened. Defense attorneys shuffle into the prosecutor's office and, in a matter of two or three minutes, dispose of the one or many cases "set down" that day. Generally, only a few words have to be exchanged before agreement is reached. The defense attorney mutters something about the defendant, the prosecutor reads the police report, and concurrence on "what to do" generally, but not always, emerges.[29]

In other words, not only are defense lawyers—typically public defenders with indigent clients—overburdened and desiring speedy resolution, but prosecutors are in a position to "act in a high-handed way" given their power to set the agenda and the defendant's likely poverty and challenges with bail and pretrial detention.[30] One common tactic involves "overcharging," whereby prosecutors either file or threaten to file charges that may not be supported by probable cause as a means to pressure the defendant to accept a plea.[31] This process was made even easier by the imposition of "mandatory minimum" sentences (discussed in the next chapter), which provide prosecutors with an even bigger threat with which they can pressure defendants to accept a plea offer. And on the federal level, Attorney General John Ashcroft articulated in a 2003 memorandum that "federal prosecutors must charge and pursue the most serious, readily provable offense"—a position that was softened slightly by Attorney General Eric Holder in 2010, who essentially changed the wording of "must" to "ordinarily should."[32] In terms of the role and practices of judges, O'Hear adds, "Perhaps more importantly, though, it is well recognized that judges routinely impose substantial penalties at sentencing on those defendants with the temerity to go to trial, sometimes doubling the punishment, or worse."[33]

On the defense side, the quality of representation for indigent defendants in the U.S. varies widely: some jurisdictions have a full-fledged public defender service (considered the highest standard, with full-time professionals devoted to criminal defense—although often with very different levels of funding, support, and resources); others have assigned counsel programs (with attorneys paid by the hour or case, but with very low amounts that hardly provide an incentive for mounting a vigorous defense); still others are structured on a contract system (with a fixed annual fee for indigent defense cases, thus providing very little incentive to expend much effort or resources). Yet even in the best of circumstances, indigent defendants rarely receive the type of zealous representation that could allow them to challenge or overcome the tremendous institutional and cultural pressure to "take the plea."

Overall, the reality of American plea bargaining is far afield from its original theory and principles. It is no exaggeration to say that for defendants, their "voluntary" decision to accept a plea is often no choice at all.

Comparative Approaches to Plea Bargaining: France and Germany

Although no country in the world practices plea bargaining as extensively as the United States, several other countries have begun to incorporate a very limited version into their legal system. Perhaps motivated by the universal overloading of court dockets, or by a sense that the American model is worth emulating in some respects, some have tinkered with their own systems and experimented with plea bargaining.[34] France and Germany, both of which have long and proud traditions of independent legal systems, have taken tentative steps to incorporate plea bargaining for the purpose of relieving the case backlogs that plague all legal systems. Yet, as discussed below, the nature of the parties and the power balance between them remain quite different from the American model of plea bargaining. Indeed, as Yue Ma writes, "despite the emergence of plea bargaining in continental law countries, no country has allowed prosecutors to gain such bargaining advantage over the accused that they are in a position to exact highly pressurized pleas from the accused."[35]

France

The French criminal justice system has a long-standing reputation of being relatively forgiving, often making use of fines and suspended sentences instead of incarceration.[36] This less punitive approach also figures into how crimes are defined, charged, and prosecuted, as well as how custodial arrest and pretrial detention are carried out.[37]

Following the "expediency principle," the role of prosecutors in the French system is not to win convictions, but to "determine a just solution to the case and present it to the judge."[38] As in the U.S., the majority of cases in France (estimates range from 50–80 percent) do not result in a criminal trial. Unlike the U.S., however, this is not due to plea bargaining, but rather because these cases are dropped for various reasons.[39] Like their American counterparts, French prosecutors can reduce a charge against a defendant—called "correctionalization"—either because they feel the penalty at the higher charge would be too harsh, or to relieve the congestion on the court calendar. Yet, as Ma writes, "The similarities between American plea bargaining and French correctionalization, however, end here. In France, there is no evidence indicating that the reduction of charges or the decision to correctionalize a crime is a result of bargains and negotiations between prosecutors and the defense. The decision to correctionalize is the unilateral decision of prosecutors."[40] Moreover, unlike in the U.S., the prosecutor's decision is completely independent of whether the defendant confesses to the crime.[41] French prosecutors also have much more limited powers in terms of dropping charges once they have been filed—which rules out the "overcharging" tactic common in American plea bargaining.[42] And they lose control of the case once it has been referred to the judge.[43]

In 2003, the French government introduced plea bargaining for the first time, for the purpose of removing some of the backlog from the overcrowded French criminal courts. The new policy allows prosecutors to offer "a reduction in penalties in exchange for a recognition of guilt and an agreement to cooperate with investigators."[44] Any agreement has to be accepted by all parties, including the judge. But this French form of plea bargaining only applies to crimes that could be punished with fewer than five years in prison, and the prosecutor must propose a sentence of under one year.[45] When it was initially proposed, the policy ran into strong resistance from all sides—prosecutors, judges, and defense lawyers. One leftist organization decried the reform as a "decline in the rights of the defense and the presumption of innocence, and the unbounded increase in police prerogatives and the marginalization of the function of judges in favor of ever more powerful prosecutors."[46] Perhaps as a result of this resistance, or the lack of a tradition of plea bargaining in France, only 21,000 of the 530,000 criminal decisions issued in 2005 were settled by a plea bargain—just under 4 percent of the total.[47]

In short, despite the recent introduction of this option, plea bargaining is rarely used in France. While it could obviously increase in the future—and institutional changes often take time to become widely accepted in practice—the landscape is certainly vastly different from the nearly universal practice in the U.S., and the principled resistance to plea bargaining is much stronger.

Germany

Germany's criminal justice system has been considered even more merciful than the French version. Since prison sentences of fewer than six months are not allowed by German law, Germany, like France, frequently gives out fines and suspended sentences instead of requiring incarceration.[48]

Until 2009, plea bargaining was formally prohibited in Germany in the sense that guilty pleas were not permitted—leading comparative legal scholar John Langbein to call Germany the "Land without Plea Bargaining."[49] Yet informally Germany had already adopted a mild version of plea bargaining since the 1970s. It began with limited application to minor offenses, but its use gradually expanded, particularly in the realm of white-collar and drug crimes.[50] In 2009 the German parliament passed a law that formally recognized and allowed for plea bargaining—under certain narrowly defined circumstances—and in 2013 the German constitutional court affirmed the law (while actually nullifying the plea bargains of three defendants, on the grounds that the standards of "justice" and "legality" had not been met).[51] In its ruling, the court "emphasized that the search for truth, the proportionality of punishment, and transparency of negotiations are important values in criminal justice and they must be respected even in the context of plea bargaining."[52] This compromise decision seems to have disappointed critics of plea bargaining who had hoped the court would ban the practice outright, while still reassuring them that plea bargaining would remain limited in scope, with numerous restrictions and constraints to prevent its overuse or abuse.[53]

In general terms, the German version of plea bargaining can take on three main forms: first, prosecutors can dismiss minor charges in exchange for the offender paying the victim, the state, or a charity; second, prosecutors (with approval of the judge) can prepare a penal order that allows the defendant to avoid a costly and embarrassing trial by paying a fine—though if the defendant rejects the offer and chooses to go to trial, prosecutors cannot increase the penalty as punishment (otherwise this would be a coercive procedure); third, in exchange for a confession, prosecutors can offer to file fewer charges and to move for a lighter sentence at trial.[54]

In the latter scenario—which most closely resembles the American model of plea bargaining—the judge takes on an active role in the bargaining process, arguably serving as a mediator between the two sides. The judge can perform an evaluative mediation by indicating to the defendant the upper limit on sentencing, with the non-binding understanding that if the defendant confesses, the judge's sentence will be lower. In contrast to the American model, a plea bargain is not an alternative to a trial—even cases with confessions must go to trial in Germany—but it can alleviate the level of evidence the prosecution would otherwise need to bring, thus reducing the length of the trial, and thereby diminishing the burden on the courts.[55] Another important distinction is that German defense lawyers are entitled to review the prosecutor's files, which thus prevents the bluffing and over-charging that often occurs in American plea bargains.[56] Finally, unlike their American counterparts, German prosecutors are required to "provide written reasons for their disposal of cases," which makes them act more responsibly and less high-handedly.[57]

Although specific statistics about the frequency of plea bargaining nation-wide do not seem to be available, the practice appears to have made greater inroads into the German system than the French one. A study of the German federal state of North Rhine Westphalia in 2011 found that about 18 percent of criminal proceedings in local courts and 23 percent in district courts were settled via plea bargaining.[58] As Frase and Weigend write, "in most respects, the German system—although closer to the French than to the American system—has more in common with American criminal justice than does the French system." Moreover, "there are increasing instances of explicit charge and sentence bargaining in Germany."[59] Yet the use of plea bargaining is much more limited and restricted in Germany than in the U.S. The crucial distinctions are that German plea bargaining can only be applied to cases that involve relatively minor crimes, it does not forgo the requirement of holding a trial, and it includes safeguards against coercion by the prosecutor.[60]

Overall, the comparison to France and Germany highlights the particularly American phenomenon of widespread and prosecutor-dominated plea bargaining. As Ma writes, although "plea bargaining has emerged in continental law countries, it remains a unique American feature that prosecutors are allowed to gain such an overwhelming dominance in the bargaining process that they can exact highly pressurized pleas from defendants."[61] Moreover, he emphasizes that the key distinction in Europe is that "continental prosecutors' discretion is subject to much stricter control and supervision than that enjoyed by their American counterparts." As a result, "despite the emergence of plea bargaining, no continental law countries have allowed plea bargaining to be conducted in a highly pressurized fashion."[62]

In short, the French and German analogues bear little resemblance to American plea bargaining, with the crucial difference being the high discretionary power and unchecked authority of American prosecutors. What accounts for this strong line dividing American and continental criminal legal systems? The next subsection briefly explores the important distinction between adversarial and inquisitorial systems, showing how the latter is structurally incompatible with the kind of plea bargaining regime that is routine in the U.S.

The Crucial Distinction between Adversarial and Inquisitorial Systems

The roots of the difference between American and continental European plea bargaining practices stem from the much larger and long-standing distinction between adversarial and inquisitorial systems. The adversarial model, exemplified by common law systems in the U.S. and U.K., involves a direct contest between two sides that argue vigorously on behalf of their position to an impartial decision-maker—either a judge or a jury (or both). It is essentially a two-party structure with two adversaries that compete to convince the judge or jury of their version of the truth, one of which wins out.[63] Importantly, when a defendant admits guilt in an adversarial system, the case is closed without a trial and the defendant is sentenced.

In contrast, in inquisitorial systems, judges play a far more important and central role in criminal cases. Rather than being passive and impartial arbiters, inquisitorial judges are responsible for fact-finding and searching for evidence. While the attorneys take on a more passive role, judges are the ones who question witnesses and seek to discover the truth.[64] In this sense, an inquisitional trial setting is closer to a mediation (with the judge as an active and hands-on evaluative mediator) than the familiar negotiation model of adversarial systems (where the judge merely supervises). Moreover, as discussed above, in inquisitorial systems a defendant's confession does not eliminate the need for a trial, thus preventing the type of plea bargaining so common in the U.S.[65]

Proponents of each side have developed arguments about why one system is superior to the other, but in the end it usually comes down to a critique by supporters of the inquisitorial model of the excessive power of adversarial prosecutors, which is rife with abuse (particularly in the case of plea bargaining), whereas proponents of the adversarial model argue that the inquisitorial system places too much power and control in the hands of judges, with few checks on their potential abuse of power.[66] As Marcus puts it,

> In choosing the means for disposing of cases with or without a full-blown trial, each model reflects its own underlying assumptions.

While the adversarial model looks to the partisan efforts of the prosecutor and defense counsel to search for the truth and to protect the public and the defendant, the inquisitorial model depends upon the even-handed initiative of the judge. Any conclusion about which model is more effective for these purposes is likely to reflect a cultural bias rather than a tested hypothesis.[67]

Without our seeking to resolve this intractable debate, it is clear that plea bargaining takes on very different forms—both in theory and in practice—in these two types of systems. And not only do the parties—judges, prosecutors, defense lawyers, and defendants—carry out quite distinct roles, but the frequency of plea bargaining is vastly different. Plea bargaining is the omnipresent norm in the U.S., whereas it remains an isolated and limited exception in France and Germany. This is not to suggest that all continental European systems are identical. Quite the contrary, as Frase and Weigend write, "the French system thus still seems to be much more inquisitorial than the German, leaving the German system located somewhere in the middle between the American and the French systems."[68] Yet in terms of plea bargaining, the American adversarial model is worlds apart from both the French and German inquisitorial systems.

Comparative Approaches to Plea Bargaining: The U.K.

If the German model of plea bargaining lies somewhere in between the French and American systems, where does the British model fit in? The U.K.'s common law system is, of course, the original source of American legal traditions, principles, and precedents, so it would be logical to expect a great affinity between the U.K. and the U.S.

The United Kingdom

At first glance, it appears that the U.K. does match up with the American propensity to use plea bargains, as over 90 percent of British convictions are now obtained through guilty pleas.[69] Yet interestingly enough, this time around it was the U.K. that "borrowed" the practice from the U.S. in the 1960s.[70] Many English judges and barristers initially disfavored the use of plea bargaining, in part because of its distinctly American flavor. In the landmark 1978 case *R v. Atkinson*, Lord Scarman stated that "plea bargaining has no place in the

English criminal law."[71] The 1970 case *R v. Turner* outlined the traditional stance of English judges, stating that "one of the core principles enunciated by [the case] was that under no circumstances was a judge to indicate that the sentence that would be imposed if an accused pled guilty would be less severe than the sentence imposed on conviction following a plea of not guilty."[72] In other words, the idea behind the ruling was that any indication of a different sentencing outcome between a trial and a plea—the very disparity that captures the essence of the American plea bargaining model—would undermine the key principle of freedom of choice.

More recently, however, in part due to efforts to make plea bargaining more transparent, public opinion has started to look more favorably upon the practice. The 2005 decision of *R v. Goodyear*, which for the first time allowed the defendant to request an indication of the highest possible sentence type that could be imposed if he or she pled guilty, seems to indicate a cultural shift toward greater acceptance of the practice.[73]

Although it would appear that the British and American models of plea bargaining are quite similar and converging—and this would be logical given the general affinity between these two common law systems—upon closer inspection it turns out that there are some clear and important distinctions between them. Most important, prosecuting barristers in the U.K. hold far less power than their counterparts in the U.S. In the U.K., the prosecuting barrister is chosen by the Crown Prosecution Service (CPS) for a single case and has no control over dispositions or briefs. This means that "With only one case, the prosecuting barrister has no backlog that the time needed to litigate this defendant's case, if not resolved by guilty plea, will exacerbate."[74] The pressure for plea bargaining is further limited by a more flexible sentencing structure as well as the lack of public prosecutors. And unlike in the U.S., British prosecutors are not motivated by professional pressures to obtain a conviction.[75] Overall, these three distinctions "have left the system unencumbered by any form of bargaining system and have left the courts free to control all the discretions associated with the administration of justice."[76] Moreover, the role of the English prosecutor is much more passive than in the U.S., as he or she "does not typically participate in making submissions as to the nature or length of sentence before the judge and does not engage in editorial comment as to the matters before the court."[77] In short, "The English prosecutor's role is limited."[78]

Another key distinction involves the role of defense attorneys. In the U.S., defense attorneys "are typically at a disadvantage in negotiating with prosecutors over guilty pleas," which can make them more inclined to recommend to their clients (whom they may not have had time to meet beforehand, due to their high caseload) that they simply agree to the prosecutor's proposed plea bargain.[79] Within the British system, in contrast, the responsibilities of the defense lawyer are divided between the solicitor and the barrister. The solicitor is responsible for preparing the defense, while the barrister, based on the information gathered from the solicitor, advises the defendant about possible plea options.[80] This practice usually leads to better preparation and ultimately more zealous representation for the defendant.

The issue of transparency provides another example of the stark contrast between British and American plea bargaining. International movements to limit prosecutorial discretion have been particularly prominent in the U.K., "where legislation and mandatory guidelines direct the actions of criminal justice agencies in almost all aspects of criminal proceedings."[81] This occurred in the 2000s, largely through the passing of "The Attorney General's Guidelines on the Acceptance of Pleas and the Prosecutor's Role in the Sentencing Exercise" to restrict prosecutorial discretion in sentencing and plea bargaining. The guidelines were then amended in 2009 to provide more "specific guidance on [. . .] a uniform and workable procedure for plea negotiations between the prosecution and defense prior to trial."[82] Overall, these new parameters aim to make legal conduct more transparent while maintaining flexibility for individual circumstances and upholding public interests and avoiding "an American-style pressure cooker."[83]

Conclusion

This chapter has attempted to explain the peculiar institution of plea bargaining, a procedure that has become the default method through which 95 percent of criminal cases in the U.S. are resolved. The tradition of American plea bargaining dates back centuries, and it has been affirmed and endorsed in recent decades by the U.S. Supreme Court. By contrasting the theory of plea bargaining—based on voluntariness as its core principle—with its common practice—based on prosecutorial discretion, power, and potential coercion or even extortion—the chapter has highlighted the contradictions and problems with this distinctly American form of adjudication. In reality, although the outcome may seem less draconian than a longer sentence imposed by a judge or jury after a full trial, plea bargaining can lead to excessive guilty pleas without consideration for the strength of a defendant's case. Moreover, since probation is the typical plea bargaining alternative to a prison sentence, this practice lays the foundation for future incarceration by later sending people to prison for probation "violations" that occur in the absence of due process.[84]

The comparative dimension has helped to show that even though some other countries have, to varying degrees, incorporated plea bargaining into their criminal justice systems, the American practice stands out as anomalous in multiple respects. The first part of the comparison focused on France and Germany, two important civil law countries that have inquisitorial, rather than adversarial, systems of justice. These two countries have incorporated "light" versions of plea bargaining in recent years and decades, but the practice is still relatively rare, and when it is applied, the procedural and substantive protections to defendants are far greater. The second part of the comparison, to the U.K.—a fellow common law country with an adversarial system that also has a high level of plea bargaining today—helps to further isolate the distinctively American features, which amount to extremely vast, broad, and discretionary powers in the hands of prosecutors who are seeking simultaneously to improve their "victory" record and reduce their case backlog.

There is still much to learn about American plea bargaining—both in terms of its own evolution and in comparative perspective. Although the Supreme Court seems unlikely to revisit this question in the future, there are grave ethical questions raised by the reality that so many plea bargains appear to be driven by such structural factors as a defendant's desire for bail or to be released from detention, which seem to be inherently coercive. Future studies will have to explore the inner workings of plea bargaining, as well as the wider effects on a society—one whose Constitution explicitly mentions the right to jury trials, no less—of having almost all cases be decided behind closed doors, under conditions that do not seem to provide defendants with the rights they are ostensibly guaranteed. The fact that countries such as France, Germany, and the U.K. provide defendants with far greater protection from coercion suggests the need to re-evaluate both the prevalence and the particular structural dynamics of American plea bargaining.

3

Sentencing

AFTER THE LEGAL process leads to an adjudication of guilt—whether by a plea bargain or a trial—the next crucial stage of the "life cycle" of criminal justice involves the sentence imposed by the plea agreement or a judge. And while all countries follow a general basic hierarchy of the severity of crimes—where minor theft is considered less serious than assault, which is punished less severely than murder—there is tremendous variation in the sentencing of crime across jurisdictions, both within the United States and especially across countries.

This chapter focuses on American sentencing practices in comparative perspective. Unlike in most of the other empirical chapters, the comparative reference point here goes beyond the three cases of France, Germany, and the U.K., as it also covers a somewhat broader array of countries based on comparable data that exist on the issue of sentencing. The cumulative body of evidence on comparative sentencing provides an overwhelming picture of the U.S. as a country that stands far apart from other liberal democracies, based on its application of frequent and relatively long prison sentences—including numerous "life" sentences and the distinctly American and increasingly common sentence of "life without parole." The chapter then turns to the particular policy changes that have taken place within the U.S. since the 1970s, tracking the specific legislative and judicial decisions that contributed to the stunning rise in incarceration rates over the ensuing decades.

Comparative Studies on Sentencing

Although the comparative study of sentencing faces numerous methodological challenges—both in terms of the varying definitions of crimes and the uneven application of sentences across jurisdictions—several studies have provided data and analyses that are useful for understanding and comparing American sentencing practices. The first subsection discusses several broader comparative projects, while the second subsection focuses more closely on paired comparisons between the U.S. and our three cases of France, Germany, and the U.K.

A Broader Comparative Perspective

The scholar who has focused most closely on the comparative dimension to sentencing and punishment has been Michael Tonry. In the introduction to his co-edited volume that includes case studies of the U.S. and five other advanced democracies, Tonry concludes that "the most dramatic difference is between the United States, which continues to use the death penalty and life sentences without possibility of parole and where prison sentences exceeding ten years are common, and the rest of the Western world, which has renounced the death penalty and where prison sentences longer than a few years are uncommon."[1]

Tonry goes on to provide some examples of the vast differences in terms of how countries apply criminal sentences. He mentions that "only a few percent of prison sentences in most countries are for terms longer than one year, while, by contrast, in 1994 [. . .] the mean average maximum sentence of persons committed to U.S. state prisons was seventy-one months."[2] More specifically, he writes:

> In some countries, for example, Germany and Austria, prison sentences shorter than six months are regarded as destructive and serving no valid penal purpose and are therefore strongly discouraged. In others, including Sweden and Finland, certainty of punishment is seen as important, but not severity, and as a result many sentences to days or weeks of imprisonment are imposed. And there are wide divergences in the use of community punishments. Community service is a commonly used prison alternative in England, Scotland, and the Netherlands, but is seldom used as a primary punishment in many other countries.[3]

These examples are instructive in several regards, not least because they help to point out that there is considerable variation *within* the European countries. Yet despite different policies and approaches, these countries are generally bound by, or supportive of, international agreements, including the

European Court of Human Rights, which has held that life sentences must allow for at least the possibility of eventual release,[4] and the United Nations Convention on the Rights of the Child, which opposes life sentences for juveniles.[5] Indeed, Tonry adds that most European countries have established a 10–15 year period as the upper limit on prison sentences.[6] And while life sentences still exist in Europe, James Whitman reminds us that they are meant to "announce the gravity of the offense to society and the offender," whereas "the actual service of sentence is governed by norms of mercy."[7]

In another comparative study, Tonry and Farrington focus on eight countries—Australia, Canada, England and Wales, the Netherlands, Switzerland, Scotland, Sweden, and the U.S. They incorporate data from a combination of victimization surveys, police records, and other police, court, and correctional sources. They examine six types of crimes—residential burglary, vehicle theft, robbery, serious assault, rape, and homicide—but data limitations force them to focus specifically on burglary (a property crime) and robbery (a violent crime). By incorporating three measures of punishment—"the number of convictions per 1,000 offenders, the probability of custody following a conviction, and the average time served in custody"—their data "permit confident conclusions to be drawn about cross-national differences in the use and severity of punishment."[8] They find that: (1) the probability of being convicted of burglary or robbery fell from 1980 to 1999 in the other seven countries, but rose in the U.S.; (2) the U.S. (in this case followed closely by Sweden and England) had the highest rate of imposing prison sentences for both burglary and robbery; and (3) the U.S. (and Australia) imposed the longest sentences for these two crimes.[9]

According to the research conducted by Marc Mauer and his colleagues at the Sentencing Project, violent offenders are punished with incarceration at roughly similar rates in the U.S., Canada, and England and Wales.[10] The difference, however, is with the *term* of the sentence. "Burglars in the United States [. . .] served an average of 16.2 months in prison, compared to 5.3 months in Canada and 6.8 months in England, and U.S. larceny offenders served about three to six times as long as those in Canada."[11] Mauer adds that the disparity in drug punishment is even wider: "Possession of five grams of crack cocaine yields a mandatory five years in federal prison in the U.S., while comparable offenders in Britain would serve between zero and six months."[12] Moreover, Frase and Weigend found in their comparison of the U.S. and Germany that even after adjusting for the higher rate of violent crimes and drug crimes in the U.S., "overall sentencing severity per crime was about three times more severe in the United States than in Germany."[13] In short, as James

Lynch writes, "in the case of property crime, it is clear that the United States incarcerates more and for longer periods of time than other similar nations. The same appears to be true for drug offenses."[14]

In a 1994 study based on 1991 data in the U.S. and England and Wales, Lynch and his co-authors found that "34% of sentenced U.S. inmates, but 4% of those in England and Wales, had a prison sentence to a term of over 10 years but less than life."[15] In other words, defendants in the U.S. were 8.5 times more likely to receive a lengthy prison sentence—and the difference has surely grown since 1991. Lynch et al. also found disparities in drug sentencing, as 24 percent of American prisoners were incarcerated for drug crimes, compared to only 8 percent of inmates in England and Wales.[16] Moreover, of those prisoners who were convicted of drug offenses, 27 percent received sentences of over 10 years in the U.S., 4.5 times higher than the 6 percent in England and Wales.[17] Overall, the comparison between the U.S. and England and Wales— which is arguably the case that should be closest to the U.S. within Europe— points to tremendous differences in the severity of sentencing.

Another major distinction involves the use of life sentences, and in particular life without parole (LWOP). One comparative study published in 2002 found that 10.7 percent of American prisoners were serving life sentences, compared to 8.4 percent in England and Wales, and only 3.1 percent in Germany.[18] More recent statistics indicate that the percentage of life sentences has risen to about 11.1 percent in the U.S. in 2012[19] and 8.8 percent in England and Wales in 2015,[20] whereas it has dropped slightly to 2.95 percent in Germany in 2010.[21] While the percentage difference between life sentences in the U.S. and U.K. may seem relatively minor, the crucial distinction involves the subsequent possibility of parole or early release—a theme that will be explored in greater detail in Chapter 6—since in the U.K. and other European countries a life sentence almost always implies the possibility of subsequent release.[22]

Unlike in Europe, LWOP sentences are now applied quite commonly in the U.S.—and this does not even include sentences of multiple life terms, or life plus a certain number of years, which effectively yields the same result as LWOP. This American reality stands in stark contrast to European countries, which apply life sentences sparingly. For example, as of the early 2000s, among the life sentences, about 25 percent of them in the U.S. were without the possibility of parole, a rate that is 50 times higher than the 0.5 percent in England, where over 99 percent of lifers will eventually be parole-eligible.[23] As of 2012, there were nearly 160,000 Americans serving life sentences, of whom nearly 50,000 (almost 31 percent) had an LWOP sentence.[24] The proportion of lifers exceeds 10 percent in 12 different states, and in New York and

California it is approaching 20 percent.[25] Moreover, of these lifers, "about a third are serving time for sentences other than murder, including burglary and drug crimes."[26]

Overall, as shown in Figures 3.1 and 3.2, the number of life sentences in the U.S. has increased by over 469 percent from 1984 to 2012, and the number of LWOP sentences has gone up nearly 400 percent as well from 1992 to 2012 — a major increase in just 20 years. These are especially striking figures when considering the permanence of such life (and especially LWOP) sentences.

Given these figures, it is safe to say that in the U.S., "life" is no longer the exception but a relatively common outcome, and in many ways this new sentencing reality crystalizes the essence of the many punitive changes in American criminal justice over this time period. Indeed, in a perceptive and trenchant analysis and critique of the prevalence of LWOP sentences in the U.S., Sharon Dolovich argues that LWOP epitomizes "the central motivating aim of the contemporary American carceral system," which is no longer concerned with rehabilitation and reintegration but instead prefers "permanent exclusion."[27]

When we turn to juveniles, the sentencing disparities are even greater. According to a comparative study of juvenile sentencing, the U.S. stands out

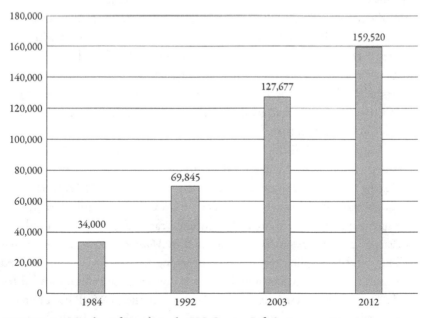

FIGURE 3.1 Number of People in the U.S. Serving Life Sentences, 1984–2012
Source: Nellis 2013

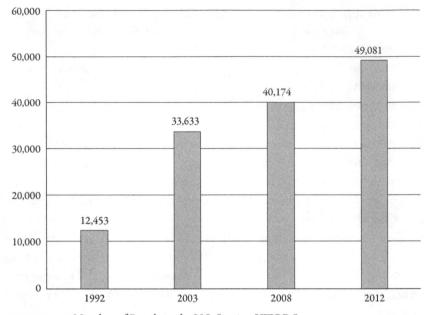

FIGURE 3.2 Number of People in the U.S. Serving LWOP Sentences, 1992–2012
Source: Nellis 2013

in terms of its widespread application of adult standards to juvenile defendants, the severity of punishment imposed on children, the lack of separation from adults within prisons, and the inability to maintain contact with their families.[28] The authors conclude that "it is clear that the USA does not follow the 'best interests of the child' principle on which the international standards are based."[29] Moreover, over 2,500 American children have been sentenced to LWOP—a sentence that is categorically prohibited from being applied to juveniles in other countries.[30] The U.S. Supreme Court has chipped away at several features of this distinctively American practice: in 2010 the Court ruled in *Graham v. Florida* that an LWOP sentence for crimes other than murder violates the Eighth Amendment,[31] in 2012 the Court held in *Miller v. Alabama* that laws carrying a *mandatory* sentence of LWOP for juvenile perpetrators were unconstitutional (although the sentence can still be applied in individual cases),[32] and in 2016 the Court decided in *Montgomery v. Louisiana* that *Miller* should be applied retroactively, meaning that juveniles who received automatic LWOP sentences now have to be re-sentenced or considered for parole. Despite these restrictions on its use for juveniles, LWOP itself remains an increasingly popular sentence in the U.S.—particularly as an alternative to capital punishment, which has faced a variety of challenges in recent times.

One of the legal reasons that helps to explain the widespread and distinctively American use of life sentences—both with and without the possibility of parole—involves the twin doctrines of felony murder and accomplice liability. Deriving from English law, felony murder attributes criminal liability for the charge of murder to anyone who was involved in the commission of a felony that resulted in another person's death—even if a defendant did not actually cause or even foresee the resulting death. In other words, the mens rea, or mental state required to demonstrate intentionality, is applied to the predicate felony, not to the death of another person. This quite expansive approach allows a group of defendants to be charged and convicted of murder as if each and every one of them had personally conducted the killing, even if only one defendant actually committed the act. To mention one evocative example that received the attention of the *New York Times*, a groggy 20-year-old man loaned his car keys to his friends before passing out after a late-night party, while they drove his car several miles away to commit a home burglary and wound up killing someone at the house. Although he was fast asleep, he received an LWOP sentence for murder.[33]

In comparative perspective, the felony murder rule is an anomaly, "a primitive relic of medieval law that unaccountably survived the Enlightenment and the nineteenth-century codification of criminal law."[34] In contrast, other countries strive to apply punishment that is proportional to a person's actual level of culpability and responsibility for the death of another—and this can of course vary widely in cases where multiple defendants were involved in a felony that led to a person's death.[35] The U.K. was the originator of the felony murder rule, which has only existed in common law countries, but it derived from an era where relatively few felonies existed, unlike in the U.S. today, where any crime punishable by a year or more in prison is considered a felony. Moreover, England and Wales abolished the felony murder rule in 1957, and Northern Ireland followed suit in 1966 (and it never existed in Scotland). In the U.S., almost all states apply some version of felony murder, and it is widely viewed as a convenient tool for prosecutors that makes it much easier to yield convictions, since they do not have to prove the mental intent required for murder, as long as they can show the defendant's clear involvement in the predicate felony.

One additional important—and obvious—European-American distinction involves capital punishment. Perhaps surprisingly, the two continents were actually quite similar for a long period of history—both in terms of early widespread use of the ultimate punishment for many types of crime and the gradual imposition of restrictions over time. As David

Garland writes, "for much of the last 200 years, America and other Western nations have marched in lockstep, continually restraining, refining, and reducing the use of the death penalty."[36] European countries eliminated capital punishment altogether in the period from the end of World War II through the 1970s (with France being the last major European country to abolish it in 1981). The U.S. seemed to be headed for a similar outcome in 1972 when the Supreme Court in *Furman v. Georgia* imposed a moratorium on executions because its inconsistent application constituted "cruel and unusual punishment," thus violating the Eighth Amendment. Yet four years later—around the same time as Nixon's "War on Crime" began to translate into higher levels of incarceration and a new "tough on crime" political movement that would thrive for decades—the Court held in *Gregg v. Georgia* that a capital sentencing scheme based on objective criteria that also took into account a defendant's record was indeed constitutional, which thereby opened the door to a resurgence in both death sentences and executions in many U.S. states. According to Garland, this American exceptionalism—and the sudden rejection of the common trajectory once shared with European countries—can be best be explained by (1) the predominance of local control of the criminal justice system, (2) regional differences within the U.S. (particularly within the American South), and (3) the tradition of "extra-legal executions"—most notably race-based lynchings—in the South.[37]

In contrast to Europe, where the decision to ban capital punishment was elite-led and actually went against prevailing public opinion at the time, the American model has been to allow individual states to create or change their own policies. As Garland writes, "In Europe and elsewhere, governing elites decided that the state ought not to kill its citizens whatever the people thought. In the United States, the Court insisted that the people should decide."[38] As a result, in the years and decades since *Gregg*, the application of capital punishment in the U.S. has displayed tremendous regional variation, as 19 states (mainly in the Northeast and Midwest) have abolished it,[39] and of the 31 states that still maintain it, those that actually carry out executions are mostly located in the South.[40] Capital punishment remains a live and "evolving" issue in many individual states, but the overall American law and practices demonstrate a sharp distinction from the European norm in this important area of sentencing policy. Moreover, the very existence of the death penalty as a possible sentence has an effect on non-capital sentencing policy and plea bargaining agreements as well. In fact, death penalty opponents in the U.S. usually frame their arguments by making the case for LWOP—a sentence that does not even exist in most other democracies, because it is considered inhumane—as the less punitive alternative. In this sense, the very existence of capital punishment in so many American states serves to "anchor" the range of possible sentencing outcomes at an extremely high level.

Sentencing in France, Germany, and the United Kingdom

Focusing a bit more closely on our three main comparative reference points—France, Germany, and the U.K.—several other scholars have contributed important perspectives on sentencing by focusing on the U.S. in paired comparisons to these countries.

Starting with the U.K., Jones and Newburn consider the extent to which the U.K. has been "Americanizing," since at first glance it seems to have been incorporating such concepts as privatized prisons, "zero-tolerance" policing, and "three strikes" sentencing laws.[41] Yet on closer analysis, they find that despite some "policy transfer," the reforms in the U.K. have been much more symbolic than substantive, unlike in the U.S.[42] Similarly, Mirko Bagaric finds that the "U.K.'s three-strike laws apply to a much more limited range of offenses and the penalty enhancements are less harsh and not always imposed."[43] And Julian Roberts shows how in 2009 England and Wales declined to adopt an American model of sentencing guidelines, choosing instead to implement a system designed to "promote uniformity and sentencing by prescribing a sequence of steps for courts to follow when sentencing an offender, while also allowing a significant degree of discretion."[44] On balance, "England operates under the rationale that proportionality should be the guiding criterion for deciding the severity of the sentence."[45]

Another distinction involves the emphasis on the maximum possible sentence in the U.K., whereas the American practice focuses on the "mandatory minimum" sentence.[46] English courts and judges often yield tremendous discretion—something that is lacking in the U.S.—and they can choose to shorten sentences, offer early releases, or grant community sentences.[47]

In a sign of its possible "Americanization," from 2005 to 2011 the U.K. also applied a sentencing practice known as Imprisonment for Public Protection (IPP), which was intended to protect the public from serious, violent offenders whose actual crimes were nonetheless not severe enough to warrant a life sentence. Instead, after serving their minimum term in prison, a person who had received an IPP sentence would have to apply for release to the Parole Board, which would approve requests only if it was satisfied that the person no longer represented a threat to public safety (and in those cases, the person would remain under a parole-like supervision for at least 10 years).[48] After discovering that the IPP sentences were being used far more frequently than was originally intended—at a rate of 800 per year, and even in some cases to people sentenced to short, two-year prison terms—the U.K. Ministry of Justice under then–prime minister David Cameron announced that it would be eliminating the IPPs, instead "introducing a range of consistent tough sentences with fixed lengths, which will see more dangerous criminals given life sentences and give victims a clear understanding of how long offenders will be imprisoned."[49]

Both sets of reforms—establishing the IPPs and replacing them with "tough" sentencing standards that impose longer mandatory sentences—suggest a shift in the British approach to punishing crime, moving the U.K. in the direction of the U.S. That said, it should be stressed that these reforms apply only to what are called "dangerous criminals" and "the most serious offenders," and are therefore much less sweeping than the sentencing policies in the U.S., which are extremely lengthy across the board, including drug and property crimes. Overall, while the sentencing practices in the U.K. certainly bear some resemblance to the American guidelines—and perhaps increasingly so—on balance they are carried out differently and yield results that are far less draconian.

Sentencing practices in France and especially Germany are even less punitive than those in the U.K., as many non-violent crimes are punished by fines and penalties rather than incarceration. With reference to France, Richard Frase points out that "the French make very sparing use of custodial penalties and punish most offenses with fines or suspended sentences."[50] He adds that "France's less punitive attitude is evidenced not only in its sentencing laws and practices, but also at earlier stages of the criminal process: in the legal definition of crimes; in the use of custodial arrest and pretrial detention; and in decisions about whether (and on what charges) to prosecute."[51] And Aharonson highlights the fact that French judges possess tremendous discretion to reduce sentences or to release prisoners at some point during their incarceration.[52] That said, the political and policy rhetoric in France—as in many countries—has certainly become harsher. But, as argued by Sebastian Roché, "Policy transfer has not reshaped French laws and practices, even though slogans are shared across both sides of the Channel and both sides of the Atlantic."[53]

Turning his comparative lens in the direction of Germany, Frase shows that while 71 percent of burglary convictions in the U.S. lead to incarceration, only 34 percent do in Germany; the corresponding figures are 63 percent for serious theft in the U.S., 26 percent in Germany; 47 percent for fraud and embezzlement in the U.S., compared to only 3 percent in Germany; 55 percent for forgery in the U.S., 7 percent in Germany. In the area of drugs, 70 percent of drug possession and 74 percent of drug dealing convictions lead to incarceration in the U.S., compared to just 8 percent and 21 percent in Germany.[54] Overall, and based on more recent data, a 2013 report from the Vera Institute of Justice shows that whereas 70 percent of all convictions in the U.S. result in prison terms, only 6 percent of convicted Germans serve jail time.[55] Moreover, "In 2006 in Germany, 75 percent of prison sentences were for 12 months or less and 92 percent of sentences were for two years or less. In addition, Germany suspended the vast majority of prison sentences that were under two years—in about 75 percent of cases, so only a very small percentage of those sentenced ever went to prison."[56] Given these distinctions, Frase concludes that "there is much for Americans to learn from the German experience with non-custodial sentencing options over the past three decades. The Germans have shown [. . .] how to deal humanely and efficiently with high-volume, low- and medium-severity crimes, most of which are committed by socially-integrated offenders for whom non-custodial sanctions are both feasible and highly cost-effective."[57]

Although other countries have discussed and perhaps enhanced their sentencing guidelines, Germany has remained steadfast in its application of relatively short sentences. Hans-Jörg Albrecht notes the "remarkable stability in the structure of criminal sactions [. . .] in Germany since the end of the 1960s, when a major law amendment gave priority to fines and significantly restricted the use of prison sentences."[58] He adds that since the late 1960s, "four out of five criminal sanctions imposed by German criminal courts are day fines."[59] What explains this remarkable—and apparently quite effective—lack of punitiveness? According to Tatjana Hörnle, since judicial practices in Germany remain at the level of an apolitical judiciary and are thereby free from political "pressure" to change, "sentencing reform is not a political issue and the sentencing reform movement has not reached Germany."[60]

Putting these various findings together, there is clearly a sharp divergence between the sentencing practices of the U.S. and otherwise comparable countries, with a pattern of across-the-board higher levels of sentencing in the U.S.—whether for property crimes, drug offenses, or violent crimes. Whereas in Europe most crimes are punished by day fines and suspended sentences, the U.S. has chosen incarceration as its solution. In short, although this was not always the case, there can be no doubt that sentencing policy in the U.S. has become by far the most draconian of the democratic world.

Changes in American Sentencing from 1970 to 2010

As explained in the Introduction, the United States did not always stand out for its punitiveness. Indeed, Tocqueville marveled about American "mildness." And American sentencing practices were actually quite close to the European mainstream before the two regions began to diverge considerably in the 1970s. This section tracks the policy changes that took place in the U.S. over the subsequent decades, which moved the U.S. away from its fellow liberal democracies by enacting extremely punitive sentencing policies.

The Pre-1970s Historical Norm: Indeterminate Sentencing

Prior to the 1970s, American sentencing policies were highly indeterminate. The prevailing scheme "stipulated a fairly broad range of sentence to allow for discretionary parole release upon evidence of rehabilitation."[61] In other words, "indeterminacy in the system referred to the relative disconnect between the length of the sentence imposed by the sentencing court and the length of sentence actually served by an offender in prison prior to release on parole."[62] This model was based on the long-since-forgotten idea that individualized punishment sanctions could lead to rehabilitation.[63]

By the early 1970s, however, both scholars and policymakers had become increasingly critical of the indeterminate sentencing model. As will be explained in more detail in Chapter 5, in a very influential and controversial 1974 article, sociologist Robert Martinson reviewed 231 studies and concluded that "with few and isolated exceptions, the rehabilitative efforts that have been reported so far have had no appreciable effect on recidivism."[64] Following the publication of the "Martinson Report," many academics abandoned the idea of rehabilitative programs.[65] Politically, both the Left and the Right turned on them as well. Liberals felt that the amount of discretion afforded to sentencing judges and parole boards left the system open to discrimination and abuse, while conservatives favored the harsher treatment of criminals.[66] As a result, the initial reforms that emerged in the 1970s—and which intensified over the subsequent decades—reflected a desire to equalize punishments and increase consistency in sentencing and parole decisions.[67] This led to a shift in the direction of determinative sentencing policies.

Determinate Sentencing

In its most basic form, determinate sentencing refers to a system without discretionary parole release for offenders.[68] In a determinate sentencing scheme, the offender must serve a statutorily determined portion of the specific sentence that was imposed by the judge. The actual length of the sentence was primarily determined by a judge, leaving parole boards with a much more limited role to play. The first two states to pass determinate sentencing legislation were Maine and California, which abolished discretionary parole release. In 1976, the California legislature went further by adopting the Uniform Determinate Sentencing Law, which prescribed a presumptive sentence—established by a sentencing committee—for certain statutory offenses, thus severely limiting the discretion of judges or sentencing officers.[69] Other states, including Indiana, New Mexico, Illinois, Minnesota, Florida, Washington, Oregon, Delaware, Kansas, Arizona, North Carolina, Mississippi, and Virginia, also went on to adopt determinate sentencing schemes.[70] Yet the actual statutory sentences for specific offenses differ across states and systems.[71]

Structured Sentencing

A further movement that has increased the harshness of sentencing policies involves structured sentencing. In a structured sentencing plan, states implement recommended or presumptive prison terms for specific offenses. "States with structured sentencing seek to narrow or guide judicial discretion in determining the length of an imposed prison term by proscribing a recommended term within the wider statutory sentence range for an offense."[72] The "structure" in this scheme refers to the state officials' attempts to introduce uniformity to sentencing according to levels of offenses. Structured sentencing took the form of presumptive sentencing in nine states: Alaska, Arizona, California, Colorado, Indiana, New Jersey, New Mexico, Ohio, and Rhode Island.[73] In these states, judges impose a prison term from within a narrowly specified recommended range, and they must cite mitigating factors or other reasons for deviating from the norm.

Other states implemented a looser form of structured sentencing through "sentencing guidelines." These states include Minnesota, Alaska, Pennsylvania, Florida, Maryland, Washington, Wisconsin, Delaware, Oregon, Tennessee, Kansas, Arkansas, North Carolina, Virginia, Ohio, Missouri, Oklahoma (later repealed in 1999), Utah, and Michigan.[74] Sentencing guidelines "specify a fairly narrow range of sentence for a convicted offender given his/her

current offense and prior record."[75] The main difference between structured
sentencing and sentencing guidelines involves the inclusion of the offender's
criminal history in the latter. The purpose of sentencing guidelines is to reduce
the disparities in sentencing between similar offenders committing similar
offenses. Sentencing guidelines can take either a presumptive or voluntary
form. In the presumptive form, which was first implemented in Minnesota in
1980, judges must impose a sentence that is within the recommended limits,
or provide written justification for imposing an alternative sentence. In such
cases, sentences that are outside of the recommended limits may be appealed
by either the defendant or prosecutor. In contrast, voluntary sentence guidelines do not require the judge to adhere to the recommended limits and do
not allow for appeals.[76]

Sentencing commissions were considered attractive for various reasons.
First, appointed commissions were set up to be independent and insulated
from political pressures that were highly responsive to electoral demands.
Second, the commission would be responsible for collecting data and developing expertise that would lead to a more informed sentencing policy.[77]
Proponents of sentencing commissions also claim that they are the best mechanism for resource management with respect to imprisonment rates, since
commissions can respond to changing needs in certain jurisdictions. And
some have argued that state sentencing commissions proved useful insofar as
making sentencing practices more accountable and being less "disparate in its
impact on minority group members."[78]

The federal government also sought to introduce sentencing guidelines in
the 1980s. Senators Ted Kennedy and Strom Thurmond cosponsored the 1984
Sentencing Reform Act, whose primary purpose was "to address the seemingly
intractable problem of unwarranted sentencing disparity and enhance crime
control by creating an independent, expert sentencing commission to devise
and update periodically a system of mandatory sentencing guidelines."[79] The
Federal Sentencing Guidelines were intended to "limit judicial discretion and
make sentences consistent via the introduction of binding regulations and
appellate review of sentences."[80] Yet these new guidelines were received with
widespread criticism, particularly from those who had to adhere to them. In
the words of Marc Mauer, the guidelines, which went into effect in 1987, carried "a heavy presumption of imprisonment for most offenders and [gave]
little regard for any mitigating circumstances involved in an offence."[81] With
the stated goal of further reducing disparities in sentencing similar offenders
for similar offenses, the guidelines essentially eliminated judicial discretion
while imposing uniformly harsh sentencing policies. Eventually, the Supreme

Court found the mandatory guidelines unconstitutional in 2005, but held that they could still be advisory, even if no longer binding. Moreover, the decision was not retroactive, and therefore did not apply to the many prisoners already sentenced under the guidelines.[82]

It is often noted that the experience of states that have implemented sentencing guidelines has been different from that of the federal government.[83] Frase argues that state guideline systems are more flexible than federal guidelines, as well as easier to apply. He criticizes the Federal Guidelines as being too ambitious, particularly for trying to "structure and define every single decision."[84] In contrast, state guidelines are relatively short documents, as many of them explicitly prefer simplicity and therefore allow for some ambiguity.[85]

Overall, the move from judicial discretion to determinate sentencing was premised on a legitimate problem, namely the vast discrepancies between sentences imposed by individual judges, as well as the potential for racist and discriminatory applications of sentences across defendants—a practice that has a long-standing history in the U.S. For this reason, in principle, a determinate sentencing plan is more "just" in that it prevents this type of variation from occurring. The problem with the application of state and federal sentencing guidelines is not necessarily that they are determinate per se (although arguably a bit more "wiggle room" for judges would have been preferable), but that the length of the fixed prison terms assigned to individual crimes were extraordinarily severe. This left many judges in the difficult position of having literally no choice but to impose sentences that they thought were vastly disproportionate to what they thought the defendants in front of them actually deserved.

Mandatory Sentencing

Another major change in American sentencing policies involves the increasing use of mandatory sentencing statutes. Indeed, "between 1975 and 2002, every state adopted some form of mandatory sentencing law."[86] Mandatory sentencing reflects determinate practices in two respects: first, it takes away case-specific discretion from the trial judge to impose any other sanction; second, it removes the discretion of the parole board to grant release.[87] A common variation on mandatory sentencing involves *mandatory minimums*, or statutes that remove the discretion of the sentencing judge to impose a sanction below the minimum. This is particularly common for five classes of offenders or offenses: "(1) repeat or habitual offending, (2) drunk driving offenses, (3) drug offenses, (4) weapon offenses, (5) sex offenses."[88] In the U.S., mandatory sentencing has often been used to produce "hyper-determinacy" in sentencing structures.[89] In other words, while in theory mandatory sentencing should result in identical sentencing for certain crimes, critics allege that it robs guideline commissions from manipulating sentences to keep up with the changing realities of their jurisdiction. This is particularly problematic in jurisdictions that are faced with the difficulty of managing large rates of drug-related mandatory sentences.[90] Trial judges often oppose mandatory sentencing laws that impose penalties far removed from any sense of justice for the specific case in their courtroom. Nonetheless, mandatory sentencing has been a prominent feature of all U.S. jurisdictions since the 1970s. Reitz concludes that "in the absence of a change in the U.S. politics of law and order, widespread repeal or defanging of such statutes are unlikely events."[91]

Another common variation of mandatory sentencing takes the form of laws targeting habitual offenders by means of harsh sentences for those who have repeatedly committed felonies. In 1980, the U.S. Supreme Court upheld a Texas verdict, which had imposed a life sentence on a man who had fraudulently used a credit card for $80, passed a forged check for $28.36, and then refused to return payment of $120.75 for having inadequately repaired an air conditioning unit.[92] Following this Supreme Court imprimatur, many other states passed similar laws. Between 1993 and 1995, 24 states implemented some form of habitual offender law. Such laws, which were implemented by states in order to introduce "greater determinacy and structure in their systems,"[93] have proven to be quite popular with the general public, and are thus politically very effective. Although Washington was the first state to pass a "three strikes and you're out" law in 1993, California's version in 1994 was much more substantial and influential.[94] According to this law, an offender with a history of at least two criminal convictions could receive a sentence of 25 years to life upon the commission of any felony—even shoplifting. The law, which was approved by California voters in a popular initiative called Proposition 184, received strong support from various correctional officers' associations, the National Rifle Association, and Republican governor Pete Wilson, who wanted to introduce harsher sentences for habitual offenders in response to the rape and murder of a 12-year-old girl, Polly Klaas.

California's original version of the "three strikes" law was atypical (and atypically harsh) in that it did not require a criminal history of violent acts, and the penalty could be applied for the conviction of any felony in the California Penal Code.[95] Other states imposed much narrower versions of the "three strikes" law. In Pennsylvania, the sentencing penalty is only invoked when an offender commits one of eight specific felonies at least three times, two of which must involve the same felony. In this version, a judge may increase an offender's sentence by an additional 25 years. Many other states that have versions of habitual offender laws have adopted similarly narrow criteria for sentencing, using strike-eligible felonies for sentencing only. The Supreme Court has given states carte blanche to determine their own version, as the Court upheld California's draconian law in 2003, in the case of a man who was sentenced to a minimum of 25 years for stealing three golf clubs, because he had prior convictions for burglary and robbery.[96] But in 2012, California voters approved Proposition 36, which limits life sentences to cases where the "third strike" was "serious or violent," while also allowing for the re-sentencing of those people who had been convicted under the previous law.[97] This latest development seems to indicate the potential for popular and political shifts away from the punitiveness of previous decades.

Time-Served Requirements

Another indicator of the movement toward determinacy in American sentencing laws involves the general increase in "time-served" requirements. Also known as Truth-in-Sentencing legislation, these laws "seek to ensure that time served by offenders is primarily determined by the length of the sentence imposed by the sentencing court rather than by the discretionary decision-making of a parole board."[98] In 1994, the federal government offered grants for prison capacity improvement for states that required offenders to serve at least 85 percent of their sentence. While these grants are no longer available, many states still require offenders to serve the large majority of their sentence before becoming eligible for release. For instance, Arizona and Ohio require violent offenders to serve nearly 100 percent of their sentence. While this percentage varies from state to state, as of 2002, 22 states have implemented Truth-in-Sentencing laws that require violent offenders to serve at least 85 percent of their sentence, and no state allows offenders to be released before serving at least 50 percent of their sentence. Overall, there has been a marked increase in the amount of time prisoners are required to serve. As Stemen et al. point out, "In 1975, offenders were required to serve an average of 70 percent of the minimum term imposed before release from prison; by 2002, this had increased to 93 percent."[99]

Drug Laws

In addition to general policy changes involving how criminal sentences are imposed and enforced, a crucial component of the vast increase in American incarceration rates since the 1970s involves the criminalization of drugs to a degree unseen and even unimaginable in Europe. While determinate sentencing and structured sentencing represent largely *procedural* changes, drug-related sentencing laws embody *substantive* changes. On the federal level, legislators repeatedly introduced drug-related mandatory sentencing proposals in the late 1980s. Mauer argues that such legislation was in response to exaggerated media reports regarding drug abuse, particularly concerning crack cocaine, which was portrayed as highly addictive and dangerous.[100] This resulted in the Anti-Drug Abuse Act of 1986, which implemented a 100-1 weight disparity between crack and powder cocaine.[101] Depending on the amount of possession, the mandatory minimum sentencing was set at 10 years (without parole) for amounts exceeding either 50 grams of crack or 5,000 grams of powder cocaine, and five years for possessions of just 5 grams of crack or 500 grams of cocaine.

Mauer suggests that continuing popular fears about drug abuse led Congress and President Reagan to pass and sign the Anti-Drug Abuse Act of 1988, "which contained yet more mandatory sentencing laws among its hundreds of provisions."[102] The Act gave renewed impetus and ambition to the "War on Drugs," as it established the White House Office of National Control Policy, and it declared a national policy of creating "a Drug-Free America" by 1995. Mauer argues that by encouraging the Anti-Drug Abuse Act of 1988, the Reagan administration succeeded in "stoking the ideological fires for tougher crime policy," which was furthered by the subsequent Bush administration.[103]

There were few policy changes over the course of the Bush and Clinton administrations, both of which pursued a "tough on crime" agenda. Meanwhile, the number of people incarcerated in American prisons continued to skyrocket. Mauer reports that from 1985 to 2000 the percentages of inmates sentenced for drug crimes increased by 402 percent in state prisons and 546 percent in federal prisons, which represented 52 percent and 28 percent of the total increase in prisoners.[104]

Perhaps surprisingly, it was during the George W. Bush administration that some pushback began to emerge, sparked initially by Republicans. In 2002, Republican senators Orrin Hatch and Jeff Sessions introduced a bill that proposed to reduce the disparity to a 20-1 ratio. Yet ultimately the Bush White House and Justice Department opposed the bill because of a fear that it would signal a retreat on the War on Drugs, and the bill stalled.[105] The momentum picked up again in the Obama administration, however, as policymakers focused on the vast mandatory sentencing disparities between crack and powder cocaine. In 2010, Congress passed the Fair Sentencing Act. Backed by a bipartisan coalition of Senators Jeff Sessions (R) and Dick Durbin (D), the law has effectively reduced the sentencing disparity to 18-1, while also removing the mandatory minimum sentence for smaller possessions (leaving only the 10-year mandatory sentence for large possessions). While heralded by many as a significant advancement in sentencing reform, some critics point out that the bill's inherent compromise has not eliminated the disparity entirely—indeed, it is still 18 times higher—and thus the reform effort remains incomplete.[106]

Conclusion

This chapter has attempted to demonstrate and characterize the vast disparities in sentencing between the United States and other advanced democracies. The comparative perspective shows that other countries are significantly less punitive than the U.S.—whether measured by the average term of sentence for similar crimes, the extensive use of life without parole and the continued existence of capital punishment as possible sentences, the range of both minimum and maximum sentences for murder, the minimum period prisoners are required to serve for a life sentence, or the minimum amount of time served for other sentences. As Aharonson writes,

> Despite the growing Americanization of political debates over crime problems in various Western democracies, these models of determinate sentencing legislation did not find a market across the Atlantic. The number of offenses liable to mandatory sentences in other Western democracies has remained significantly lower than in the United States. European systems did not adopt "truth in sentencing" laws or similar statutory mechanisms to restrict the early release of prisoners. And no other country has imported the American version of numerical sentencing guidelines.[107]

In sum, the U.S. clearly stands out as the most extreme case within the comparative sentencing picture.

Moreover, what is especially striking about the punitive sentencing structure in the U.S. is that it is a relatively recent phenomenon. Indeed, it is important to recall that at the beginning of the 1970s, the U.S. was not particularly out of line with other comparable democracies. Yet over the ensuing decades, specific policy and judicial decisions—on both the federal and state levels—moved in the direction of determinate, structured, and mandatory sentencing laws, with fewer opportunities for individualized sentencing or "time served" reductions, and based on the newfound priority of criminalizing drugs. As a result of these conscious choices, which other advanced democracies did not pursue, the sentences served by an ever-increasing number of American prisoners lengthened dramatically. This massive and growing disparity in sentencing has been an important component of the larger picture of American punitiveness in comparative perspective. The next set of chapters takes us from the legal process of sentencing to the conditions within prisons.

4

Prison Conditions

PREVIOUS CHAPTERS HAVE shown that different countries vary tremendously in terms of the investigative and prosecutorial procedures they follow, the types of crimes they punish, and the severity of sentences they impose. Yet once defendants are convicted and sentenced, there is often an implicit assumption in the literature on comparative punishment that "prison" means the same thing in different contexts. The fundamental underlying feature of prisons everywhere, of course, is that inmates are deprived of their liberty of movement—albeit to varying degrees—and forced to follow the rules and standards of prison officials. But are prison conditions really equivalent? Is it in fact a similar experience to be locked up in the United States as opposed to Sweden, or in California instead of Minnesota? Although common sense says that the answer must be no, the recent literature has devoted relatively little attention to the conditions under which prisoners in different jurisdictions are confined.

This chapter takes a step in that direction, with the goal of shedding light on how American prison conditions compare to those in other democracies in the world. The analysis reveals that American prisons are significantly more crowded, cramped, unsanitary, unhealthy, inhumane, and violent. The value of this comparative perspective is to show that there are alternative forms of incarceration that work and are successful—both in terms of keeping prisons safe and calm, and for preparing inmates for their eventual reintegration into lawful society upon their release.

The first section focuses specifically on prison conditions in the U.S. It starts by providing a general overview of the situation in American prisons, showing that overcrowding and violence are the two dominant themes. It then briefly reviews the key Supreme Court rulings over the past several decades related to prison conditions in the U.S., covering "failure-to-protect" claims, medical and psychiatric care, conditions of confinement, and the use of force against prisoners. The common, underlying theme in these holdings has been the Court's tremendous *deference* to prison officials, particularly on the grounds of maintaining the security of correctional facilities.[1] All of this leads to a potential turning point, derived from the May 2011 Supreme Court ruling in *Brown v. Plata*, in which Justice Kennedy, writing for a narrow 5-4 majority, described some of the conditions in California prisons that he found shocking. Yet it took over 20 years of ongoing litigation in a major state, where constitutional violations were clearly established by 2001, for relief to be granted. Moreover, the spirited dissents from Justices Scalia and Alito revealed the strong resistance to reforming the current situation, and the high judicial tolerance for tough prison conditions in both federal and state facilities. Although in this case the Court did find that these conditions violated the Eighth Amendment's prohibition of "cruel and unusual punishment," it shows just how extreme the conditions have to be in order to trigger such a finding—and this by the thinnest of margins.

The following section expands beyond the U.S. to develop a comparative perspective on the American situation. It starts by introducing what might be viewed as the opposite extreme from the U.S., namely prison conditions in Scandinavian countries, which are extremely humane and non-punitive. Then it turns to additional countries from Western Europe, with special focus on our three main comparative cases: France, Germany, and the U.K. But rather than address each country separately, the section is organized thematically, looking at such issues as living space, facilities, food, relations between guards and prisoners, contact with the outside world, voting, and health care. Overall, this comparative analysis presents a very different picture of prison life, where inmates do not wear orange jumpsuits and live in constant fear, and where they have rights, opportunities, and rehabilitation. Indeed, from this vantage point, American prisons appear to be some of the harshest and scariest places in the democratic world.[2]

Prisons in the United States

Any assessment of "American prisons" must begin with the recognition that there is really no such thing. There are instead 50 different state systems, each of which includes both local jails (typically for defendants awaiting trial and those sentenced to under a year) and state prisons, along with a broad federal system that runs many types of facilities located in most of the states. Within prisons, there are various levels of security for incarcerated people, ranging from minimum- to medium- to maximum-security (sometimes with even more variation within each of these categories), along with several "supermax" prisons. Many facilities actually combine prisoners who have different security levels, with relatively little segregation by level of security.[3] Moreover, within the same general category of prison—even in the same state—there can be tremendous variation in the living conditions for prisoners, depending on the specific facility's leadership and resources. Prisons and jails are also of all different sizes, and they are located in many different types of geographical settings.

Accepting the important caveat that tremendous variation exists, it is nonetheless possible to generalize about the situation within American prisons.[4] The analysis in this chapter does so by focusing on the "average" conditions in medium- and maximum-security settings. It therefore does not explore in detail the extremes, since neither the minimum-security prisons that tend to house a much smaller number of (generally white-collar) prisoners nor the "supermax" experience of near-complete sensory deprivation can be treated as typical. Yet the reality that emerges from this analysis is that while there may be some circumstances where conditions are relatively harmonious, the overwhelming majority of American facilities remain extremely dehumanizing and unsafe places to live.

The established literature about American prison conditions highlights two primary features: overcrowding and violence. Cavadino and Dignan refer to "a general *crisis of conditions* within the American prison system," whereby 41 percent of facilities are "under court decrees to change conditions of confinement, limit the numbers of inmates or correct their policies or procedures."[5] Yet even in the cases where the prisoners have "won" the court battle, it is then left to the prisons or states to administer the relief, which often never comes. And in most cases brought by inmates, the U.S. courts, led by the Supreme Court, have sided with the prison officials, leaving prisoners to fend for themselves within often dangerous and sometimes horrific conditions. The situation is so dire that the United Nations Committee against Torture has expressed "public concern with regard to the brutal treatment of inmates in some USA penal institutions."[6]

What exactly goes on inside of most American prisons? Practices vary, of course, but most still share the same underlying characteristics. Sharon Dolovich provides a powerful summary of their "key features":

greatly restricted movement; limited media access to the facility; strict limits on visits and communication with family and friends on the outside; minimal access to or control over personal effects; a lack of privacy vis-à-vis staff or other prisoners; limited access to meaningful work, education, or other programming; little if any concern for the self-respect of the incarcerated; an "us" versus "them" dynamic between the incarcerated and custodial staff; and increased reliance on solitary confinement for the purpose of punishment or control.[7]

Dolovich goes on to argue that prisons have created a "self-generating" system that "*produces* the very conduct society claims to abhor, and thereby guarantees a steady supply of offenders whose incarceration the public will continue to demand."[8] And she adds that such a process "operates to create a class of permanently marginalized and degraded noncitizens."[9]

How does this occur? In the extreme cases of "supermax" prisons, inmates are kept in complete isolation and sensory deprivation for 23 hours a day, with very real threats of physical violence by guards, including the use of pepper spray, tasers, or restraints.[10] Within most facilities, at all levels of security, there is now a paucity of drug treatment, education, or training programs, meaning that inmates are even less prepared to function in "normal" society upon their eventual release.[11] Meanwhile, work opportunities within many federal and state prisons are limited. Where they do exist, the demand for them is great, despite wages of approximately $0.12 to $0.40 per hour in federal prisons and roughly $0.13 per hour in many state facilities—which allows for great savings by the prisons, which can avoid hiring outside contractors, while often generating significant profits for the state enterprises that use prison labor.[12] Moreover, the fact that prisons are often (and usually intentionally) located far away from where inmates' families live, combined with strict limits on visiting and extremely expensive options for collect telephone calls,[13] means that most prisoners are bereft of social ties to the outside world.[14] And medical care is extremely poor, aggravated by unhygienic conditions that can lead to diseases such as HIV, hepatitis C, staph, and tuberculosis.[15] All of this creates psychological damage, which Craig Haney calls "prisonization," whereby the overcrowded and miserable conditions create lasting mental anguish and trauma, resulting in people being more angry, tense, and violent than they were before.[16]

In addition to these difficult and traumatic prison conditions, there is also the omnipresent risk and reality of sexual violence and rape. As Dolovich writes,

In many facilities—especially the overcrowded ones—the threat of rape motivates a gendered economy of respect, in which the more masculine one appears, the more respect one gets, and thus the greater one's protection from victimization. Sexual predators, by their predation, prove themselves to be men, and those prisoners who appeal to correctional officers for protection will often be told to "fight or fuck." In such a climate, even those not otherwise prone to violence must be constantly prepared to fight. Those unable to defend themselves can escape their dilemma only by "hooking up" with more powerful prisoners, who will protect them from violent rape by other prisoners in exchange for unlimited sexual access and other "wifely" duties like cooking and cleaning. This last resort, sometimes referred to as "protective pairing," has also perhaps more aptly been described as "sexual slavery." [17]

Although these circumstances do not necessarily characterize all prisons and all prisoners, the reality of prison rape is so horrific that even a conservative Congress in 2003 passed the Prison Rape Elimination Act (PREA).[18] The psychological cost of the constant fear of rape, and the resulting culture of "hypermasculinity" that reigns in prisons, is dehumanizing and devastating.[19]

The Supreme Court's Key Rulings on Prison Conditions (Pre *Plata*)

Before tracing the history of legal rulings with regard to prison conditions, one should acknowledge the distinctively American feature that affords prisoners the *right* to sue the prisons in which they are confined. In cases where courts look favorably upon prisoners' lawsuits, this right provides genuine power and leverage to a class of people who are otherwise entirely powerless. Even though that right was significantly reduced by the passage of the Prison Litigation Reform Act in 1996, there is a strong—and occasionally successful—tradition of prisoner litigation that has directly influenced prison conditions over time.[20] That said, the pattern over the past several decades has been to establish a high standard of deference to prison officials that usually works against prisoners who sue to protest their treatment and conditions.

Although much of the responsibility of implementation has depended on state and federal judges,[21] the Supreme Court has set national standards and practices on most issues related to prison conditions. In the area of First Amendment rights, although there were several earlier cases as well, the crucial case of *Turner v. Safley* established the Court's general approach to the rights of prisoners.[22] In *Turner*, the Court held that when a prison regulation impinges on a prisoner's constitutional rights, the regulation is nonetheless valid as long as it is "reasonably related to legitimate penological interests." More specifically, if prison officials can articulate a "valid, rational connection," the courts will defer to their judgment. The argument supporting this conclusion was that "courts are ill equipped to deal with the increasingly urgent problems of prison administration and reform."[23] In other words, *Turner* established an explicitly deferential standard that treats prison officials as "experts" who should not be second-guessed by the courts.[24]

This approach set an important and lasting precedent that has made it extraordinarily difficult for prisoners to protest their conditions, since prison authorities can justify most conditions based on security grounds. For example, in *Thornburgh v. Abbott*, the Court supported a warden's right to restrict prisoners from receiving certain publications;[25] in *Block v. Rutherford*, pretrial detainees were prohibited from having contact visits;[26] and in *Overton v. Bazzetta*, restrictions on visiting privileges were found to be constitutional because they had a "rational relation to legitimate penological interests [. . .] regardless of whether [prisoners] have a constitutional right of association that has survived incarceration."[27]

The Court has also built a very deferential body of work with regard to four specific areas of Eighth Amendment litigation: (1) "failure to protect," (2) medical and psychiatric care, (3) conditions of confinement, and (4) the use of force against inmates by prison officials.

The crucial case in the related areas of failure to protect and medical and psychiatric care was *Farmer v. Brennan*,[28] but the doctrine originated in *Estelle v. Gamble*,[29] an earlier case in which the Court considered the complaint of a prisoner who was punished for not performing his work duties after he had suffered a serious back injury. In *Estelle*, the inmate was not allowed to sleep in the area assigned by a doctor, could not receive his prescribed medication for four days, and was put into solitary confinement where he suffered from blackouts and chest pains. Despite these facts, the Court denied the challenge and established the category of "deliberate indifference" to a substantial risk of serious harm, which required demonstrating the prison officials acted "with a sufficiently culpable state of mind." In *Farmer*, the Court clarified and applied this standard to a failure-to-protect case, which represented the first time that it had addressed the issue of prison rape. The Court held that a prisoner could not prevail on a claim of Eighth Amendment violation unless he or she could demonstrate that a prison official actually "knows of and disregards an excessive risk to inmate health or safety." In practice, such a ruling creates the near-impossible standard of the prisoner having to *prove* a prison official's actual knowledge and disregarding of a risk of harm, a claim that could simply be dismissed by that official's (self-protecting) statement to the contrary.[30] As a result of *Farmer*, prisoners face extremely high barriers to litigation, even in situations where they have clearly and indisputably been victimized.

The Court has also established its doctrine in cases about the conditions of confinement. In *Rhodes v. Chapman*, the Court set a crucial precedent that enabled future overcrowding of prisons when it held that the double-celling of inmates (even in tiny cells that have living space that is "about the size of a typical door") did not violate the Eighth Amendment, since "the Constitution does not mandate comfortable prisons."[31] According to Justice Powell's majority opinion,

> Conditions of confinement, as constituting the punishment at issue, must not involve the wanton and unnecessary infliction of pain, nor may they be grossly disproportionate to the severity of the crime warranting imprisonment. . . . But conditions that cannot be said to be cruel and unusual under contemporary standards are not unconstitutional. To the extent such conditions are restrictive and even harsh, they are part of the penalty that criminals pay for their offenses against society.[32]

The holding in *Rhodes* was mixed: on the one hand, it established a low bar of "minimal civilized measure of life's necessities" that effectively ruled out many possible claims for living conditions that most people would find unbearable; on the other hand, it kept the door open to future challenges by prisoners to the conditions of their confinement—thus allowing claims related to clean water and air, extreme temperatures, and adequate bedding, clothing, sanitation, and food to be heard.[33] In *Wilson v. Seiter*,[34] the Court went a step further by applying the "deliberate indifference" standard from *Estelle* and *Farmer* to cases about conditions of confinement. Justice Scalia wrote that a "prisoner claiming that the conditions of his confinement violate the Eighth Amendment must show a culpable state of mind on the part of prison officials." This standard—which is by definition almost impossible to prove—has made it extremely difficult for inmates to raise legal challenges to any aspect related to their conditions.

Another area of established prison law involves the use of force against inmates by prison officials. In *Whitley v. Albers*,[35] the Court ruled in favor of prison officials who used deadly force to quell a prison riot. It held that deliberate indifference was too low a standard for evaluating the use of force when exigent circumstances suggested that security was a competing concern. In such situations, correctional officers must make decisions in haste under frightening circumstances, and the appropriate standard in such situations should be whether the officers acted "maliciously and sadistically," thus bringing the standard beyond "intentional" or even "purposeful." In *Hudson v. McMillian*,[36] the Court actually found that prison guards *had* used excessive force with a malicious and sadistic state of mind, but this was primarily because of the "smoking gun" that a supervisor had told the guards "don't have too much fun" before they beat up an inmate. *Hudson* shows just how difficult it can be for a prisoner to demonstrate an unconstitutional use of force by correctional officers, since most cases will not have such a smoking gun, and officers can simply provide a convenient justification that invokes security.

These lines of prison law cases have evolved in parallel with one another, demonstrating the bleak chances of prisoners who protest against the conditions under which they are confined. This futility was further exacerbated by two developments in 1996. In the first, the Court ruled in *Lewis v. Casey* that a class action on behalf of Arizona prisoners who alleged a lack of access to the courts because of their inadequate law library did not prove "actual injury" and therefore had no legal standing.[37] As a result of this ruling that effectively held that prisoners are not guaranteed the right to a law library, many prison libraries reduced their collections.[38] The larger effect—of both this decision itself and the subsequent reduction in library resources—was to limit the ability of inmates to present legal grievances.

The second development of 1996 went even further, as Congress passed the Prison Litigation Reform Act (PLRA), which was intended to reduce the amount of "frivolous" lawsuits filed by prisoners.[39] Proponents of the PLRA argued that lawsuits by and on behalf of prisoners were not serious, took up valuable court time and resources, and resulted in the micromanagement of prisons by the judicial branch.[40] What turned out to be false stories spread about lawsuits by prisoners—who were supposedly complaining about crunchy versus smooth peanut butter and filing grievances about the color of towels provided—were widely exploited in the campaign against the right of prisoners to litigate.[41] Other arguments emphasized that prisoner lawsuits were without merit, wasted taxpayer money, tied up federal courts "to the detriment of more worthy litigation," and undermined the transition to harsher conditions of confinement.[42] This "campaign of misinformation" enabled the passage of the PLRA, which has severely restricted prisoners' access to courts and reduced the powers of federal courts to ameliorate bad prison conditions.[43]

Among its many features, the PLRA specifies that a court "shall not grant or approve any prospective relief unless the court finds that such relief is narrowly drawn, extends no further than necessary to correct the violation of the Federal right, and is the least intrusive means necessary to correct the violation of the Federal right."[44] While these standards might not sound unreasonable, they introduce tremendous subjectivity in a process that is already characterized by high deference to prison officials, thus leaving prisoners with little chance of prevailing. The PLRA also prohibits inmates from recovering for psychological injury while in custody without verifiable accompanying physical harm—a step that essentially downplays the psychological violence and damage that occurs within prisons. In addition, the PLRA sets up an "exhaustion" requirement, forcing prisoners to exhaust all possible administrative remedies—pursuing to completion all inmate grievance and appeal procedures, even though these are usually hopeless—before being able to challenge a condition of their confinement in a federal court. Overall, the PLRA has made it very difficult for prisoners to reach federal court, since the odds of missing a deadline or procedural step are substantial, particularly with the very limited legal resources available to inmates. As demonstrated by Margo Schlanger's important research, since the passage of the PLRA, both the number of challenges filed and the success of those cases have diminished substantially.[45]

On the whole, this section has shown that the legal avenues available to American prisoners who wish to challenge their conditions of confinement are quite limited. This adds to the already grim general picture of prison conditions depicted in the previous section. We now turn to a (potentially) major recent Supreme Court case that seems to have expanded the rights of prisoners in California.

The Window on California Prisons Exposed by *Brown v. Plata*

In a rare victory for prisoners' rights advocates, the Supreme Court ruled on May 23, 2011, that a California court's order to reduce the long-term overcrowding in California prisons from nearly double its design capacity to a maximum of 137.5 percent of capacity within two years was constitutional. Writing for a narrow 5-4 majority, Justice Kennedy—joined by Justices Breyer, Ginsburg, Kagan, and Sotomayor—was particularly struck by the state of California's prisons: "For years the medical and mental health care provided by California's prisons has fallen short of minimum constitutional requirements and has failed to meet prisoners' basic health needs. Needless suffering and death have been the well documented result."[46] Kennedy's more specific observations focused on the overall conditions, the lack of mental health treatment, and the insufficient medical care.

In general terms, Kennedy addressed the pernicious effects of overcrowding, which "has overtaken the limited resources of prison staff; imposed demands well beyond the capacity of medical and mental health facilities; and created unsanitary and unsafe conditions that make progress in the provision of care difficult or impossible to achieve."[47] He was also disturbed by the use of gymnasiums as prison dormitories where cells are already full: "Prisoners are crammed into spaces neither designed nor intended to house inmates. As many as 200 prisoners may live in a gymnasium, monitored by as few as two or three correctional officers."[48]

In terms of mental health, Kennedy wrote that "Prisoners in California with serious mental illness do not receive minimal, adequate care. Because of a shortage of treatment beds, suicidal inmates may be held for prolonged periods in telephone-booth sized cages without toilets. A psychiatric expert reported observing an inmate who had been held in such a cage for nearly 24 hours, standing in a pool of his own urine, unresponsive and nearly catatonic. Prison officials explained they had 'no place to put him.' "[49] Moreover, not only does it take up to 12 months to receive mental health care, but "Mentally ill inmates 'languished for months, or even years, without access to necessary care' and 'suffer from severe hallucinations, [and] they decompensate into catatonic states.' "[50]

Turning to physical illness, Kennedy was also shocked by the "severely deficient care" in California's prisons: "A correctional officer testified that, in one prison, up to 50 sick inmates may be held together in a 12- by 20-foot cage for up to five hours awaiting treatment."[51] He also added that "A prisoner with severe abdominal pain died after a 5-week delay in referral to a specialist; a prisoner with 'constant and extreme' chest pain died after an 8-hour delay in evaluation by a doctor; and a prisoner died of testicular cancer after a 'failure of MDs to work up for cancer in a young man with 17 months of testicular pain.' "[52] He then quoted from the District Court, which found that "it is an uncontested fact that, on average, an inmate in one of California's prisons needlessly dies every six to seven days due to constitutional deficiencies in the [California prisons'] medical delivery system."[53] And finally, he mentioned that "Overcrowding had increased the incidence of infectious disease, and had led to rising prison violence and greater reliance by custodial staff on lockdowns, which 'inhibit the delivery of medical care and increase the staffing necessary for such care.' "[54]

To illustrate the conditions he described, Kennedy also included three photographs, reproduced here, which show the prison conditions that he found so objectionable.[55]

FIGURE 4.1 Mule Creek State Prison (August 2008)

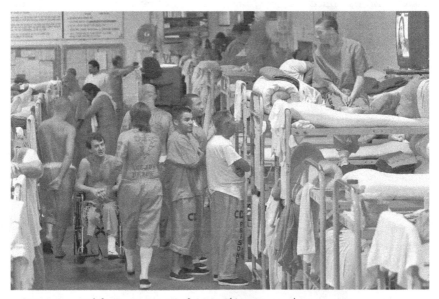

FIGURE 4.2 California Institution for Men (August 2006)

FIGURE 4.3 Salinas Valley State Prison (July 2008), Correctional Treatment Center (dry cages/holding cells for people waiting for mental health crisis bed)

Following this examination of California's prison conditions, Kennedy concluded that since the government has an obligation to provide "food, clothing, and necessary medical care" to its prisoners, "If government fails to fulfill this obligation, the courts have a responsibility to remedy the resulting Eighth Amendment violation."[56] The Court therefore upheld the original three-judge panel's order to reduce overcrowding, thus overcoming the tremendous obstacles of the PLRA in this particular case.

Plata, which one expert called "the biggest and most consequential prison case in almost two decades,"[57] clearly represents a victory for prisoners' rights, and it may herald a change in criminal sentencing strategies.[58] Indeed, the powerful discussion of the Eighth Amendment's emphasis on "dignity" could send a signal to lower courts to be less deferential to prison officials when reviewing cases dealing with prison conditions.[59]

On the other hand, the spirited dissents by the late Justice Scalia (joined by Justice Thomas) and Justice Alito (joined by Chief Justice Roberts) suggest that there may be tremendous resistance to further change in this direction. Scalia argued that the Court was overreaching its scope and authority, while Alito emphasized the public safety risk of releasing prisoners.[60] Neither seemed particularly concerned with the prison conditions themselves. This raises the question of whether there are *any* conceivable prison conditions that the dissenters would find objectionable or actionable.

The fact that a majority of the Court held that California's overcrowding problems had led to mental and physical health problems that were so severe and horrific that they warrant the release of up to 46,000 prisoners can be viewed as an encouraging development for supporters of prisoners' rights. Yet the ruling still sets an extremely high bar for determining that prison conditions violate the Eighth Amendment—and even so, the decision only passed with the thinnest possible majority. This leaves open the question of whether this ruling might encourage future prison reform through the court system, or whether it will be a one-time decision that will have little practical impact beyond this case. And in California, the effect of the mandated reduction in the state prison population has already been counterbalanced somewhat by the state's "realignment" policy, which has transferred many inmates from state prisons to local jails, while also creating a "jail-building boom" under the slogan "local is better."[61]

Overall, conditions in American prisons (and jails) are bleak. Not only do prisoners live in constant danger and fear, but they have few legal avenues to pursue grievances about the conditions to which they are subjected.[62] While the *Plata* ruling offers a ray of hope to those in favor of more humane prison conditions, it is far too early to speak of a sea change. American prisons remain highly punitive, terrifying, and dehumanizing places. The next section incorporates a broader comparative perspective that sheds more light on the situation in the U.S.

A Comparative Perspective on Prison Conditions

Outside of the U.S., most advanced democracies run prisons that provide greater space, privacy, and security, with fewer restrictions on movement, and without forcing inmates to wear demeaning orange jumpsuits or other uniforms. Indeed, in most circumstances the mere fact of being in prison is viewed as the punishment, without needing added discomfort, humiliation, and fear. And the very purpose of prison is to rehabilitate and reintegrate criminals by helping them to develop the maturity, education, and skills that will help them stay away from prisons in the future. Moreover, rather than preventing former prisoners from finding jobs and housing after their release, as is typically the case in the U.S., many countries actually help them to become productive members of society.

That said, the same point made above about the wide variation among "American prisons" applies to carceral institutions all across Europe as well. There is no single standard, and there are many different types of facilities, conditions within them, and rights and opportunities provided to prisoners. And even though the analysis below emphasizes their relative moderation in comparison to the high degree of punitiveness in the U.S., this does not mean that there are no examples of decrepit or inhumane settings, incidents or fear of violence, or abuse of the otherwise considerable rights afforded to prisoners in Europe. And one should always remain skeptical about the articulation of abstract principles that may be very different from the realities in practice. Nonetheless, even while maintaining these important caveats in mind, the analysis below highlights an undeniable and unmistakable difference between the conditions in "average" American and European prisons.

Unusually Humane: The Scandinavian Model

Although the main focus of the comparison in the book is to France, Germany, and the U.K., on the issue of prison conditions, the Scandinavian countries deserve particular attention, since they represent the opposite extreme to the U.S., as they are unusually humane.[63] Indeed, Finland, Norway, and Sweden have very low prison population rates, averaging about 70 per 100,000 people, roughly 10 times fewer per capita than in the U.S. The actual physical prisons are typically much smaller structures, "often with 100 inmates or fewer," which of course makes them much easier to manage.[64] In contrast to the U.S., where prisons are often built in faraway rural areas, so as to break ties between inmates and family/visitors, most prisoners in Scandinavia are sent to facilities that are close to their homes and families. In short, "The Nordic approach to punishment, the setup of their prisons, and the public perception of the purpose of the penal system are fundamentally different than the US."[65] Moreover, "the framework of the Nordic Prison System serves to rehabilitate inmates to directly address recidivism."[66]

Inside Nordic prisons, the conditions are very different from their American counterparts. The starting point is the ethos that the temporary "loss of liberty" is the only punishment.[67] The prisons are all state run, and prisoners "have direct impact into prison governance."[68] There is also a close working relationship between academics and prison officials in terms of what policies best help inmates cope with prison and prepare them for a return to society. In closed prisons, which house about 75 percent of all prisoners, the facilities display clear differences to American prisons:

> What strikes any visitor familiar with Anglo-American prisons is the personal space and relative material comfort of most prisoners. There is no "prison smell" in Scandinavia—the combined aroma of poor personal hygiene, "slopping out" practices, food preparation and cigarette fumes. "Double-bunking" is quite uncommon. Prisoners have televisions in their cells, usually state-provided. Most cells have internal sanitation.[69]

Moreover, the cells and common areas are relatively quiet, and most prisoners either work or receive a full-time education. The food is also "nutritious and generous, with ample servings provided," and inmates have some opportunities for cooking and "self-catering." Even high-security prisons allow for conjugal visits, for which the prisons "provide accommodation where partners and children can stay free of charge for weekends—usually at monthly intervals—with the prisoners on an unsupervised basis." In short, inmates are treated humanely, with opportunities to live, grow, and prepare for their future lives outside of prison.

A striking feature about prisons in Scandinavia is the existence of "open prisons," which house about a quarter of all inmates. These are typically where prisoners who are nearing the end of their sentence will develop "the foundation for inmate rehabilitation; allowing the offenders more freedoms, more relaxed surroundings, fewer security measures, and more programs aimed at societal reintegration."[70] Open prisons have few (and sometimes no) fences or walls, no bars on the windows, and prisoners can sometimes even lock their own doors. "After the prisoners finish work or classes, they are free to walk around the prison grounds and sometimes into local communities." If their sentences are relatively short, they may even be able to continue their prior employment, and some can even drive to and from the prison and their place of work. In Finland, open prisoners can actually receive fair wages, which allows them to pay for food and to support their families or the victims.[71]

The Scandinavian situation is quite exceptional, of course, due in large part to a strong culture of equality that makes the "highly symbolic spectacles of punishment" that characterize other countries unnecessary and inappropriate in the Scandinavian cases.[72] Moreover, the strong welfare state in these countries provides support to the downtrodden and needy, rather than leaving them to fend for themselves. And while inmates are incarcerated, they receive both educational opportunities (including university degrees) and help to "locate and secure jobs within the public sector that will maintain them following their release."[73] As a result, despite crime rates that have followed trends that are similar to those in other European countries,[74] "Scandinavian social and cultural arrangements seem to have insulated these countries from the law and order politics that this generated in Anglo-American societies in particular, and which allowed similar philosophical shifts to be overlaid with more punitive intents."[75]

Thus far the chapter has explored both American and Scandinavian "exceptionalism," which are based on relatively harsh and humane treatment of prisoners, respectively. The following subsection turns to other West European countries and models of prisons and punishment.

Prison Conditions in France, Germany, and the U.K.

Despite the significant cross-national variation in prison conditions—shown so clearly in the contrast between American and Scandinavian prisons—there are few systematic comparative analyses of prison conditions in different countries upon which to draw. Nonetheless, based on the relatively limited information available, it is possible and instructive to explore how the prison conditions in our three main comparative reference points compare to the two models presented above.

It should be pointed out that within each country—and particularly in France and the U.K.—the domestic analysis and debates about prisons can be quite critical of the conditions. And one should therefore be very careful not to exaggerate the quality of life within European prisons. In absolute terms, those conditions can be extremely unpleasant, and even miserable in some cases. Many English and French prisons are located on extremely old (even historic) premises that are run down, and where such basic amenities as heat, plumbing, and hygiene function poorly.[76] Movies such as the award-winning French film *A Prophet* depict violence, organized crime, and abuse of the system's weak spots. And news stories about terrorist events often stress the formative impact of prison experiences on their perpetrators, especially when they are immigrants.[77]

In France, the conditions of certain particularly dilapidated prisons have even resulted in major public debates that led to policy reform. In January 2000, Véronique Vasseur, the head doctor at the main Paris jail "La Santé," launched a firestorm with the publication of a bestselling book. Her account, written in the style of a personal diary detailing her daily observances and experiences, expressed her indignation—which later that year led to her resignation in protest—at the unsanitary, unhealthy, and unsafe conditions throughout the notorious prison that was founded in 1867.[78] Just as striking as the horrific setting that she deplored was the national reaction to her account. The massive publicity and outrage resulted in a national parliamentary inquiry, the closing of some of the prison's most dilapidated housing blocks, and most recently a complete closing from 2015 to 2019 while the entire prison receives an €800 million "modernization."[79] Meanwhile, on the opposite end of France, a 2012 report about "Les Baumettes," a notoriously run-down prison in Marseilles, led to a national debate and measures for renovation and reform.[80] In other words, while the conditions in some French prisons are undoubtedly atrocious, this simple fact resonates with both the public and politicians, who have pushed for reform and improvements—thus contrasting starkly with the American situation.

Overall, when engaging in these Euro-American comparisons, it is important not to treat European prisons—particularly in France and the U.K.—as comfortable and peaceful settings. Prison is still prison, after all. Nonetheless, while being mindful of this important caveat, the analysis that follows shows that when viewed in *relative* terms, the conditions in most prisons in the three European countries—and within advanced democracies in general—are considerably safer, more sanitary, and more humane than those in the U.S. The rest of the section briefly addresses specific categories of prison conditions—covering living space, facilities, food, relations between guards and prisoners, contact with the outside world, voting, and health care—drawing on examples from each of our three main countries (and sometimes a few others).

Living Space

Given their relatively low rates of incarceration, few countries have the same problem of overcrowding that characterizes so many American prisons. Unlike the U.S. since the *Rhodes* decision, most countries do not allow the double-celling of inmates—much less triple-celling or the use of mass dormitories in gymnasiums. For example, many West European countries explicitly maintain a "one prisoner, one cell" policy,[81] although in practice that is not always followed—particularly in France and the U.K. In France, there is actually a long-standing formal guarantee of single-celling in place since 1875, yet in recent years overcrowding has resulted in a 114.5 percent occupancy rate (and the rate is even higher in remand prisons, or jails, reaching a national average of 133.5 percent[82]), meaning that some inmates are double-celled. Even so, the government has repeatedly introduced plans—even if these have been pushed back several times—to fulfill the constitutionally-mandated promise of single-celling.[83] In the U.K., overcrowding has also become a problem, and approximately 25 percent of prisoners there share cells that were originally designed for one person.[84] And Germany does not have an overcrowding problem, as its prisons are actually underpopulated—for reasons explained in the previous chapter on sentencing. None of these countries has anything remotely resembling the large dormitory-style open spaces that characterize some of the extremely overcrowded American prisons.

In short, even though systematic cross-national information on celling practices is not available, and France and the U.K. both struggle with the consequences of prison overcrowding as well, the U.S. stands out with its common practice of grouping as many prisoners as possible into already-crammed spaces.

Facilities

Although practices vary widely across facilities, particularly those housing different types of offenders, other countries do not appear to keep their inmates confined to the same extent as American prisons. In the U.K., over a third of the prisons are open facilities (called "training prisons"), which have no fences or walls, and where the objective is to rehabilitate.[85] Even within closed facilities, many have solid doors instead of metal bars, thus making cells more quiet and comfortable.[86] Prisoners can sometimes even lock their own cells, control the temperature and lights, and furnish and decorate their "rooms" as they wish.[87] In many European countries, inmates have no limits to their personal belongings, provided they fit in the available space.[88] And in most European countries prisoners are not required to wear uniforms, and friends and relatives can bring them clothing (and the facility will provide inmates with standard clothing if they do not have or cannot afford their own clothes).[89]

For example, in Germany, "prisoners are allowed individual expression and a fair amount of control over their daily lives, including the opportunity to wear their own clothes and prepare their own meals; and, in order to instill self-worth, both work and education are required and remunerated."[90] Moreover, "respect for prisoners' privacy is practiced as a matter of human dignity." France abolished prison uniforms in 1983,[91] and it allows prisoners to wear their own clothes, whereas England and Wales since 2013 "require all convicted male prisoners to wear a prison uniform for the first two weeks of their sentence," but then this requirement is removed.[92]

Solitary Confinement

In terms of gross numbers, the U.S. holds more people in solitary confinement than each of the three comparable countries has total prisoners, and the use of solitary—whether in "segregation" units within American state or federal prisons or special "supermax" prisons that consist only of solitary confinement—has been increasing significantly over the past decades. According to a 2014 study by David Cloud for the Vera Institute of Justice, "From 1995 to 2005, the number of people in solitary confinement nationally increased by 40 percent, from 57,591 to 81,622 people, and the most recent estimates suggest at least 84,000 individuals live in conditions of isolation, sensory deprivation, and idleness in U.S. jails and prisons."[93] A 2015 study by the Yale Law School Liman Program and the Association of State Correctional Administrators estimates that "between 80,000 and 100,000 people were in isolation in prisons as of the fall of 2014," and these figures do not include people held in solitary confinement within jails.[94]

As for the conditions within solitary confinement, according to another study by the Vera Institute,

> At the same time, conditions of isolation have become increasingly severe. Evidence shows that holding people in isolation with minimal human contact for days, years, or even decades is exceptionally expensive and in many cases counterproductive. Correctional systems also use segregation to sanction prisoners who have committed relatively minor violations within prison, despite evidence that long-term segregation can create or exacerbate serious mental health problems and antisocial behavior among incarcerated people, have negative outcomes for institutional safety, and increase the risk of recidivism after release.[95]

In short, the U.S. leads the way—in both quantity and "quality"—in applying a practice that the UN and many observers and psychologists have considered torture.[96]

This is not to say that solitary confinement does not exist in European prisons. The key difference, however, is that the practice remains both relatively rare and relatively short in duration. In England and Wales, segregation units do not exist in all prisons, and when they do, they are used "fairly sparingly," usually as punishment for specific disciplinary offenses, and with a maximum of 21 consecutive days.[97] French prisons all have solitary confinement areas, and they are used as a disciplinary tool, for a maximum of 30 days.[98] In

Germany, the practice is very rare, as "German corrections staff are trained to rely on the use of incentives and rewards, with an emphasis on positive reinforcement; disciplinary measures—such as solitary confinement—are used sparingly."[99] Overall, unlike the American regime where solitary confinement remains a widespread and often long-term practice, segregation in European prisons seems to serve the specific purpose of isolating targeted individuals for a short period of time as an incentive to cease their harmful behavior.

Food

Prison food is particularly difficult to compare because all countries tend to exaggerate the nutritional value, quality, and portions of the food they serve. For example, in the U.S. there are official guidelines and policies on nutrition, but they are seldom followed, and most American prisoners express widespread dissatisfaction with mass-produced and tasteless "prison chow."[100] And in some cases extreme cost-saving measures have led to bland and nutritionless meals that sometimes even take the form of the dreaded prison "loaf" that allegedly meets minimum nutritional standards but has a consistency and taste that most find repulsive.[101]

In England and Wales, the regulations require the serving of food that is "wholesome, nutritious, well prepared and served, reasonably varied and sufficient in quantity," but apparently the quality falls short. In fact, a 2006 study on the nutritional content of prison food uncovered that "although prisoners were offered meals that contained recommended quantities of most vitamins and minerals, there were some notable exceptions which could affect prisoners' health."[102] These included high salt content and lower levels of dietary fiber and whole grains.

Similarly, French prisons guarantee multiple hot meals that reach minimal standards of nutrition, balance, and taste. In theory, they "must provide each prisoner with a diversified diet, well cooked and presentable meals, which meet guidelines regarding nutritious need (in terms of quantity and quality) and standards for food hygiene."[103] Moreover, the menu "must take into account a prisoner's age, health, the type of work he does during the day, and, as far as possible, his religious and philosophical beliefs."[104] In reality, of course, the food quality can vary, and the portions can be insufficient for some.

Although it is difficult to accurately measure the distinction between policy and practice in terms of prison food, some clear contrasts can be made. For example, many German prisoners can cook their own meals, and in Spain, prisons even have grocery stores that sell such products as coffee, fresh fruits, and fresh vegetables.[105] Overall, while keeping in mind that it is doubtful that anyone *anywhere* would rave about the high quality of food in prisons, it does seem that the cost-saving logic of American prison budgeting has created a particular pressure that negatively impacts food quality—arguably to a greater extent than in our European comparative cases.

Relations between Guards and Prisoners

It is difficult to generalize about the way in which prison guards treat inmates, since obviously there can be exceptions in all directions within any given prison, much less across a country. Yet it is clear that the training, preparation, and incentives for being prison guards in European systems are very different from the U.S.

Contrary to the picture of American prison dormitories—invoked by Justice Kennedy's ruling in *Plata*—that have two or three guards for 200 inmates, other countries have a more balanced ratio, thus allowing the officers to interact with prisoners more, without feeling outnumbered or threatened. The ratio in Sweden and Ireland is about one guard to one inmate, and in the Netherlands, the guards actually outnumber the prisoners.[106] Moreover, in the "training prisons" in England, correctional officers have a stake in the eventual success of the inmates, as their job performance is measured in part by the rehabilitation of prisoners.[107] Some facilities in France have also "adopted a collaborative model intended to enhance the relationship between inmates and staff."[108] And in Germany, "corrections staff are professionals who undergo extensive training that is more akin to that of social workers and behavior specialists in the U.S."[109]

In general, many European prisons rely on what is sometimes called "dynamic security," which refers to security created by direct interpersonal engagement between staff and prisoners.[110] This is quite different from what might be called the "static security" logic of American prisons, which impose regular lockdowns and other ways to physically separate prisoners from staff and from each other. Altogether, the European model suggests a very different—and far less mutually antagonistic—relationship between prisoners and guards than currently exists in the U.S.

Contact with the Outside World

A distinctive feature of American prisons involves the disconnect between prisoners and the outside world.[111] Other countries, however, are not nearly so restrictive. In many countries, prisoners have unlimited access to telephones, and in some cases phones are even installed within cells.[112] Some countries, including France, do not censor written correspondence, and many countries do not restrict prisoners' reading material (and in Sweden, inmates can check out materials from public libraries).[113] Regular visitation is also permitted and encouraged in many countries, and most allow for direct physical contact during those visits.[114] Spain, like the Scandinavian countries, even allows for private conjugal visits, as does France in some facilities that have special accommodations for couples and families.[115]

Many countries also allow their prisoners to participate in work or education programs that take place outside of the prison walls. France and England both allow some prisoners—particularly those who are close to the end of their terms and will soon be released into society—to work unsupervised, as long as they return by a specified time and follow the rules of the program.[116] The goal of such programs is to facilitate their reentry after the prison term.[117] When they do work, most prisoners have the opportunity to receive standard (albeit usually low) wages—a stark contrast to the pittances that American prisoners receive, which often amounts to a few dollars a week for a full-time job. And most European countries, including France and the U.K., regularly approve inmate requests to visit a sick relative or attend a funeral—often without an escort.[118] And some countries, including the U.K., even allow prisoners to take "vacations" from prison, which often means that they can attend major family events and spend a short time in the outside world before returning to prison.[119] Again, these examples are far removed from the realities of American prisons, where inmates remain extremely isolated and disconnected from their families and the larger society.

Voting

In the U.S., prisoners are banned from voting in all states except Vermont and Maine—in many states they lose their right for long after they have served out their sentences and have been released into society.[120] Within the European context, prisoners' right to vote is mandated by Article 3 of the European Convention on Human Rights, and every EU country except for the U.K. applies this right, either by letting prisoners travel to the polling stations or by bringing the ballots to the prisons.[121] In Germany, since the reform of the Criminal Code in 1969, a person's status as a convicted criminal and prisoner has no bearing on his or her right and ability to vote.[122] France allows prisoners to vote unless they were specifically stripped of this right as a part of their sentence. That said, transportation to a polling station is not provided, which requires a prisoner to "mandate" another person—who must be registered in the same municipality—to vote on his or her behalf, thus adding a layer of complication to the voting process that in practice makes it more difficult to carry out.[123] The U.K., in contrast, seems aligned with its American counterpart, steadfastly defying the European Court of Human Rights by refusing to allow people to vote while they are incarcerated.[124]

On the whole, despite the British exceptionalism within the European context, the distinction between American and European prison voting practices remains clear and glaring.[125]

Health Care

The topic of prison health care is so large that it almost warrants a chapter in its own right. One of the main attributes of the current prison crisis in the U.S.—and certainly the one that most shocked Justice Kennedy in his *Plata* ruling—is the extremely poor health care in prisons. Ironically, while the larger public debate in the U.S. rages about whether citizens can be required to have health insurance, American prisoners constitute the one population to which the state—whether federal, state, or local governments, depending on the jurisdiction of a given prison—*must* provide universal health care. Yet the inadequacy of this care hardly gives prisoners a reason to celebrate their complimentary health services. The reality of prison overcrowding has had significantly detrimental effects on the quality of health care services offered to inmates.[126]

Meanwhile, the costs of prison health care have skyrocketed, as the Government Accountability Office estimates that prison medical costs have been rising at an *annual* rate of 21 percent.[127] It is difficult to determine actual costs and who really pays for prison health care, but in 2001 prison health care was estimated at $3.3 billion, or 12 percent of total prison operating expenses.[128] In a nutshell, while American prisoners have an Eighth Amendment "right" to medical care—which, as explained above, is really only a right against deliberate indifference to serious medical needs, that is, the right not to be intentionally and maliciously tortured—in practice, the care is extremely poor. Whether in terms of mental health, communicable diseases, elderly care, or women's health in female prisons, prisoners receive substandard and often dangerous quality of treatment and care.

This bleak depiction of American prison health care becomes even more disturbing when placed in comparative perspective, since other democratic countries have found solutions to the treatment of inmates that appear to be much more effective and humane.[129] While France, Germany, and the United Kingdom each displays its own national peculiarities, the variations in prison health care services between them are clearly "of degree" and not "of kind." Indeed, these three European countries all guarantee a continuity of health care to prisoners that is roughly comparable to what they would receive in free society, as part of each country's national health care system. Inmates can thus receive regular screenings, assessments, and treatment for various diseases ranging from ordinary illnesses to tuberculosis and HIV, in order to prevent further contamination and the spreading of disease within prisons and beyond them.[130] And the European countries often use community-based approaches to mental health, rather than following the American model of letting the mentally ill deteriorate further within a prison environment.[131] In Germany, therapists can even prescribe treatment including "open or relaxed correctional settings, vacation leaves, release preparations, visitors, correspondence, as well as free-time planning."[132] And in all three countries, prison physicians have more influence in terms of opposing certain types of punishment that would be psychologically harmful to prisoners.[133] Overall, these comparisons provide suggestions and alternatives for the U.S. that—although difficult to implement in the very different American health and prison systems—would greatly benefit the health and safety of both inmates and the communities to which they will eventually return.

Overall, this comparative analysis of prison conditions shows that despite their sometimes decrepit physical state—and the obvious reality that prison is still a harsh environment anywhere—conditions in French, German, and British prisons come much closer to the Scandinavian "humane" model. Indeed, these European countries share the general purpose of using prisons primarily to incapacitate criminals (without adding further punishment, suffering, or humiliation) and to rehabilitate them (and thereby help them to eventually reintegrate into society). This broader comparative perspective highlights the vast and consistent extent of the American anomaly.

Conclusion

The data on prison conditions remains necessarily scattered, as data are compartmentalized within individual facilities that are difficult to access. And there is tremendous variation across individual facilities, much less across countries, thus making it difficult to generalize. Yet a comparative analysis reveals striking cross-national differences. This perspective shows that not only is the U.S. the most punitive country in the world in terms of the numbers of prisoners per capita, but the conditions within those prisons are particularly inhumane and unsafe.

These findings show that when comparing criminal justice policies across countries, one should not assume that the end result of "prison" is the same. Indeed, few prisoners in advanced democracies outside of the U.S. wear uniforms and live in such cramped and violent conditions. Many actually receive education, job training, family visits, mail privileges, and even short vacations. These policies have been imposed by national governments, in close consultation with both scholars and prison officials, with the goal of establishing practices that preserve the rights and dignity of prisoners, while helping to prepare them for a safe and productive return to society.

This is a far cry from the current system that has been implemented in the U.S. over the past four decades, with the stamp of approval not only of "tough on crime" legislators seeking reelection, but also of the Supreme Court. Indeed, despite the important fact that in the U.S. prisoners have the right to sue the prisons that confine them—whereas in France it took a doctor's exposé to reveal deplorable conditions and effect change—the Court has almost always responded with "deference" to prison officials. This deference has essentially given prisons carte blanche to act with impunity and to impose an increasing number of punitive restrictions on inmates—even those that may be physically and psychologically damaging. This, combined with the fact that the American prison population has increased by 372.5 percent from 1971 to 2008 (an increase that was over nine times higher than the modest 40.8 percent increase in European countries in that same time period), has created the combustible situation that led to the remarkable *Plata* ruling, which represented a rare "win" for prisoners.[134]

Although it remains to be seen whether *Plata* will serve as the first major step in reversing the tide and moving toward an increase in compassion for the plight of American prisoners, the attention given to the case has certainly helped to shed light on the horrific conditions in many prisons. As this chapter has shown, those interested in new solutions for American prisons would be well served to look at the models in most other advanced democracies, which maintain prison systems that are not only more humane, but also more efficient and successful in terms of rehabilitation. While it would obviously be unrealistic and naïve to advocate the wholesale importation of these models to the U.S. in a flash, this chapter suggests that other—and better—ways of organizing and running prisons already exist.

5

Rehabilitation

WITHIN THE BROAD field of criminology, there are long-standing tensions and debates about the purpose of punishing crime, the most prominent theories being incapacitation, deterrence, retribution, and rehabilitation. Modern prisons were established with the objective of serving all four functions: to remove individuals who have broken the law and victimized others from the free population (thereby making society safer overall), to dissuade other potential lawbreakers from committing crimes that would likely send them to prison (thereby preventing crime), to punish offenders who have caused suffering in the lives of others (thereby extracting "just deserts"), and to transform people from criminals into law-abiding and productive citizens who can eventually return to society (thereby "correcting" people's criminal defects). Whereas the first two approaches have more to do with the criminal justice system and sentencing policy, the last two involve the organization and purpose of prisons themselves—the subject of this chapter. In essence, should prisons primarily be locations of punishment or rehabilitation?

Until the mid-1970s, rehabilitation was central to the mission of American prisons. This explains the widespread use of the terms "corrections" in American prison parlance and in the institutional name of many modern prisons (while older prisons are often called "penitentiaries," derived from a previous era when prisons were considered a locus of religious penitence). Yet over the course of the subsequent decades—and parallel to the similar developments taking place in the various other realms discussed in previous chapters—the "tough on crime" movement not only put into question, but eventually eliminated any serious systematic attempts to treat prisons as sites of human transformation and improvement. Instead, just as plea bargaining practices and sentencing policies were sending massive numbers of people to increasingly overcrowded prisons, the very purpose of prison shifted overwhelmingly in the direction of punishment, and the principles of rehabilitation and correction became empty slogans of another era.

One of the most important early sparks that ignited the relentless "tough on crime" movement in the 1970s originated in a set of academic findings and analyses that were misappropriated and dragged into the political fray, leading to vastly unintended consequences. The centerpiece of this transformation was a 1974 article published by sociologist Robert Martinson. Based on his analysis of existing research on the connection between rehabilitation programs and recidivism rates, Martinson concluded that few rehabilitation programs were actually effective. Shortly after publishing his results, Martinson was thrust into the limelight, as his findings provided precisely the "scientific" imprimatur that the leaders of the "tough on crime" movement sought to justify their new punitive approach to building prisons and inflicting punishment. And even though numerous critics—including Martinson himself just five years later—refuted Martinson's original research and findings and denounced the policy changes that it helped to spawn, the concept of rehabilitation has never since recovered in the U.S.

This chapter takes a fresh look at the abandonment of rehabilitation in American prisons. As with previous chapters, it begins with a detailed examination of the situation in the U.S., before turning to a comparative perspective. The first major section evaluates the state of research on the possibility of rehabilitation in American prisons. It revisits the arguments and findings of the original Martinson report and its subsequent critics, showing that in reality rehabilitation programs were *not* the failure that they were made out to be. And it argues that the consequences of the "tough on crime" movement's punitive approach have actually reduced public safety and been considerably more expensive than would have been the case under properly administered rehabilitation programs.

The second major section addresses comparative perspectives on rehabilitation, based on the European countries of France, Germany, and the U.K. It shows how the French and German models in particular have maintained and actively supported the rehabilitative ideal and associated programming and opportunities in order to prepare inmates for a productive return to society, whereas the U.K. falls somewhere in between its fellow European neighbors and its fellow Anglo-Saxon former colony. This European belief in the importance of rehabilitation emphasizes not only a utilitarian approach to reducing future crime in society, but also a sense of moral obligation to undertake efforts to improve people—and their chances to succeed when they return to society—as individual human beings. Overall, this comparative perspective provides an alternative model and vision that helps to show that the American abandonment of rehabilitation was neither necessary nor well served.

Finally, the conclusion draws on the evidence from the earlier sections to argue for a renewed appreciation and implementation of rehabilitation programs within prisons—while being cognizant of the difficult economic reality that such programs will cost money in the short term, even if they yield great savings and rewards in the longer term. The chapter thereby attempts to "rehabilitate rehabilitation" by demonstrating the inadequate and mistaken justification for having abandoned it as a goal, while also showing the complete failure of the punitive American model that replaced it. Given recent discussions about the cost-effectiveness of the current use of prisons, the time is ripe for a more nuanced evaluation of "what works" and "what doesn't work" that is devoid of ideological motivations, while seeking to better understand the potential for both rehabilitating inmates and reducing societal costs. And the comparative perspective on rehabilitation suggests the need to move beyond utilitarian arguments by also considering the moral implications of how society treats and helps people who have gone astray but still have hope of becoming productive citizens.

The Decline and Death of Rehabilitation in the United States

This section traces the decline and death of the concept of rehabilitation in American prisons. It starts by synthesizing the key findings of the Martinson report and re-evaluating some of his original evidence. It also considers the main arguments made by critics of the report, many of whom found the original studies Martinson had reviewed to be so methodologically weak that they did not warrant any broader conclusions one way or another, much less a consistently negative interpretation. It then turns to subsequent research on rehabilitation, much of which has demonstrated that certain programs do, in fact, have positive effects. These studies suggest that rehabilitation can indeed work—when applied carefully, to targeted and appropriate populations, with competent and motivated staff, and in the right settings. Finally, the section shows the failure of the American "tough on crime" approach to improve public safety and reduce costs. It presents evidence suggesting that the national recidivism rate has actually risen in recent decades, and it complements the picture of the violent and dehumanizing conditions in American prisons presented in the previous chapter.

The Martinson Report and Its Critics

The story behind the Martinson report is nearly as thorny as its aftermath. Robert Martinson was originally hired in 1967 by Douglas Lipton, the research director of the New York Division of Criminal Justice, to collaborate on a comprehensive review of all 231 studies that measured the effectiveness of criminal rehabilitation programs. Lipton, Martinson, and Judith Wilks co-authored a 1,484-page report in 1970, but—for reasons unknown—the state declined to publish it for several years.[1] During this time, Martinson surreptitiously—without the knowledge of his co-authors, who were not willing to circumvent the state authority that had commissioned the report—proceeded to write and eventually publish a synthesis of the report, with only his name on it, in the Spring 1974 issue of *The Public Interest*. The article, which went on to be known as the "Martinson report" without any recognition of his collaborators, caused a sensation in the field of corrections and criminal justice, contributing to the major policy changes that emerged in the years and decades to come.

The substance of the Martinson report itself was clear and straightforward: "With few and isolated exceptions, the rehabilitative efforts that have been reported so far have had no appreciable effect on recidivism."[2] Based on the 231 studies that he (and his initial collaborators) had reviewed, Martinson went on to debunk hypotheses about the virtues of educational and vocational programs, individual or group counseling, or intensive parole supervision. Martinson did add an important caveat—one that was overlooked or willfully ignored by the "tough on crime" movement that so eagerly hyped up Martinson's findings—stating, "It is just possible that some of our treatment programs *are* working to some extent, but that our research is so bad that it is incapable of telling." Yet Martinson's stark and oft-quoted conclusion was that "I am bound to say that these data, involving over 200 studies and hundreds of thousands of individuals as they do, are the best available and give us very little reason to hope that we have in fact found a sure way of reducing recidivism through rehabilitation."[3] Although Martinson himself embedded his statements in caution and caveats, the conclusion to his article's title—"What Works?"—was commonly quoted and interpreted as "Nothing Works."

To be sure, the ideas articulated in the Martinson report were not altogether new. The 1960s brought about not only general distrust of public institutions but also dissatisfaction with the prevailing indeterminate sentencing structure, which was viewed as unsystematic and haphazard. Moreover, according to Francis Cullen, an attack on rehabilitation "was initiated several years earlier and had far more to do [than the Martinson report alone] with a declining trust in the state to exercise its discretionary powers, especially in the courts and in prisons, in a humane and equitable way."[4] Crime became a highly politicized issue, as conservative politicians promised to restore law and order by increasing punitive policies. Over time, this also led to an undermining of the social welfare aspect of corrections and the accompanying elimination of Pell grants and educational programs for inmates in order to make prison "more painful."[5]

Yet the timing and message of the Martinson report hit a nerve with American politicians and the general public. The repeated occurrence of prison riots in Attica, San Quentin, and other institutions, combined with a rising fear of crime and criminals, catapulted Martinson to national prominence, as he appeared on *60 Minutes* and was quoted in numerous newspaper and magazine accounts. As a result, the impact of the report spun out of control and took on a life of its own.

Although the tenets of the anti-rehabilitation movement were already established, the tremendous publicity surrounding the Martinson report galvanized its supporters, giving new energy—and "scientific" credibility— to the nascent "tough on crime" movement that would transform American criminal justice over the ensuing decades. It was invoked by those who drafted and passed new state laws, including California's Uniform Determinate Sentencing Law—signed in 1976 by Governor Jerry Brown—which became a model for numerous other states, by explicitly claiming that "the purpose of imprisonment is punishment" and removing any mention of rehabilitation.[6] The spirit of the Martinson report also fed into the federal Sentencing Reform Act of 1984, which essentially eliminated federal parole, based on the notion that prisoners could not be rehabilitated. And it provided the intellectual foundation—sometimes explicitly, often implicitly—of many other changes that have contributed to the massive increase in incarcerated Americans, as well as the meager opportunities for prisoners who have served their time.

While the public and political reaction to the report fueled a more punitive approach to corrections, the response from the academic community was much more circumspect. Indeed, scholars have raised many challenges to the accuracy of the report, and they have especially disagreed with the policy conclusions that it spawned. Yet, as James Q. Wilson writes, "While the debate in corrections journals raged, the public view, insofar as one can assess it from editorials, political speeches, and legislative initiatives, was that Martinson was right."[7] Given this major disjuncture—along with the current questioning of the American incarceration model that has been sparked by recent budgetary crises—a review and revisiting of the scholarly literature on rehabilitation is warranted.

In a 2006 book that provides a wide-ranging and synthetic analysis of "what works in corrections," Doris MacKenzie argues that Martinson's main contribution was not to show that nothing worked, but rather that there was little hard evidence to tell what, if anything, was effective. She points out that most of the studies that Martinson examined concerned interventions that lacked "program integrity," which she defines as "a clearly defined rationale [. . .], qualified and trained staff to deliver the program, treatment methods shown to be effective, and a consistent protocol."[8] Moreover, many of the programs that Martinson examined were "so poorly conducted from a research design point of view that it was impossible to tell what the outcomes meant."[9] She adds that "no conclusions about the effect of the programs could be made because the research designs were so poor."[10] In short, MacKenzie shows that "Martinson's conclusion that nothing works was really a critique of the poorly designed studies of inadequately implemented programs."[11]

Looking more closely at the studies Martinson reviewed, we can identify some patterns that suggest that he tended to draw the most negative conclusions possible from each study he evaluated. In some cases, Martinson identified two studies of a certain type of treatment or program that came to different conclusions, and based on this apparent "contradiction" he dismissed the entire approach as being invalidated. For example, Martinson considered the question of whether minimum security institutions were more effective than maximum security prisons. He highlighted that "an American study by Fox (1950) discovered that for 'older youths' who were deemed to be good risks for the future, a minimum security institution produced better results than a maximum security one,"[12] yet he then contrasted it with a British study that found that youths under 16 in the U.K. fared better in facilities in which they were totally confined rather than in less restrictive partial physical custody arrangements. Based on these two seemingly contradictory findings—and without considering that the first one might have still been correct—he reached the conclusion that "In short, we know very little about the recidivism effects of various degrees of security in existing institutions; and our problems in finding out will be compounded by the probability that these effects will vary widely according to the particular *type* of offender that we're dealing with."[13] In other words, based on these two imperfect and problematic studies—one of which did in fact show a strong positive relationship—Martinson's report essentially dismissed the possible benefits of medium security arrangements. Although Martinson's own words were

actually somewhat cautious and not categorical, the subsequent interpretation of his work by the "tough on crime" movement was to include medium
security on the list of "nothing works." And the implications of such a conclusion are vast, as it helped to fuel—or at least to justify or rationalize—greater
punitiveness by using higher levels of security in American prisons.

Similarly, Martinson put into question arguments about probation and
the use of a remand home as an alternative to imprisonment, based on his
analysis that "Two studies from Britain made yet another division of the
offender population, and found yet other variations. One (Great Britain,
1964) found that previous offenders—but not first offenders—did better
with *longer* sentences, while the other (Cambridge, 1952) found the *reverse* to
be true with juveniles."[14] Once again, based on a simple juxtaposition of two
studies, the Martinson report—perhaps unintentionally, or based on an exaggerated (mis)interpretation of his findings—undermined an entire segment
of rehabilitation theory.

In his analysis of other studies, Martinson was often selective or misleading in his portrayal of the findings and the original authors' interpretations.
For example, one study compared the adult arrest records of patients who
had received psychiatric treatment with those who had not, finding that
psychiatric treatment had no effect in reducing recidivism. But the authors
had concluded that this was the case not because therapy never works, but
rather because the particular patients treated at the clinic "represented the
poorest risks for any kind of treatment program."[15] Yet Martinson dropped
the authors' caveat and interpretation and simply characterized the results
as follows: "Adamson (1956), on the other hand, found no significant difference produced by another program of individual therapy."[16] Martinson also
dismissed arguments about the effectiveness of "group therapy" based on a
particular study that was methodologically flawed and included a very small
sample of boys of very different ages, stating that "a study by Craft (1964)
of young males designated 'psychopaths,' comparing 'self-governing' group
psychotherapy with 'authoritarian' individual counseling, found that the
'group therapy' boys afterwards committed *twice* as many new offenses as the
individually treated ones."[17] In short, these examples show that Martinson's
reanalysis was at the very least unbalanced, and perhaps even intentionally
misleading.[18]

After the publication of "What Works?" other scholars raised concerns
about its accuracy. In 1975, Ted Palmer challenged Martinson's results by
reviewing a number of the original studies.[19] He found that up to 48 percent
could actually be classified as reducing recidivism.[20] Palmer was among the first

to argue that certain types of interventions worked in certain situations. More specifically, he found that "a larger number of favorable than unfavorable/ambiguous results were noted in relation to the use of (a) probation rather than prison and (b) small caseloads and intensive supervision. The numbers were about equal in the case of (c) group counseling within residential settings and (d) psychotherapy within the community."[21] More recently, Andrews et al. claimed that "reviews of the literature have routinely found that at least 40 percent of the better controlled evaluations of correctional treatment services reported positive effects."[22] These analyses directly contradicted Martinson's conclusion that it was impossible to tell what, if anything, worked for rehabilitation programs. Instead, Palmer posed the question differently: "Which methods work best for which types of offenders, and under what conditions or in what types of settings?"[23] It was precisely this type of question that the subsequent literature on prison rehabilitation began to address.

Post-Martinson Research on Rehabilitation

Although rehabilitation quickly went out of fashion following the publication of the Martinson report, scholars in the field of criminology continued to create and monitor programs in order to see if they had any effect. Two Canadian psychologists, Paul Gendreau and Robert Ross, questioned the underlying belief of the "nothing works" doctrine. Summing up their findings, they wrote:

> Our reviews of the research literature demonstrated that successful rehabilitation of offenders had been accomplished, and continued to be accomplished quite well.... [R]eductions in recidivism, sometimes as substantial as 80 percent, had been achieved in a considerable number of well-controlled studies. Effective programs were conducted in a variety of community and (to a lesser degree) institutional settings, involving predelinquents, hard-core adolescent offenders, and recidivistic adult offenders, including criminal heroin addicts. The results of these programs were not short-lived; follow-up periods of at least two years were not uncommon, and several studies reported even longer follow-ups.[24]

Given Martinson's pessimistic conclusions about the ineffectiveness of rehabilitation, Gendreau and Ross's finding that some programs had resulted in a decline in recidivism of up to 80 percent was particularly striking.

More specifically, Gendreau and Ross applied a "learning theory" approach that asserted that offenders—like everyone else—acquired attitudes, beliefs, and behaviors. They disagreed that "criminal offenders are incapable of re-learning or of acquiring new behaviors."[25] Their work involved two major research reviews covering the years 1973–1978 and 1981–1987. Their findings led to three major conclusions. First, programs could not be expected to be effective if they lacked integrity. Programs with weak conceptual foundations or those that used untrained staff were more likely to fail. For Gendreau and Ross, the important question was "to what extent do treatment personnel actually adhere to the principles and employ the techniques of the therapy they purport to provide?"[26] Second, they argued that programs that were untargeted to meet specific criminogenic needs were also likely to fail. In this context, criminogenic needs refer to "known predictors of recidivism that are amenable to change (e.g., antisocial attitudes and behaviors)."[27] In contrast, their studies found that behaviorally-oriented programs, such as those with incentive structures, were especially effective. This type of program had been ignored by Martinson's report. Third, they found that the individual nature of offenders required different methods, rather than a "one size fits all" approach—particularly with regard to the level of risk for reoffending. For example, treatment interventions were best suited for high-risk offenders, whereas structured learning programs were more appropriate for offenders with low intellectual abilities.[28]

Such studies fueled a renewed "what works" discussion—this time almost exclusively relegated to academia, as the policy world was no longer interested in considering the possible effectiveness of rehabilitation—and led to a search for the principles of effective intervention. As noted by Gendreau, in order to move beyond Martinson's damning report, it became necessary to ask: "what are the principles that distinguish between effective and ineffective programs?"[29] Four core principles have emerged from the post-Martinson literature. First, interventions should "target the known predictors of crime and recidivism for change."[30] These known predictors can either be static or dynamic.[31] Static predictors refer to the criminal history of the offender and cannot be changed, whereas dynamic predictors—sometimes called criminogenic needs—involve behaviors and values and can be changed. Understanding these two types of predictors is important for identifying potentially effective treatments. If the major predictors are static, then one might assume that interventions are likely to be ineffective. However, research shows that most predictors are actually dynamic. These predictors include "antisocial/procriminal attitudes, values, beliefs and cognitive-emotional states," "procriminal associates and isolation from anti-criminal others," and other antisocial personality traits such as impulsivity and risk taking.[32] Consequently, programs that target these aspects are likely to be more successful.

A second principle is that "the treatment services should be behavioral in nature."[33] In other words, they should be targeted at changing the antisocial attitudes, personalities, and associations of the offenders. Such interventions should "employ the cognitive behavioral and social learning techniques of modeling, graduated practice, role playing, reinforcement, extinction, resource provision, concrete verbal suggestions and cognitive restructuring."[34] These interventions should include positive reinforcement, since negative reinforcement programs—such as those associated with punishment programs—are not likely to be successful. Additionally, treatments are likely to be ineffective if they are "less structured, self-reflective, verbally interactive, and insight-oriented approaches."[35] Cognitive behavioral programs typically have two aims. They first attempt to change the faulty cognitive beliefs of the offender. Then they facilitate learning new cognitive skills. For offenders, faulty cognitive beliefs include attitudes that justify antisocial behaviors. Thus, effective cognitive behavioral programs will help offenders to identify their faulty cognitive beliefs, identify goals, present alternative pro-social beliefs, and help them to implement these new values. Cognitive behavioral programs demand a therapist-patient relationship, either individually or within a group setting that can be prolonged through repeated episodes of positive reinforcement. In the same way that cognitive behavioral programs are successful in reshaping the belief system of the offender and therefore are effective at reducing recidivism rates, educational programs, if designed properly, can be effective. A recent meta-analysis found that "there is sufficient evidence to say that the results from the adult basic education, GED preparation, and post-secondary education programs effectively reduce future offending."[36]

The third principle states that "treatment interventions should be used primarily with higher risk offenders, targeting their criminogenic needs for change."[37] The reason for this is twofold. First, as discussed above, higher-risk offenders, in contrast to Martinson's line of thinking, are actually receptive targets for intervention. Second, lower-risk offenders, unlike hardened criminals, are unlikely to repeat their criminal actions. This finding suggests that having lower-risk offenders undergo intervention treatment is a waste of resources, and it may also inflict unintended consequences, such as exposing them to higher-risk offenders in group settings.[38]

Finally, the fourth principle incorporates "a range of other considerations [that], if addressed, will increase treatment effectiveness."[39] These include a number of program integrity issues, such as training, quality of service, and monitoring and evaluation. It also includes "specific responsivity," or making sure that the type of treatment is appropriate for the learning style of the offender.[40]

In short, the post-Martinson study of rehabilitation has developed principles that point to the effectiveness of behavioral programs that are well targeted and carefully carried out.

Despite these academic developments, the American political winds were blowing in the opposite direction for several decades. The "tough on crime" movement, to which Martinson's report had provided "scientific" legitimacy, produced a series of correctional programs that have placed greater controls on offenders, including longer sentences, intensive and punitive supervision programs, and juvenile boot camps. In contrast to programs based on the principles mentioned above, control-oriented correction programs operate on the perplexing theory that increasing the severity of punishment or extent of supervision will make offenders less likely to commit crimes. Indeed, research has shown that deterrence-oriented interventions are ineffective, and they can even raise recidivism rates.[41] Similarly, intermediate sanctions—a method introduced in the 1980s that uses intensive supervision probation, or "boot camps"—have been ineffective.[42]

Some scholars have called for "evidence-based correctional treatment services" in order to figure out more systematically what works in certain circumstances.[43] According to this approach, most offenders would benefit from discretionary decisions made by thoughtful and responsible corrections officers. Along similar lines, Ann Chih Lin argues that the key variable for prison rehabilitation programs is their "implementation" by prison administrators. In order to be successful, these programs must be implemented in a way that creates "prison environments that encourage prisoners to rehabilitate themselves, and that encourage staff to help the prisoners along."[44] Such environments rarely exist, however, in the current political and prison climate.

As an epilogue to the story of how the impact of the Martinson report spun out of control, it is worth noting that even Martinson himself disagreed with the way in which his article was interpreted and used by the "tough on crime" movement. In 1979, five years after the publication of "What Works?" and in a remarkable concession to his academic critics, Martinson published a follow-up article in the *Hofstra Law Review*, in which he wrote that "contrary to my previous position, some treatment programs do have an appreciable effect on recidivism. Some programs are indeed beneficial;

of equal or greater significance, some programs are harmful."[45] Moreover, he went on to add:

> The most interesting general conclusion is that no treatment program now used in criminal justice is inherently either substantially helpful or harmful. The critical fact seems to be the *conditions* under which the program is delivered. For example, our results indicate that a widely-used program, such as formal education, is detrimental when given to juvenile sentenced offenders in a group home, but is beneficial (decreases reprocessing rates) when given to juveniles in juvenile prisons. Such startling results are found again and again in our study, for treatment programs as diverse as individual psychotherapy, group counseling, intensive supervision, and what we have called "individual/help" (aid, advice, counseling).[46]

Finally, in an extraordinary retraction of the key argument derived from his influential 1974 article, Martinson discussed his earlier oft-quoted conclusion ("with few and isolated exceptions, the rehabilitative efforts that have been reported so far have had no appreciable effect on recidivism") and wrote that

> On the basis of the evidence in our current study, I withdraw this conclusion. I have often said that treatment added to the networks of criminal justice is "impotent," and I withdraw this characterization as well. I protested at the slogan used by the media to sum up what I said—"nothing works." The press has no time for scientific quibbling and got to the heart of the matter better than I did. But for all of that, the conclusion is not correct. More precisely, treatments will be found to be "impotent" under certain conditions, beneficial under others, and detrimental under still others.[47]

Retractions of any kind are rare in the social sciences. But to see such a direct self-correction by the author of a major and widely celebrated public report is truly astonishing.

Yet Martinson's 1979 reversal received little attention in the policy community, and his revised arguments were essentially ignored by the massive anti-rehabilitation movement that his 1974 article had helped to justify. In fact, the impact of the Martinson report had gone far beyond what Martinson had originally intended, and in some ways in the opposite direction, since he had not advocated greater punitiveness. Apparently these developments led

Martinson to depression and despair, as his "life spiraled downward."[48] Five years after the initial publication made him a (perhaps accidental) celebrity, and only several months after publishing the "correction" to his own analysis and a "withdrawal" of his conclusions, Martinson committed suicide by jumping out of a fourteenth-story window.[49]

In the end, merely five years after the initial publication of the Martinson report, its findings had been refuted by multiple critics, including the author himself. Yet by then, the damage was done, and the scientific support for rehabilitation failed to capture the public imagination, while the punitive measures continued to increase over the course of the 1980s, 1990s, and 2000s. Although it is possible that Martinson's report was simply "in the right place at the right time," and that another study would have served the same purpose, it certainly became the touchstone document, and the "nothing works" slogan nicely captured the new movement's views and policies. Meanwhile, public opinion adapted to this new message, as the percentage of Americans who believed that "the primary purpose of prison should be rehabilitation" declined from 73 percent in 1970 to 26 percent in 1995.[50] As the incarceration rates skyrocketed—from about 400,000 in 1975 to 750,000 in 1985 to over 1.5 million in 1995 to nearly 2.3 million by 2005—and prisons increasingly served as overcrowded human warehouses, rehabilitation shifted further and further into the background of prison administration.

Evaluating the Punitive Model in Practice

Given that the primary justification for abandoning prison rehabilitation programs in the 1970s and 1980s was their alleged failure to reduce recidivism, it seems only fair to evaluate the current "tough on crime" model using the same measure. Although recidivism rates remain a tricky and elusive concept that can only be captured by means of a major study with tremendous resources, the U.S. Department of Justice's Bureau of Justice Statistics conducted such an undertaking at three points in time—focusing on prisoners released in 1983, 1994, and 2005—in an attempt to capture the "national" recidivism rate. The first involved an analysis of 108,580 prisoners released from prison in 11 states, the second tracked 272,111 prisoners from 15 states, and the third monitored 404,638 from 30 states. Figure 5.1 below shows the percent who were re-arrested within three years, both on aggregate and broken down into four different types of crimes: violent, property, drug, and public order.

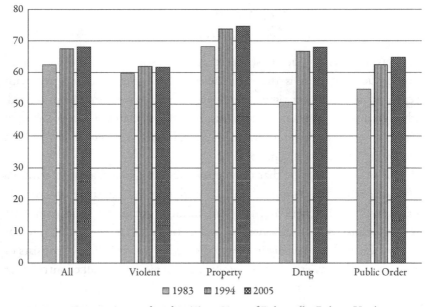

FIGURE 5.1 Percent Arrested within Three Years of Release (by Release Year)

Sources: Langan and Levin 2002; Durose, Cooper, and Snyder 2014 (based on BJS data)

The figure shows that the overall recidivism rate has gone up from 62.5 percent to 67.8 percent, with corresponding increases in each of the four specific categories as well—most notably an increase from 50 to 67.9 percent in drug crimes. One should be cautious in interpreting these results, since unfortunately we do not have an earlier baseline from the early 1970s to compare to, but clearly the level of recidivism has been increasing over the past several decades—even if the rate of increase has tapered off somewhat at an extremely high level. Put differently, at the very least, these data do not in the slightest way lend credence to the argument that the current punitive model has been lowering recidivism rates.[51] In other words, if recidivism rates serve as the measure for evaluating the effectiveness of prison rehabilitation, the current model can be declared a complete failure.[52]

Looking more closely within American prisons, we see that not only have most educational, vocational, training, drug treatment, and mental health programs been terminated, but—as shown in Chapter 4—the conditions themselves are appalling, characterized by overcrowding and violence. Moreover, the medical care in American prisons is abysmal, with disease and illnesses of all kinds running rampant, and the societal health consequences are detrimental and vast.

Keeping Rehabilitation Alive:
The Comparative Perspective

Previous chapters have demonstrated that outside of the U.S., most advanced democracies run prisons that provide adequate space and security, with greater privacy and more rights, and fewer restrictions on movement. Indeed, although there are certainly exceptions, in general, the mere fact of being in prison is viewed as the punishment in and of itself, without needing added discomfort, humiliation, pain, or fear.

This is not to suggest that these countries have found a magic formula to make recidivism disappear, and indeed they all continue to struggle with constant challenges and frequent failures. Although recidivism rates are unfortunately not measured across countries due to vastly different methodologies[53]—especially in terms of whether a new "offense" consists of imprisonment, conviction, arrest, or a technical violation—all countries face challenges with preventing former criminals from returning to a life of crime. Yet, in stark contrast to the U.S., not only has the concept of rehabilitation neither diminished nor died, but in many European countries the objective has actually been reinvigorated in recent years.[54] In fact, the main priority and primary purpose of prison remains to rehabilitate and reintegrate criminals by helping them to develop education and skills that will keep them away from prisons in the future. As a result, most prisons maintain targeted programs and plans for each prisoner's eventual rehabilitation and societal reentry.

This section shows how France, Germany, and the United Kingdom did not follow the American abandonment of rehabilitation. This has occurred on both the national and EU levels. In fact, in the wake of the 2015 and 2016 terrorist attacks in Paris and Nice, one might have expected a surge in punitive actions—longer prison sentences and harsher conditions—against terrorists and potential terrorists (or those who "look like" them). Instead, EU Counter-Terrorism Coordinator Gilles de Kerchove has explicitly argued against such measures, calling instead for rehabilitation measures that serve to "de-radicalize" individuals, rather than imposing long and harsh prison sentences.[55] The following subsections briefly summarize the status of rehabilitation in French, German, and British prisons, respectively.

France

Reintegration has long been the guiding principle of the French criminal justice and prison systems. As with many state functions in France, prison regulations are centralized, under the national Ministry of Justice, which also follows European-level rules and court decisions. According to the latest French law on prisons, from November 2009, the purpose of prisons is to enhance "integration or reintegration of prisoners and the prevention of recidivism, in due respect of the interests of society and the rights of victims."[56]

From the very beginning of a convicted person's sentence, administrators make an effort to help inmates maintain family ties. Other than for a small number of extremely dangerous cases, or prisoners who require specialized care, "the institution must be as close as possible to the place of residence of the prisoner's relatives, in order to help him maintain social bonds and to make social rehabilitation easier."[57] In terms of cultural and professional activities, there is much variation across facilities, as some provide a rich array of programs, while others have only sparse offerings.[58]

An important feature of the French prison system is that each inmate receives an individualized "project of execution of sentence" (PEP), which is an official written document that must "describe every action that the convict promised to do during his detention to help his rehabilitation." The PEP, which is revised annually, is established and agreed upon by both the prison administration and the inmate; it specifies such activities as classes, training, employment, and discussion groups.[59]

Prisoners in France also have the opportunity to leave the prison occasionally. "An authorization to leave the establishment for a few days (usually 3 days, and up to 10, exceptionally) can be delivered to maintain familial links, to prepare to social rehabilitation (to follow some procedures, look for a job, a housing, etc.) or serious circumstances (relative severely ill or passed)." Other circumstances, such as voting, having a job interview, or a medical appointment, can result in a day-long leave. Such opportunities will vary depending on the length of the person's sentence and the percentage of it served, and in some cases they will require supervision by prison staff, but "in general, a leave of several days can be given to the convict when he has gone through half of his/her sentence (two thirds in case of recidivism)." Moreover, "leave of one day can be given without any other condition to convicts with a sentence of less than five years, and after half of the sentence for the others."[60]

In short, the French criminal justice and prison systems continue to view rehabilitation as the main purpose of a prison sentence. Given that very few prisoners actually spend the rest of their lives in prison—because of sentencing and parole policies that are considerably shorter and more forgiving than in the U.S.—prison officials take their rehabilitative functions seriously. French judges also play an important role in the process. Unlike in the U.S., where the trial judge's role effectively ends once the sentence is pronounced and the convicted person is incarcerated, judges in France stay connected to the reintegration plan, consider requests for leniency or shortened sentences based on both good behavior and demonstrated need, and generally work together with the prison authorities to pursue the common goal of preparing convicted criminals for a productive life after they have served their time.[61] Overall, while France still faces numerous problems in terms of prison conditions, available programming and resources, and ultimately recidivism, the commitment to rehabilitation remains firm and the efforts genuine.

Germany

Like France, Germany's prison system focuses on the principles of "resocialization" and "rehabilitation," and this commitment is enshrined in law. This constitutional guarantee provides prisoners with "an economic and social right to state resources directed towards their resocialization."[62] Indeed, Germany's Prison Act states that "the sole aim of incarceration is to enable prisoners to lead a life of social responsibility free of crime upon release, requiring that prison life be as similar as possible to life in the community (sometimes referred to as 'the principle of normalization') and organized in such a way as to facilitate reintegration into society."[63] Whereas the broader goal of protecting society remains, the German Federal Constitutional Court treats that objective as "resolved best by an offender's successful re-integration into society," rather than by long-term incapacitation or subjection to harsh prison conditions.[64]

As discussed in Chapter 3, the result of this German approach is that prison sentences are meted out quite sparingly, and not at all in cases that would lead to a sentence of under six months. And for those who are incarcerated within German prisons, the "conditions of confinement—in particular, treatment and disciplinary approaches—are less punitive and more goal-oriented."[65] This means that everyday life within German prisons is structured in a way to maximize rehabilitation, as the "principal goal of incarceration is to help inmates lead more independent, productive lives in society once released. As a result, life in prison aims to inculcate fundamental skills that offenders will need in the community."[66] Moreover, even the facilities themselves "are designed with features that are conducive to rehabilitation, such as moderate temperatures, lots of windows and light, and wide hallways."[67]

Every inmate in Germany receives an "individual reintegration plan" that is based on a detailed assessment, conducted by prison administrators but with the participation of the inmate, in order to help him or her "create tools and plans for re-entry."[68] This plan involves "specific workplace or training placement with individualized goals and tools for measurement."[69] It is developed at the beginning of a person's sentence, and it is regularly revisited by both parties, thus providing attentive care for each individual inmate. In addition, many prisoners in Germany receive access to "work-day releases," which allow them to attend training or educational courses, and even to "sample" a job on the outside—one that many will continue to hold after their release.[70]

Overall, Germany presents the strongest example of the rehabilitation model in action. With a relatively limited number of prisoners—as a result of much less reliance on incarceration, and shorter terms for those who are sentenced—German prisons do not suffer from the same overcrowding as in other countries. But this also means that the people who are incarcerated have usually committed more serious crimes, which would presumably make them more difficult to rehabilitate. Yet the German commitment to rehabilitation remains steadfast, as judicial and prison officials have the resources and means to devote considerable effort to the eventual transformation of prisoners into citizens.[71]

The United Kingdom

As in several other respects explored in previous chapters, in terms of rehabilitation, the U.K. fits in somewhere in between continental European countries and the U.S. Incarceration rates in British prisons are on the high end for Europe (though still five times lower than in the U.S.), and they have been overcrowded for decades. As a result, whereas the open prisons in the U.K. do provide a model for less punitive conditions where rehabilitation is still practiced, the opportunities in closed British prisons have diminished considerably. As Silvestri writes, "Overcrowding and churn make consistent provision and attempts at rehabilitation and treatment more difficult and often unrealistic."[72]

For example, although in principle efforts should be made to house inmates within close proximity to their families, in reality "there is no requirement that prisoners should be held within a fixed distance of their home and nothing to prevent them being transferred to another prison; in fact, the secretary of state in England and Wales has discretion to hold prisoners 'in any prison.' "[73] As for programming, inmates receive opportunities to "engage in a range of activities during their time in custody, in order to facilitate 'order and control, rehabilitation and resettlement,' " including education, exercise, behavior modification programs, rehabilitation services, and prison industry and other employment. But these opportunities are uneven and often limited.[74] And Genders shows that rehabilitation in British prisons is treated as a means to protect the public, rather than to help individual inmates.[75]

One bright spot is that since 2006, the U.K. has also allowed a charity called Prison Radio Association to create a National Prison Radio channel for inmates, which is "aimed at lowering reoffending rates" and allows for presentation and production by prisoners.[76] According to a Prison Radio Association spokesperson, "Equipping prisoners with skills and confidence is crucial in bringing down reoffending rates. Prison radio offers a unique, innovative and effective way to communicate with prisoners and engage them in education, debate and community."[77] Most important, the prison radio station "also gives convicts something essential to successful rehabilitation: hope."[78] A survey of British prisoners showed that 99 percent of them have heard of National Prison Radio, 76 percent listen to it, and 37 percent do so every day; moreover, 85 percent agree with the statement "National Prison Radio helped me think about making a positive change to my life."[79]

Overall, the concept of rehabilitation has been weakened in the U.K., even if not to the extent of the U.S., where it has almost disappeared entirely. There are certainly bright patches where rehabilitation lives on—such as in open prisons, particular facilities that have more programming resources available, or with the National Prison Radio project—but overall the cumulative effect of both constant overcrowding and high recidivism has taken its toll on the rehabilitative ideal.

Conclusion

One of the main arguments against prison rehabilitation programs is that they are expensive to run and maintain. And this may be true—at least in the short term. Whether situated in the U.S., France, Germany, the U.K., or just about anywhere else, a prison administrator today will find it nearly impossible to come up with funds in an already-tight budget to add educational, professional training, or drug treatment programs.

Given the trajectory of rehabilitation in the U.S., any appeals to national, state, or local legislative bodies for extra funding for prison rehabilitation programs will almost certainly be dismissed or even ridiculed. Yet the short-term costs of annual budgets should also be put into the larger context of the long-term costs of recidivism and future incarcerations, as well as the continued perpetuation of crime on society with recidivism rates nearing 70 percent. Since 95 percent of prisoners "will eventually be released and will return to communities,"[80] might it not be more sensible and efficient to implement programs that are shown to be effective in reducing recidivism and crime, even if they cost more in the shorter term?

This question brings us back to the academic research on rehabilitation. If political leaders are genuinely concerned with reducing crime, improving public safety, and bringing down costs, they would be well-served by leaving behind the facile "nothing works" approach and instead re-engaging with the now-vast literature on the effectiveness of rehabilitation programs, as well as the experience and practices of other countries—particularly France and Germany. This would lead to a prioritization of prison programs that are (1) based on strong conceptual foundations and run by competent and trained staff; (2) behaviorally oriented, usually making use of incentive structures to motivate participants; and (3) targeted to specific categories of offenders who can benefit from certain types of programs.[81]

It might be too ambitious to expect a complete transformation of the punitive American model of the past several decades. But, at the very least, the evidence presented above and the continuation of rehabilitation in other countries should call for the incorporation of certain state-funded pilot programs in existing prisons, with the goal of expanding them if they continue to be effective. Any justification of these programs will need to include reminders of the high costs of crime and recidivism on society, which go well beyond the already staggering $80 billion annual cost of the prison industry itself. But if the programs are indeed effective in bringing down recidivism, there will be a reduced need for prisons, thus lowering the economic costs of prisons. And, in turn, perhaps prison overcrowding could thus be alleviated somewhat, which would thereby reduce the violence and mental health problems that result from the cramped and decrepit conditions that characterize so many American prisons.

The lessons learned from the French and German models raise another dimension that goes beyond treating prison reform as utilitarian cost-benefit calculations. It will entail a larger societal rethinking about the morality of how the downtrodden in American society should be supported and treated. Should they be left to rot in prison cells, forgotten by the communities around them, or should they be given a second chance—or, for many, a first real chance—to become skilled, responsible, and productive members of society? Are prisons a final resting place, or can they be a location for penitence and renewal? These are major questions that get at the heart of American identity and belonging, but they still lie far outside of the mainstream political conversation. Restoring rehabilitation as a central objective of criminal punishment involves taking political risks, but the reward could be a more humane society that supports people who once committed serious mistakes but have since shown the willingness and ability to choose a new path.

6

Parole

THE ATTENTION THUS far in the book has focused mainly on the widening of the front "entrance" gates to prison. This chapter now turns to the simultaneous—but less well known—narrowing of the back "exit" doors. Indeed, while the numbers of American prisoners has skyrocketed, the corresponding rates of those released on parole has been quietly but steadily decreasing. Figure 6.1 reproduces a chart from the Introduction, showing the total American correctional population from 1981 to 2006, and indicating corresponding numbers of people on probation, in prison, and out on parole—each of which extends from zero on the chart. The figure shows sizable increases for all three forms of supervision, most notably an approximately fourfold increase in probation and prison sentences. A closer look at the parole line, however, shows that while the parole population increased from about 250,000 to 600,000 over this 25-year period, almost all of that increase occurred before 1990, and the line has actually remained relatively flat since the early 1990s. This disjuncture took place despite the fact that probation and prison rates continued on their earlier trajectory, which should have, in theory, led to more parole-eligible prisoners over time. In other words, something different happened with parole, and in fact the lack of a major increase in parolees has directly—and by definition—contributed to the continued rising levels of prisoners.

In particular, the granting of *discretionary* parole, which was once widespread and routine, has diminished considerably. Many states have eliminated discretionary parole altogether. Where it still exists, parole boards now routinely deny applicants, even after they have served their minimum sentence, and even if they have had "good behavior" within prison. And some states are reducing the frequency with which inmates can even apply for parole, thus further reducing their chances of getting out. Meanwhile, "compassionate release" of prisoners at the very end of their lives is extremely rare, even

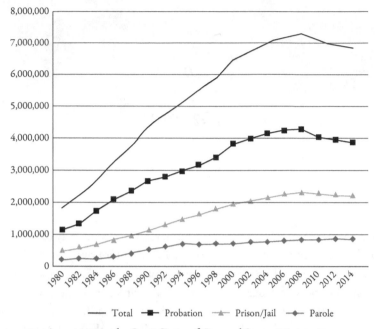

FIGURE 6.1 Americans under Some Form of Carceral Supervision, 1980–2014
Source: Bureau of Justice Statistics (BJS)

when there is clearly no risk to public safety.[1] Much of this "back end" reform has been occurring methodically, state by state, with little fanfare or focused attention on the overall pattern and cumulative effect.

This chapter explores the changing nature of American parole in comparative perspective. The first major section focuses on the United States, showing in particular the harsh turn that took place in the 1970s, and providing some of the institutional, political, and cultural reasons for it. The second major section considers the comparative models from our three European cases, and it demonstrates the extent of American exceptionalism in terms of parole, since France, Germany, and the U.K. continue to enforce regular, generous, and humane policies on early release and parole. Finally, the conclusion speculates about the possibility for changing the punitive political climate that has led to the current impasse on parole in the U.S.

The Gradual Disappearance
of Discretionary Parole in America

The section describes and explains the trajectory of American parole policies and practices, whereby—over the span of just several decades—discretionary release evolved from being an everyday occurrence to a relatively rare event. It starts by reviewing how parole has evolved historically within the U.S. It then traces the empirical developments in the granting of parole, leading to the crucial distinction between mandatory and discretionary parole, and showing the virtual disappearance of the latter, especially in states where the process is politicized. The chapter goes on to develop a multifaceted argument that attempts to account for this de facto end of discretionary parole. The argument emphasizes a combination of factors such as revisions to sentencing policies, the elimination of parole boards, and the fear that most elected officials have of being labeled "soft on crime," as well as the indirect effects of prison conditions on inmates.

The Origins and Early History of Parole in the United States

The world's first known parole system was developed in 1840 by Captain Alexander Maconochie while running the English penal colony at Norfolk Island, close to Australia. Labeled a visionary by some, he developed a system intended to provide prisoners with an element of positive conditioning.[2] Maconochie's method of parole was implemented at Norfolk Island, and eventually his system spread throughout Europe.[3]

By 1865, Americans involved in penal reform were "well aware" of the parole reforms occurring in Europe, and they were particularly impressed by the joint methods of indeterminate sentencing and the "mark system" for determining an inmate's classification for release.[4] The first American parole system was implemented in 1876 by Zebulon Brockway, a Michigan penologist, who proposed a two-pronged strategy: indeterminate sentencing coupled with parole supervision. Upon being appointed superintendent of the Elmira Reformatory for youths in New York, Brockway was able to put these ideas into practice. As Joan Petersilia explains, Brockway's ideas "reflected the tenor of the times: the beliefs that criminals could be reformed and that every prisoner's treatment should be individualized."[5]

Brockway's indeterminate sentencing and parole supervision spread rapidly across the U.S. New York led the way in 1907, as it "became the first state to formally adopt all of the components of a parole system: indeterminate sentences, a system for granting release, postrelease supervision, and specific criteria for parole revocation."[6] At the federal level, parole legislation applying to inmates in all three federal penitentiaries was enacted in 1910.[7] By 1927, all but three states (Florida, Mississippi, and Virginia) had implemented a comparable parole system, "and by 1942, all states and the federal government had such systems."[8]

According to Petersilia's overview and synthesis, as parole systems continued to gain legitimacy into the mid-1900s, the practice of granting parole
became widespread and routine. Over time, parole was not simply being used
to support particularly promising prisoners, but it had become "a standard
mode of release from prison, routinely considered upon completion of a
minimum term of confinement." Whereas in its early stages, parole had been
viewed as a "practical alternative to executive clemency," it eventually morphed
into a "mechanism for controlling prison growth." Nonetheless, it retained
a rehabilitative core, which incorporated promises of "help, assistances and
surveillance." This "rehabilitation ideal," which was widely influential up until
the late 1960s, promoted the belief that the purpose of incarceration was not
punishment, but rather to change criminal behavior.[9]

Support for rehabilitation began to erode quite quickly by the 1970s,
and demands for reforms in parole became increasingly prevalent. Petersilia
identifies three major criticisms of the U.S. parole system that emerged at this
time. First, many people believed that there was little scientific evidence that
parole release and supervision actually had an appreciable impact on recidivism.[10] Second, many argued that parole and indeterminate sentencing were
unjust and inhumane, particularly since prisoners were often "unwilling participants" and were left in a constant state of uncertainty regarding their eventual release. Third, indeterminate sentencing and parole systems rendered too
much "uncontrolled discretion" to prison authorities—who were not subject
to outside scrutiny—resulting in release decisions that appeared to be inconsistent and discriminatory.[11] In short, by the end of the 1970s, analysts on
both ends of the political spectrum were calling for major reforms to the rehabilitation ideal and the parole system in practice.

The next section moves from historical developments to empirical reality,
and it seeks to trace the frequency with which parole has been granted over
the past four decades. This will then set the stage for an analysis of how and
why the use of discretionary parole has diminished so sharply since the 1970s.

Empirical Changes in the Use of Parole since the 1970s

Tracking empirical changes in the use of parole is no easy task. Analysts must
distinguish and differentiate between several different types of parole, and
there is wide variation in definitions, measures, and statistical reporting across
states and the federal government. This section presents several different ways
of conceptualizing and measuring parole, starting with simple aggregate clas-
sifications that provide a useful but limited picture of the changes in parole

over time, and then moving to the crucial distinction between mandatory and discretionary parole. The undeniable empirical reality that emerges from this section is that while mandatory parole for prisoners sentenced to a fixed range of terms has increased, the use of discretionary parole has plummeted over the past four decades, to the point that it barely even exists in any meaningful form today.

Aggregate Measures of Parole

At the highest level of generality, one can tally the total number of people who are out on parole at a given time. Figure 6.2 presents the number of Americans on parole at the end of each year, from 1980 to 2014. Although the figure shows that the number of parolees has steadily gone up (at least until around 2010), these statistics provide only a limited account of the parole story.

Rather than tabulate the total number of people out on parole at a given time, another way of measuring changes in parole is to compare the total number of new admissions to the total number of releases from federal and state prisons. Over the course of the past four decades, both numbers have increased dramatically, with a slight but steady gap in favor of admissions, which obviously explains why the overall numbers of prisoners has increased

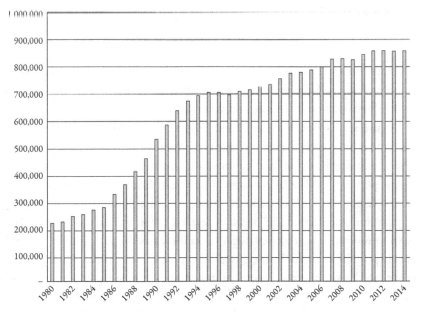

FIGURE 6.2 Adults on Parole, 1980–2014
Source: Bureau of Justice Statistics (BJS)

Table 6.1 Number of Sentenced Prisoners Admitted to and Released
from State and Federal Jurisdiction, 2000–2008

Year	Admissions			Releases		
	Total	Federal	State	Total	Federal	State
2000	625,219	43,732	581,487	604,858	32,259	569,599
2001	638,978	45,140	593,838	628,626	38,370	590,256
2002	661,712	48,144	613,568	630,176	42,339	587,837
2003	686,437	52,288	634,149	656,384	44,199	612,185
2004	699,812	52,982	646,830	672,202	46,624	625,578
2005	733,009	56,057	676,952	701,632	48,323	653,309
2006	749,798	57,495	692,303	713,473	47,920	665,553
2007	742,875	53,618	689,257	721,161	48,764	672,397
2008	739,132	53,662	685,470	735,454	52,348	683,106
Average annual change, 2000–2007	2.5%	3.0%	2.5%	2.5%	4.7%	2.4%
Percent change, 2007–2008	−0.5	0.1	−0.5	2.0	7.3	1.6

Note: Totals based on prisoners with a sentence of more than 1 year. Totals exclude transfers, escapes, and AWOLS

Source: Sabol et al. 2009, p. 3 (based on BJS data)

over that time period. By 2008, as shown on Table 6.1, the figures had nearly converged at the federal level, and the gap was essentially closed at the state level (albeit with considerable variation across states).[12]

Figure 6.3 provides yet another perspective on the same general finding, by focusing more closely on the contrast between the number of people incarcerated (including both jails and prisons, on the state and federal levels) and the parole population. The figure shows that while during the 1980s the number of people paroled increased roughly along a similar slope to the overall prison population, the increase in parolees leveled off in the 1990s. Indeed, from 1980 to 1990 the incarcerated population increased by 128 percent, while the parole population actually increased by 141 percent. In the following decade, however, the incarcerated population continued its steep increase, whereas the parole population leveled off. For example, from 1993 to 2000, the prison population in the U.S. went up by 42 percent while the parole population stayed relatively flat at 8 percent growth. In other words, after a decade of roughly parallel growth between the incarcerated and parole populations, the

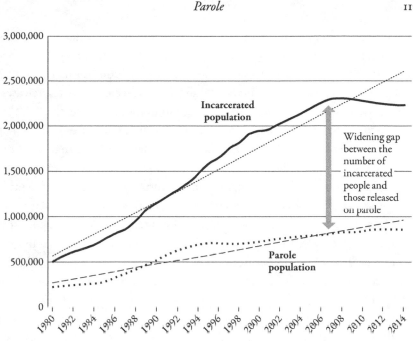

FIGURE 6.3 Incarcerated and Parole Populations, 1980–2014
Source: Bureau of Justice Statistics (BJS)

rates of growth—represented by the thin dotted trendlines on Figure 6.3—
have increasingly diverged, creating a widening gap between the number of
people incarcerated and those released on parole.[13]

While useful for providing a large-scale overview, such general statistics
tell us little about what specific changes have taken place in the realm of
parole, much less why they have occurred. In order to better understand the
empirics of parole, we need to break it down into subcategories that capture
the quite different circumstances under which people can be released.

The Crucial Distinction between Discretionary and Mandatory Parole

Analysts who focus on the distinctions between types of parole typically
begin with the larger concept of "method of release from prison," which can
include several different categories: (1) *discretionary parole*—which is typically what most people view as parole—takes place based on a decision made
by a parole board, pending approval by the governor, that reviews a prisoner's application for release after that inmate has served the minimum time
of sentence; (2) *mandatory parole*, which involves the automatic release of
a prisoner—conditional to certain parole requirements—who has served a

determinate sentence (minus any credit for "good time," which some states still offer); (3) *expiration of sentence*, which occurs when an inmate has served the full maximum sentence and must be released unconditionally, without any parole or reporting requirements; and (4) "other conditional releases," which is a residual category for pardons, commutations, and deaths.

Historically, discretionary parole was the norm, as all states and the federal government followed the "reformatory" model of prisons that sought to rehabilitate criminals and to use the parole process as both motivation for reform and a means of evaluating the person's future ability to function safely and productively in society. In recent decades, however, discretionary parole has fallen out of fashion, as prisons have explicitly shifted their function from rehabilitation to warehousing and punishment. Figure 6.4 shows that in 1977, over 72 percent of prison releases were through discretionary parole. Yet this number dropped precipitously over the ensuing years and decades, reaching a low of 19 percent in 2010. At the same time, the percentage of releases from mandatory parole, unconditional release (expiration of sentence), and other conditional releases have increased steadily, as discretionary releases have become increasingly rare.

Once the standard means for considering whether to release inmates from prison, discretionary parole has decreased dramatically over a short time period of several decades, to the point that it is now an unlikely outcome. What accounts for this striking change?

Explaining the Decline of Discretionary Parole

Numerous factors have influenced the decline of discretionary parole in the U.S. Collectively, these institutional features and the changing political climate help to present a more complete picture that allows us to understand why, in the span of just a few decades, discretionary parole in the U.S. went from being the norm to the exception.

Changes in Sentencing Laws

One of the original sparks for the decline in discretionary parole occurred when states moved from indeterminate to determinate sentencing schemes. As in many other areas, nationwide state-by-state changes in sentencing began in California.[14] In 1976, the California legislature passed the Uniform Determinate Sentencing Law, and then-governor Jerry Brown (who once again became governor in 2011) eagerly signed it into law. The objective was to do away with an indeterminate sentencing structure—with such vague

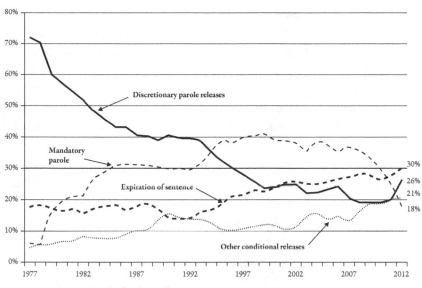

FIGURE 6.4 Method of Release from U.S. State Prisons, 1977–2012

Source: Petersilia and Threatt 2017

Note: This figure updates a figure from Petersilia 2003, p. 59 (with updated BJS data)

and wide-ranging sentences as "five years to life" for burglary—that had been roundly criticized by both the Left (who viewed it as racially and socioeconomically discriminatory, since white prisoners were paroled more readily than black inmates) and the Right (who claimed that it was too lenient and "soft on crime" by granting so much power to judges and parole boards). Under the new determinate sentencing law, prison terms were firm—and generally much higher than before—based on sentencing guidelines established by the legislature. Soon after California made its shift, many other states instituted similar determinate sentencing laws, most of which were in line with the tough-on-crime attitude of the early Reagan era. As a result of these new mandated sentences, judges found themselves with considerably less discretion to provide options for early parole, and the courts lost the ability to recommend or enforce timely parole hearings.[15]

Alongside this change in sentencing structure, many states also established other types of sentencing policies. Mandatory minimum sentences emerged in response to the perception that the low end of an indeterminate sentence was far too lenient—particularly when overcrowding would sometimes compel prisons to release large numbers of inmates who might otherwise have stayed longer—and mandatory minimums required prisoners to serve a much higher amount before being eligible for any type of release. Moreover, "truth in sentencing" laws restricted inmates' eligibility for parole or good-time credits by requiring them to serve a major portion—usually 85 percent—of their sentence. These guidelines were created in response to federal pressure and incentives from the 1994 Crime Act, whereby, "in response to prison crowding and public dismay with the early release of prisoners, the U.S. Congress authorized incentive grants to build or expand correctional facilities through the Violent Offender Incarceration and Truth-in-Sentencing Incentive Grants Program."[16] As a result, by 1999, 28 states and the District of Columbia had adopted sentencing guidelines that force violent prisoners to serve no less than 85 percent of their sentences, three had an even more draconian 100 percent minimum requirement, four had a 50 percent requirement, and six others included other requirements in between.[17]

Over several decades, the U.S. Supreme Court has not impeded the decisions by states and the federal government to restrict inmates' right to parole—usually based on the notion that correctional professionals are more qualified than courts and judges to determine prison "security," rules, and punishments. Moreover, in a 2011 ruling, the Court specifically prohibited federal courts from granting habeas relief to a state prisoner by overturning a state parole board decision. In its per curium opinion, the Court held that "There is no right under the Federal Constitution to be conditionally released before the expiration of a valid sentence, and the States are under no duty to offer parole to their prisoners."[18] This decision has helped to continue to legitimize determinate and lengthy sentencing laws.

As a direct and intentional by-product of the more strict sentencing laws that emerged over the course of the 1970s, 1980s, and 1990s, convicted criminals have been serving more time in prisons. According to a Department of Justice report, the mean time served increased significantly from 1990 to 1999 across all categories of criminals—whether first-time offenses, murders, violent or sex crimes, drug offenses, property crimes, or public order offenses.[19] And these longer sentences led to a corresponding lengthening of the time served before parole releases occurred as well. Moreover, the study found that "inmates released by parole boards served longer than those released by mandatory parole."[20] In other words, the changes in sentencing laws that occurred over several decades in most states have had a direct and negative impact on the granting of discretionary parole.[21]

The Abolition of Parole Boards

As a continuation of the trend set by California with its move away from indeterminate sentencing, many other states went even further by abolishing discretionary parole altogether. By 2001, 16 states—Arizona, California, Delaware, Florida, Illinois, Indiana, Kansas, Maine, Minnesota, Mississippi, North Carolina, Ohio, Oregon, Virginia, Washington, and Wisconsin—had completely eliminated all possibility of discretionary release, and four more states—Alaska, Louisiana, New York, and Tennessee—had ended it for "certain violent offenses or other crimes against a person."[22] In these states, mandatory parole became the only realistic option for release from prison.

Largely as a result of these changes, 16 states saw their total parole populations plummet in the 1990s—Mississippi's fell by 52 percent, North Carolina's by 68 percent, and Washington's by 98 percent. On the other side, over half of all paroles (including both discretionary and mandatory) came from California, New York, Pennsylvania, and Texas, and these four states accounted for 64 percent of the parole growth that occurred between 1990 and 2000.[23]

On the federal level, when Congress passed the Comprehensive Crime Control Act of 1984, it eliminated parole for all offenses, effective after November 1987. As a result, prisoners sentenced after 1987 have no possibility of receiving discretionary parole in their lifetime. The U.S. Parole Commission still exists for the purpose of considering parole eligibility for inmates sentenced prior to 1987 (and for District of Columbia inmates sentenced prior to 2000, when the District of Columbia Board of Parole was eliminated), but the numbers are obviously dwindling.[24] For example, the number of federal hearings declined from 947 in 2004 to 858 in 2005 to 785 in 2006.[25] Eventually, as the existing prisoner population continues to age and die out, these numbers will decline to zero.

Increased Time between Parole Applications/Hearings

Another major reason for the decline in discretionary parole has to do with the frequency with which inmates are allowed to apply for it.[26] In the past, parole-eligible inmates could apply annually, or at least relatively frequently, but more recently there have been moves to lengthen—sometimes significantly—the "set off," or amount of time that passes in between parole applications. Once again, California has been leading the charge. In November 2008 the voters of California passed Proposition 9, the Victim's Bill of Rights Act of 2008, commonly known as "Marsy's Law." In addition to having an impact on the role of victims in the parole process,

> Marsy's Law changed the default time for the date of the next parole hearing from a single year to fifteen years. It changed the amount

of time that could be set between parole hearings from 1–5 years to 3–15 years. It altered the standard for deciding when to set the next hearing, shifting the burden from the state on justifying why the inmate continued to be a threat to public safety necessitating a longer time before the next hearing, to the inmate in showing the nonexistence of reasons why he or she continues to be a threat to public safety. It also gave the board less discretion in setting parole hearings, only allowing parole hearings to be initially set at either 3, 7, 10, or 15 years.[27]

The breadth of these changes is large scale and sweeping, from an already quite strict starting point.

Although it has only been in existence for several years, Marsy's Law has already had a clear and noticeable impact on parole proceedings in California. Whereas before Marsy's Law, about half of parole denials were set for renewed consideration in two years or less, and 70 percent of them were set at three years or less,[28] in 2009, 63 percent (4,229 of 6,760) of denials set new hearings for five years later. In short, "the passage of Marsy's Law has nearly doubled the amount of time set between parole hearings (from about 2.5 years to about 5 years), and is a highly significant determinate of the length set between parole hearings."[29]

It remains to be seen if other states will follow California's model. Oregon seems to be doing so, as the legislature passed a bill in 2009 that reduces the frequency with which prisoners can apply for parole from every 2 years to every 10 years.[30] If past practice on other issues related to sentencing and parole is a guide, other states may well begin to lengthen the set off in between their parole applications as well, which would further reduce the level of discretionary parole that gets granted.

The Toxic Politics of Parole for Elected Officials

While it is impossible to distinguish institutional changes from politics— since by definition those very institutional reforms were set by political officials—an underlying dimension to the striking decline in American parole is its political dynamic. Simply put, political officials are terrified of being blamed for the potential criminal "relapse" of an inmate who was released on their watch.

Since 1988, most elected officials live and work under the long shadow of George H.W. Bush's infamous "Willie Horton" advertisement, which helped secure Bush's victory over Michael Dukakis in the 1988 presidential election. The ad—nominally produced by an independent organization called

"Americans for Bush" but clearly created by top Bush campaign strategists[31]—essentially blamed Dukakis for the crimes committed by Horton, who had been authorized to leave prison for a weekend as part of a furlough program that used to exist in Dukakis's home state of Massachusetts. The ad was misleading and false in numerous respects,[32] but it was extraordinarily effective, helping to shape the outcome of a presidential race and transforming the political climate on race and crime throughout the country.[33]

As a result of the undeniable power of that ad, most politicians, prosecutors, and elected judges have become afraid of taking part in decisions that would lead to the release of prisoners, in fear that one of them might go on to commit a violent crime, thus likely costing that official his or her job. In the context of presidential commutations and pardons during his last year in office, President Obama called such executive actions "risky" while explicitly mentioning Horton: "You commute somebody and they commit a crime, and the politics of it are tough. And everybody remembers the Willie Horton ad. And so the bias I think of my predecessors and, frankly, a number of my advisers early in my presidency is, be careful about that."[34] Referring specifically to the effect of the ad on parole policies, Sharon Dolovich argues,

> Politicians' fear of being "Willie Horton'ed" has arguably had a direct and serious impact on parole in the United States. Although the parole structure differs among jurisdictions, in many states the Governor has considerable control over the process, whether indirectly through the appointment of parole board members or directly through veto power over their decisions. Many state executives have preferred to dramatically curtail the granting of parole rather than risk the single mistake that might threaten their career.[35]

In short, politicians have decided that their career risk, if a paroled person commits another crime in the future, is more important than the freedom and lives of the overwhelming majority of people who will continue to fester in prison after being denied a chance at the parole that their original sentence was intended to provide them.

The transition from pre-"Willie Horton" to post-"Willie Horton" was stark, as illustrated by the following two examples. Well into the 1980s, the norm for life sentences was that people would typically be released—often after as few as 12 years. In fact, in upholding and justifying a Texas court's decision to impose a life sentence on an inmate who had passed a bad check—based on the larger principle that courts should not review prison sentences—former chief justice William Rehnquist stated in 1980 that Texas had a "relatively liberal policy of granting 'good time' credits," which meant that lifers "become eligible for parole in as little as 12 years."[36] In other words, a life sentence for what most would consider a relatively minor—and certainly non-violent—crime seemed acceptable to Rehnquist and other conservative justices because in reality the prisoner would be released in just over a decade. In contrast, in 1999, as a newly-elected Democrat trying to outflank the political right by showing his "toughness" on crime, California governor Gray Davis declared that he would not parole a single person convicted of murder—whatever the circumstances of the crime, however many years the inmate had served, and regardless of the person's actions and conduct while in prison.[37] As a result, it became nearly impossible to secure parole release (even for those convicted of lesser crimes than murder) in California during Davis's five years in office. In just a short period, the "Willie Horton" phenomenon crystallized the changing political climate from one of accepting the reality of early parole to fervent and hostile opposition to it.

The role of state governors in the parole process deserves special explanation. In many states that still grant discretionary parole, parole applicants must successfully pass two key steps, neither of which is easy or straightforward: (1) being recommended for parole by the parole board, and (2) having that recommendation be approved by the governor. In California, for example, in the 28 months leading up to the end of 2001, the parole board recommended parole in only 48 out of 4,800 cases, corresponding to an extremely low rate of 1 percent. Yet, despite this tremendous "selectivity," Governor Davis wound up *reversing* 47 of those 48 recommendations.[38] As a result, the successful parole rate in that period was 0.02 percent. Although the rates of both parole board recommendations and gubernatorial approvals increased slightly after Davis left office in a recall election in 2003, the California Board of Paroles still denied 98 percent of the parole petitions it heard in the 2000s,[39] and while in office from 2004 to 2010, Governor Arnold Schwarzenegger reversed 60 percent of them, while remanding another 20 percent for further review.[40]

While the Willie Horton story resonated on all levels of national and local politics, the lesser-known but equally powerful case of Reginald McFadden transformed the politics of Pennsylvania. As Adam Liptak put it succinctly, "Reginald McFadden is the reason lifers no longer get pardons in Pennsylvania."[41] McFadden had been pardoned by the state's Board of Pardons in 1992, a decision that was approved by then-governor Robert Casey in 1994, with a positive vote by Lieutenant Governor Mark Singel. At the time, Singel was the front runner in the gubernatorial race to succeed Casey, but his support for McFadden's pardon proved costly when McFadden went on to commit several brutal murders in New York shortly after getting out of prison. Singel's opponent, Tom Ridge, hammered away at Singel's support for McFadden's release and went on to defeat Singel handily. After becoming governor, Ridge "did not commute a single lifer's sentence in his six years in office."[42] The same story played out in numerous other states, whether directly or indirectly, and whether involving state executives, local officials, prosecutors, or even judges. The ultimate message delivered was that being perceived or labeled as "soft on crime"—particularly by having "supported" in even the loosest sense a criminal—was political suicide.

One of the few recent politicians to defy this larger trend was Mike Huckabee, Arkansas governor from 1996 to 2007. Apparently based on his religious beliefs, Huckabee had "a history of supporting pardons and commuting sentences of violent offenders," and he "helped to free more Arkansas prisoners than were freed from all of Arkansas' six neighboring states—combined."[43] Yet the political tides eventually caught up to Huckabee as well, not long after his surprising presidential bid in 2008 had left him as one of the main front runners for the 2012 Republican nomination. Maurice Clemmons, whose 95-year prison sentence for aggravated robbery had been commuted by Huckabee in 2000, went on a violent rampage in Washington State, killing four police officers.[44] Huckabee subsequently received harsh criticism from all political sides, and he eventually declared that he would not seek the 2012 nomination. Although it is unclear the extent to which the backlash from the Clemmons debacle contributed to Huckabee's withdrawal, Huckabee certainly did not make any political friends based on his pardons.

In short, the effects of this "tough on crime" political climate on discretionary parole, as well as pardons and commutations, have been both vast and clear. Parole is a toxic political issue for elected officials, and very few of them—or their politically appointed delegates on the parole boards—have been willing to take a chance on parolees.

The Increase in Life Sentences

In addition to the legislative changes that resulted in more determinate sentences, mandatory minimums, "truth in sentencing" policies, and the elimination of parole boards, this political dynamic also had a profound effect on the use of term-to-life sentences and other high-term or LWOP sentences that effectively guarantee that an inmate will never spend a single living day outside of prison. In the evocative words of Adam Liptak, "in just the last

30 years, the United States has created something never before seen in its history and unheard of around the globe: a booming population of prisoners whose only way out of prison is likely to be inside a coffin."[45]

As discussed in Chapter 3, the lifer prison population has grown dramatically over the past few decades, with almost 160,000 people currently serving life sentences (nearly 50,000 of whom have LWOP).[46] The increase in lengthy and life sentences occurred at the same time as prisoners' chances for parole began to dwindle. From 1941 to 1974, an average of 12 lifers received parole each year, yet "in the last 24 years, by contrast, a *New York Times* analysis found that while the number of lifers shot up, the number of lifers who were paroled declined to about seven per year—even using the most liberal of definitions."[47] It is therefore not surprising that inmates can expect to serve ever-longer periods of time in prison. Even in a short six-year time span from 1991 to 1997, the Sentencing Project estimated that "Persons admitted in 1991 could expect to serve an average of 21.2 years, a figure which rose to 29 years by 1997. Thus, in contrast to popular imagery which sometimes portrays lifers as serving short prison terms, the average life sentence today results in nearly three decades of incarceration."[48]

This "popular imagery" of relatively easy parole is not restricted to an uninformed public. Recall the quotation above by Chief Justice Rehnquist from 1980 about lifers receiving parole after just 12 years. More recently, the Michigan state bar's 2002 survey of 95 current and retired judges revealed that "on average, the judges had expected prisoners sentenced to life with the possibility of parole to become eligible for parole in 12 years and to be released in 16 years. In July, a Michigan appeals court echoed that, saying that many lawyers there used to assume that a life sentence meant 12 to 20 years."[49] The reality, however, is quite different. As put somewhat hauntingly by Walter Ray, the chair of Georgia's Parole Board, "There's a popular misconception that life in prison doesn't mean all of one's natural life. In just the last year, there are 21 Georgia lifers who are no longer around to tell you otherwise. If they could, they'd let you know that parole for a life sentence is a rare commodity." In short, the explosion of various forms of life sentences—whether term-to-life or de facto life or life without parole—has resulted from the same "tough on crime" political dynamic, and it has contributed to the further withering away of discretionary parole.

Prison Conditions

A final factor that may help to explain the decline in discretionary parole has to do with the overcrowded and violent conditions within contemporary

American prisons—discussed in detail in Chapter 4—and their detrimental physical and psychological effect on inmates. Due to the severe overcrowding in most prisons, many inmates experience conditions that Justice Thurgood Marshall once anticipated would create "serious mental, emotional, and physical deterioration."[50] As a result of lack of privacy, a near-absence of communication with family, friends, and the outside world, the perpetuation and non-treatment of substance abuse and addiction, the lack of attention to physical and mental illness, and the reality and fear of physical and sexual violence, prisoners live in an environment that is hardly conducive to self-improvement and reform. Moreover, given the change in emphasis from rehabilitation to punishment discussed in Chapter 5, prisoners' chances to acquire education and job training have been reduced, leaving most of them vastly under-skilled and undereducated, and thereby resulting in more likely rejections at their parole hearings.[51]

In the words of Sharon Dolovich, as a result of extremely long sentences served in overcrowded and dangerous prisons, "the experience of living under the conditions that currently define life in many of the nation's prisons and jails can leave at least some people resembling the image of the angry, unstable, anti-social, and potentially dangerous deviant that already justifies mass incarceration."[52] Since many prisoners have to resort to violence—or at least episodes of violence—in order to survive and function under such conditions, their violent behavior makes them even less likely to receive parole—thus perpetuating a cycle of continued incarceration that is not attenuated by parole.

In short, although the effect is more indirect than with the institutional and political changes discussed above, the conditions in many of the higher-security American prisons are so terrifying and unsafe that they have greatly exacerbated the difficulty that so many inmates face when seeking to be released on parole.

A Comparative Perspective on Parole and Early Release from Prison

Now that the decline and virtual elimination of discretionary parole in the United States has been established, this section turns to a wider comparative perspective in order to provide insights into this American transformation. The comparison to the cases of France, Germany, and the U.K. highlights the extent of American exceptionalism on the issue of parole. Indeed, all three countries maintain a strong commitment to parole and early release, albeit with certain reservations and conditions. And in stark contrast to the U.S., the process remains depoliticized, and thereby protected from the dangers of penal populism and political fearmongering.

France

France has a long-standing tradition of parole that dates back to 1885 and continues—in modified and even expanded form—today. Originally it served as a "disciplinary measure" that was intended to induce inmates to maintain discipline while in prison and to avoid recidivism by not violating the terms of their release.[53] In the 1970s the system evolved to allow for parole for inmates who "presented serious evidence of social readaptation," which meant primarily having reasonable job prospects.[54]

Today, France provides three distinct methods for potential early release from prison. The first is a conditional release (liberté conditionnelle), whereby inmates can serve the rest of the term of their sentence in freedom outside of prison, but under clearly circumscribed conditions, such as electronic surveillance (usually ankle bracelets), restricted movement and curfews, substance abuse treatment, and requirements for regular meetings with a judge or reinsertion officer.[55] Conditional release can be granted by judges who evaluate the inmate as being safe to return to society, and the restrictions imposed allow for a more gradual and controlled reintegration process.[56] Similar to American parole or probation, one slip-up by the conditionally released person can lead to a return to prison for the remainder of the sentence.

The second—and much more desirable from an inmate's perspective—type of release involves a sentence reduction (réduction de peine) based on both good prison behavior and reintegration potential.[57] After having served at least 50 percent of their sentence, French prisoners have the right to request a hearing with a judge (or panel of judges) and prison officials, with an attorney provided to them, wherein they can make their case for having served their debt (both to the victim and to society) and being ready to return to life on the outside as a productive citizen. Inmates can request as many hearings as they wish, as frequently as they desire—though obviously an abuse of this process may not be wise for the inmate since it will likely irritate the forces that hold the keys to their freedom. The hearings take place within the prison, through a formal and dignified procedure, and such reductions are frequently granted.[58] This opportunity to leave prison early serves as an important motivational factor for good prison behavior and taking advantage of educational and programming opportunities within the prison.[59]

The third means for early release has to do with compassion for illness or old age. The objective is to allow prisoners the opportunity for a dignified death with loved ones. Even formerly violent criminals will be afforded such an opportunity when the end is (with certainty) very near. And many prisoners will be granted requests for compassionate release when they are in poor health and struggling, and apparently do not represent a danger to others. Unlike in the U.S., where such compassionate release (rare as it is)[60] can sometimes be granted on rather cynical economic grounds, namely that the prison or state does not want to pay for the costly medical treatment that may be required to keep the prisoner alive, the universal health care system in France means that all people will receive the same treatment, whether in prison or on the outside.

Importantly, within the French context, the parole and early release processes are entirely judicial matters that have very little political traction.[61] Although politicians sometimes complain about decisions made by judges— and former French president Nicolas Sarkozy once publicly denounced judges for their excessive leniency, which sent a chill down their spines[62]— the fact that judges in France are appointed through a meritorious academic procedure rather than elected or retained through political campaigns and elections has insulated them from such pressures. And while they are certainly worried about making a mistake by freeing someone who may go on to commit another violent crime, the consequences are not directly imposed on them or their careers, which means they do not remain paralyzed by fear. They can therefore exercise their best judgment and attempt to balance multiple factors when making such weighty decisions.

Overall, the French parole process and debate are radically different from those in the U.S. It is exceedingly rare for prisoners to have to spend the rest of their natural lives behind bars. The expectation is that all but the most violent and rebellious inmates will be released at some point before the end of their sentence, perhaps even as early as the halfway point. This reality thereby reflects a constructive motivation process whereby prisoners can remain hopeful about having the opportunity to return to their families and society.

Germany

German practices and principles are similar to those applied in France. Procedures for conditional release are fairly routinized, with different criteria based on the inmate's age, status, and the length of sentence. Most adult prisoners will be conditionally released after serving two-thirds of their sentence, and first-time offenders with a positive reintegration likelihood can be released after serving as little as half.[63] Juveniles typically serve between one-third and five-eighths of their sentence, and the conditions of their release are often less restrictive. Prisoners who were given a life sentence can be released after a minimum of 15 years, though the process and decision are discretionary. Although the decision to release any individual inmate is made only when the person is deemed likely to successfully reintegrate into society, "the exclusion of all risk is not required—a 'justifiable' degree of risk is accepted."[64]

An important distinction is that "Early release in Germany is always conditional," meaning that the remaining sentence can be reinstated if the person commits another crime or does not comply with the requirements of the release.[65] Beyond this conditional release program, German prisoners have few opportunities to leave prison early, as there are very limited "good-time" provisions in the German system.[66]

The status of life sentences occupies a paradoxical position in German law. On the one hand, the Federal Constitutional Court does allow for the possibility of a life sentence; but on the other hand, such a sentence is only deemed constitutional if "the prisoner was given a realistic and legally-based opportunity to be released."[67] In practice, this has resulted in the suspension of the time remaining on a life sentence if the prisoner has already served 15 years and if "the gravity of the offender's guilty does not necessitate that he continues to serve his sentence." The latter clause is interpreted as whether there is a "good prognosis" for a successful release and reintegration.[68]

As in France, decisions on early release are made by judges, and then probation services handle the necessary supervision process afterward. Any violation of the terms of a conditional release can lead to its revocation, thus requiring the finishing of the original sentence within prison, which occurs in roughly 30 percent of the cases of conditional release in Germany.[69]

Overall, parole in Germany is routine and commonly applied. Inmates rarely have to finish their full sentences—especially those with a life sentence—but their return to society is conditional on avoiding further violations and infractions. The emphasis remains on creating positive incentives for successful reintegration and avoiding recidivism, thus enhancing safety both within prisons and in society at large.

The United Kingdom

Although in other respects, the U.K.'s traditions and practices lie in between the Continent and the U.S., on the issue of parole, the U.K. appears to be more European than American. Indeed, early release policies in the U.K. are generally quite regular and often automatic, thus maintaining the strong incentive among prisoners for a productive return to society.

The U.K. has a long history of granting prisoners automatic early releases, a practice that was codified in 1948 as requiring two-thirds of the sentence to be served, before leading to an automatic release without conditions or follow-up requirements.[70] The 1967 Criminal Justice Act, which came about during the height of rehabilitation, instituted a Parole Board that reviewed applications by prisoners who had completed between one-third and two-thirds of their sentence.[71] This practice was then made slightly more restrictive in the 1991 Criminal Justice Act, which required that "any person serving a sentence of four years or more would serve half of their period in custody—whereas previously it had been a third—and would then become eligible to apply for early release."[72] The 1991 reform instituted a "two fold approach of automatic and discretionary conditional release," which added a form of discretionary parole supervision (with a probation officer) that followed the automatic release.[73] This form of conditional release was solidified further by the 2003 Criminal Justice Act, which distinguished between its application for determinate sentences (which allowed automatic early release at the halfway point) and indeterminate sentences (where a court would set the minimum time before the prisoner would be eligible for parole). Although these early release policies are firmly established and lasting, it is worth noting the emergence of recent debates about whether to eliminate the automatic halfway point release for people convicted of "the most serious child sex offences and terrorism-related offences."[74]

Throughout these various changes in parole and release policies, the U.K. has maintained a steadfast belief in the utility of allowing prisoners to be released before the end of their sentence.[75] This shows the U.K.'s lasting commitment to rehabilitative ideals and practices. And the consistency of this parole practice throughout multiple reforms over the decades provides a stark contrast to the highly politicized and contentious parole process in the U.S.

Overall, the comparison between the status of parole in the U.S. and the practices in our three European countries yields a stark and striking contrast. The U.S. stands in complete isolation in terms of having either eliminated or drastically reduced the possibility for automatic early release. Most notably, the U.S. has essentially eliminated the practice of allowing inmates to review discretionary parole based on good behavior, rehabilitation, and presenting a low risk of danger to society.

Conclusion

When Jackie Lee Thompson, then 15, was sentenced to life with the possibility of parole for murder in 1970, a Pennsylvania judge told him, "You will always have hope in a thing of this kind. We have found that, in the past, quite frequently, if you behave yourself, there is a good chance that you will learn a trade and you will be paroled after a few years." Indeed, at the time, a life sentence in Pennsylvania typically meant less than 20 years behind bars. In 2005, 35 years later, Thompson was by all accounts a model inmate, who had received an associate's degree in business and learned the skills of carpentry, bricklaying, electrical work, plumbing, and welding. In support of his parole application, the father of the girl he had killed "begged" the parole board to release him, and a retired facilities manager from the prison even offered him lodging and a plumbing job. Yet the Pennsylvania Board of Pardons denied him.[76]

The same scenario applies to so many other American prisoners today. Jerald Sanders, a "small-time burglar" whose crimes were always non-violent, was sent away for life in Alabama after stealing a bicycle worth $60.[77] Santos Reyes was convicted of perjury for taking the written driver's test for his illiterate cousin, and was sentenced under California's "three strikes" law on the basis of a juvenile burglary conviction from over two decades earlier and an adult armed robbery conviction over 15 years before. After turning down a plea agreement for a four-year sentence because he thought he could disprove the perjury, Reyes received a sentence of 26 years to life.[78] Charles Lohn was paroled in 1988 after serving 20 years for an armed robbery in Michigan. Although he remained crime-free and held a paying job, a family crisis led him to neglect reporting to his parole officer for a few months, and he was returned to prison, with the recommendation that he receive "another try at parole in the not too distant future." But after Michigan adopted a "life means life" policy in the 1990s, Lohn has been denied parole repeatedly, despite now being in his sixties.[79] These are just a few of the countless human stories of people who have been caught in the dual machinery of increased length of incarceration and decreased frequency of parole.

In all likelihood, Thompson, Sanders, Reyes, Lohn, and many others like them would not go back to a life of crime if they were to be released on parole. It is well-known that most violent crimes are committed by people in their youth, and "most prisoners become markedly less violent as they grow older."[80] Indeed, the recidivism rate among inmates paroled from a life sentence is 20.6 percent, significantly lower than the 67.5 percent re-arrest rate of all offenders after their release.[81] And within California, "the incidence of commission of serious crimes by recently released lifers has been minuscule, and as compared to the larger inmate population, recidivism risk—at least among those deemed suitable for release by both the Board and the Governor—is minimal."[82] In Maryland, over 130 lifers have been released after the state Court of Appeals decided in an extraordinary 2012 case, *Unger v. Maryland*, that in the 1970s Maryland juries had been given faulty instructions, and the state decided to release many of those convicted rather than hold new trials many decades later. Virtually all of the men and women released after *Unger* had previously applied for parole, and some had actually been supported by the parole commission—but all were ultimately denied by the governor. So far, with a recidivism rate of 0 percent despite having been supposedly the "worst of the worst," the *Unger* releases provide "living proof that lifers can be welcomed back into the community with great success."[83]

Yet the political climate in the U.S. today does not forgive politicians (including prosecutors and judges) who take any chances. Even if the odds could be brought down to a fraction of a percent, most elected officials fear that one single mistake will cost them their careers. As a result, they consciously make a choice that is personally safe for them, while ensuring that countless more prisoners are refused the second chance that they had supposedly been promised once they paid back their "debt to society."

The economic costs of maintaining a system that has essentially eliminated discretionary parole are indeed staggering. According to one estimate, "Imposing a life sentence carries with it a potential cost to taxpayers of $1 million."[84] On a larger scale, "By a conservative estimate, it costs $3 billion a year to house America's lifers. And as prisoners age, their medical care can become very expensive."[85] Moreover, the human and societal costs of the intergenerational cycle of incarceration are unquantifiable and unfathomable.

Perhaps a movement for reform will emerge from those who were once swept up by the punitive turn of the 1970s and 1980s but have since changed their minds. Jerry Brown, who in his first stint as California governor in the 1970s presided over the shift to determinate sentencing that sparked a series of further "tough on crime" reforms in California and nationwide, now admits that "there was no empirical evidence to justify the change, it was based on mood," and he argues that the laws need "radical surgery."[86]

On a similar note, the man who set in motion Pennsylvania's movement against parole, Ernest Preate Jr., is leading the charge to reverse the amendment he once "helped create and supported." Having been the lone dissenter who was outnumbered by the parole board majority in the Reginald

McFadden case, Preate, then the state attorney general, pushed for a constitutional amendment—which ultimately passed in 1997—that requires a unanimous vote of the board, among other tougher measures.[87] But after serving a year in prison himself for mail fraud, he got a chance to meet older lifers and he subsequently changed his position quite radically. Claiming that he "never foresaw the politicization of this process and the fear that has crept into the process," Preate now supports a proposal to allow lifers over the age 50, who have served over 25 years in prison, to be considered for parole.[88]

The political climate that has reigned in the past four decades in the U.S. stands in stark contrast to the policies and practices in Europe, where parole and early release remain regular, widespread, routine, and well-supported. American parole practices are unlikely to change unless they become radically depoliticized, or unless political candidates have the courage and the skill to make a convincing popular argument that mass incarceration has gone too far—whether because of the financial or human costs. And both political leaders and the public will have to engage the question of whether prisoners deserve another chance to rejoin society as contributing members, or whether the state should continue locking them up and throwing away the key for the rest of their lives.

7

Societal Reentry

WHEN A PERSON walks out of prison—whether from having reached the
end of the sentence, getting granted parole, being exonerated after a wrongful conviction, or any other method of release—the struggle is far from over.
Readjusting to society creates enormous challenges, both in terms of the former inmate's ability to cope with changing social circumstances and to be
accepted by that person's family, community, and larger society as a "returning
citizen" with rights and opportunities. In theory, the process should be standard across jurisdictions and countries, since the end of a sentence—however
short or long, and whatever the conditions and experience inside—should
mean that the convicted person's "debt to society" has been paid, and a new
life can begin. In practice, however, there is tremendous variation in the "collateral consequences" of a prior criminal conviction and how these will impact
the person's new, post-prison life.

Previous chapters have already highlighted the consistently vast differences between the U.S. and our set of European countries in terms of the conditions of prisons, opportunities for rehabilitation, and preparation for life
on the outside. This chapter shows that these disparities are compounded by
what is perhaps the most egregious discrepancy of all: the effect of people's
status as ex-prisoners on their life chances once released. In the U.S., former
prisoners—along with the millions of people who were convicted of a crime
but received probation, without even going to prison—face considerable
restrictions on their ability to live as productive citizens. In other words, the
"scarlet letter" of formerly incarcerated people almost never goes away. And
in this sense the U.S. once again stands alone in comparison to other democracies in the world, where the punishment for crime consists of the temporary
removal from society, and once that time has been served, former prisoners
find their citizenship and other rights—some of which they had even maintained while in prison—fully restored.

This chapter describes the "collateral consequences" that accompany a person convicted of a felony after being released from prison. It starts by focusing on the U.S., laying out the severe consequences of a prior criminal record on people's citizenship (their right to vote, run for office, and serve on juries), employment, and housing. In doing so, the section highlights the ongoing measures to reduce some of the collateral consequences in the U.S., which might allow for more of a genuine "second chance" than is currently the case. The next section turns to the comparative cases of France, Germany, and the U.K., where the support for societal reentry is much more sustained (even if not always successful), and the consequences of a prior record much less debilitating. The European comparison helps to show just how far the U.S. still has to go, while also pointing to other methods that could serve as models within the debate about American reform.

Societal Reentry in the United States: The Enduring Scarlet Letter

All 50 states and the District of Columbia impose some form of felon exclusion laws. This section explores the harsh restrictions imposed in many states. It starts by addressing the restrictions on citizenship—primarily voting, but also running for office and serving on juries—which have distinctive racial overtones and historical implications given the disenfranchisement of numerous African Americans. It then turns to employment restrictions, showing that a felony record usually serves to disqualify prospective applicants from achieving gainful employment. And finally it considers the obstacles in the realm of housing, which forces many people (and their families) into difficult situations and even homelessness. In all three areas, a person's prior criminal conviction is deemed to be a "public matter" in the U.S., rather than an "individual right of informational privacy," as in Europe.[1] Overall, these factors present a bleak picture of societal reentry in the U.S., showing that many people's new lives are almost doomed before they even start, which helps explain the high failure and recidivism rates.[2]

Restrictions on the Rights of Citizenship

As described in Chapter 4, the U.S. is one of the only democratic countries that does not allow prisoners to vote while they are incarcerated.[3] In many U.S. states, the deprivation of voting rights continues well beyond release from the prison gates, thereby revealing the "dark side of American liberalism," based on exclusionary politics.[4] As stated by the American Civil Liberties Union (ACLU) in a well-researched comparative report entitled "Out of Step with the World: An Analysis of Felony Disfranchisement in the U.S. and Other Democracies," "post-incarceration disfranchisement in the United States is simply on a completely different scale."[5] Jamie Fellner and Marc Mauer add that "No other democratic country in the world denies as many people—in absolute or proportional terms—the right to vote because of felony convictions."[6] According to the ACLU report, "the disqualification [. . .] pursues no defined purpose, and affects millions."[7] Moreover, granting the right to vote would arguably serve a safety as well as civic purpose, as studies have indicated that recidivism rates are half as low among "returning citizens" who vote.[8]

As Mauer points out, "American disenfranchisement policies are extremely broad and can be traced back to the nation's founding."[9] In 1974, the U.S. Supreme Court declared in *Richardson v. Ramirez* that the deprivation of the right to vote for ex-offenders does not violate the Fourteenth Amendment's Equal Protection Clause.[10] While this long-standing tradition, with the Supreme Court's constitutional imprimatur, may sound like justification for maintaining the policy, Mauer reminds readers that at the American founding, women, African Americans, poor people, and illiterates were also excluded, and the following centuries saw the gradual and painstaking extension of suffrage to these groups who had previously been marginalized from American democracy. Former felons constitute the last category to remain excluded today.[11]

According to a 2016 report from the Sentencing Project, not counting Maine and Vermont (which do not restrict incarcerated people from voting), 14 states and the District of Columbia restore voting rights immediately after a person's release from prison,[12] 4 more maintain the restriction for released prisoners who are still on parole,[13] another 18 also exclude those on felony probation (in addition to those on parole) from the voting process—even if they have not been incarcerated,[14] and the remaining 12 states maintain all of these restrictions plus an additional post-sentence period as well.[15] Among these 12, there is variation in terms of the length of the voting prohibition, depending sometimes on the type of crime, whether it was a first or repeat offense, or by the date of the crime.[16] All maintain lifetime bans in some situations, but many of them allow for a process whereby people with past criminal convictions can have their individual rights restored. Overall, the number of people disenfranchised by these restrictions has been growing steadily since the mid-1970s, in lockstep with the massive increase in incarceration—from under 1.2 million in 1976 to over 3.3 million in 1995 to about 4.7 million in 2004 to almost 5.9 million in 2010, and surpassing 6 million in the 2016 presidential election.[17]

Among scholars and policy analysts, the reaction to felon disenfranchisement has grown increasingly pronounced and critical. Not only did the number of people affected skyrocket, but the breadth of types of crimes has expanded as well, since "felony" can refer to many different types and levels of crime. Considering the vast extent of what might be considered relatively "minor" crimes that count as felonies—for example, in Kentucky this would include "trafficking of eight ounces or more of marijuana, theft of property lost, mislaid, or delivered by mistake valued $300 or more, stealing a motor vehicle registration plate, and tampering or interfering with a horse race"[18]— many opponents to this policy have realized that the civic consequences are far disproportionate to the severity of some of the crimes. Even a somewhat more sympathetic analysis that views the practice of felon disenfranchisement as "legitimate" in certain cases (for serious crimes and under specific circumstances) concludes after careful investigation that "there are very few instances in which disenfranchisement is defensible."[19]

Many have also attacked the racial implications and consequences of felon disenfranchisement, pointing out the historic significance of large numbers of African Americans losing the vote—the very right that took centuries of anguish, perseverance, and conflict to acquire—as a result of criminal records.[20] Indeed, the racial imbalance in terms of the effects of these felony restrictions is particularly striking. Although African Americans comprise 12 percent of the general population, they constitute 44 percent of the population with felony records.[21] As a result, while 2.3 percent of the overall population is disenfranchised, over 7 percent of the African American community cannot vote.[22] In Florida, Kentucky, and Virginia, over 20 percent of black adults are disenfranchised.[23]

The political effects of felon disenfranchisement are potentially very high—on local, state, and even national levels. According to a 2002 study, such voting restrictions likely changed the results of seven different U.S. Senate races between 1970 and 1998.[24] It is also very likely that if "a fraction" of the 600,000 disenfranchised people in the state of Florida[25] had been allowed to vote in the 2000 presidential election, Al Gore "would have carried Florida and won the White House."[26]And the same may well have applied to Hillary Clinton in 2016.

Although the numbers have still been increasing due to the rising incarceration rates, it should be noted that in recent years the tide has been turning, as a number of states have recently repealed or loosened their restrictions some-what, thereby allowing approximately 800,000 people to regain their voting rights.[27] Perhaps legislators have been buoyed by the fact that 80 percent of Americans think that former prisoners should be allowed to vote, and over 60 percent would extend those rights to those on parole or probation.[28] More such changes may be on the horizon, as there seems to be genuine movement against maintaining these strict restrictions on the restoration of full citizen-ship rights after release from carceral control. This remains a "live" issue in Virginia, as Democratic governor Terry McAuliffe issued an executive order in April 2016 that unilaterally restored the voting rights to over 200,000 peo-ple with felony records, but then in July the Virginia Supreme Court sided with the Republicans who hold a majority in the state legislature by voiding the declaration.[29] In response, Governor McAuliffe stated that he will follow the court's ruling against a blanket restoration, but is nonetheless proceeding by individually signing restoration orders for each eligible citizen, beginning with nearly 13,000 in August 2016.[30]

On the federal level, Senator Ben Cardin and Representative John Conyers have introduced the "Democracy Restoration Act," which seeks to restore federal voting rights to 4.4 million former prisoners and maintain those rights for people on probation.[31] It remains to be seen whether the bill will generate enough support to pass. In the meantime, despite the recent loosening of some restrictions, felon disenfranchisement remains a common practice in most states.

Most U.S. states also restrict the citizenship rights of former felons in two other areas besides voting. Seventeen states and the District of Columbia link the right to run for office to the right to vote.[32] People who are unable to vote may not run for public office—until both rights are restored simultaneously. Five states add an additional waiting period.[33] For example, in Georgia former prisoners must let 10 years pass after the completion of their sentence before they can run for office. Finally, the most draconian exclusion takes place in the states of Alabama, Arkansas, Delaware, Indiana, and Pennsylvania, which flat out deny convicted felons the opportunity ever to run for office.[34]

The majority of states also impose restrictions on the "civic duty" to serve on a jury—another area that has a long history of intentional exclusion of African Americans. The rationale for this practice is that convicted felons will have a "prodefense/antiprosecution pretrial bias that would jeopardize the impartiality of the jury process."[35] A total of 31 states and the federal court system bar all people with a felony criminal record from jury service.[36] As a result, 6 percent of the American adult population, and 30 percent of all black men, are excluded from potential jury pools. Of the states that do not sub-scribe to lifetime exclusion, seven deny convicted felons the opportunity to sit on a jury until they have been unconditionally discharged. Four states require convicted felons to wait a period of time—ranging from 1 to 10 years—before being eligible for jury service.[37]

Overall, these findings show that American "returning citizens" often do not receive the full benefits of citizenship for quite some time, if ever.

Restrictions on Employment

People with a criminal record also face significant challenges acquiring gain-ful employment.[38] Despite the fact that unemployment is highly correlated with recidivism,[39] most U.S. states have created onerous barriers to employ-ment for ex-felons. Under American licensing laws, it is considered a privi-lege (as opposed to a right) for individuals to engage in certain occupations. Regulatory licenses are considered an "exercise of the state's police powers designed to protect the public's health, safety, and welfare."[40] In 1898, the U.S. Supreme Court held in *Hawker v. New York* that it was not a violation of due process to disqualify citizens from certain types of employment on the basis of criminal convictions.[41]

Today, the laws of every U.S. state, as well as multiple federal statutes and numerous municipal ordinances, explicitly state that a prior felony convic-tion is a disqualifying factor in the majority of occupations that require a regulatory license.[42] A study by James Hunt conducted in the 1970s revealed that there were 1,948 separate statutes that treated an arrest or conviction as a disqualifying factor with regulated employment.[43] In some cases, even a mis-demeanor will serve as an automatic disqualification. Other policies indicate that a conviction is just one negative factor that employers may evaluate in addition to other potentially mitigating factors. However, many statutes treat a prior conviction as an absolute, permanent, and final restriction on access to the type of occupation in question.[44] These include law, real estate, medicine, nursing, physical therapy, and education, among others.[45]

Regulatory license statutes screen for both "competence" and "character," and many licensing agencies treat a felony conviction as ipso facto proof of an applicant's absence of good moral character. Because the terms in these statutes are often vaguely defined, licensing agencies have "broad and almost untrammeled discretion."[46] Although the U.S. Supreme Court has acknowl-edged that these statutes are ambiguous, courts have generally "not sustained challenges that such statutes are unconstitutionally vague."[47]

People with a criminal record are also excluded from certain forms of public employment with state and federal agencies. A 1994 study by Bill Hebenton and Terry Thomas indicated that federal and state law barred ex-offenders from employment in approximately 350 occupations, which employ some 10 million persons.[48] And six states—Alabama, Delaware, Iowa, Mississippi, Rhode Island, and South Carolina—impose a permanent ban on all forms of public employment, which thus rules out the largest potential employer.[49]

Job applicants with a criminal record also face challenges in the private employment market. A mid-1990s survey of employers in five major cities conducted by Harry Holzer found that two-thirds "would not knowingly hire an ex-offender, and at least one-third checked the criminal histories of their most recently hired employees."[50] And now that most criminal records are easily available online, involving little effort, time, and cost for the employer, the incentive to conduct these criminal background checks is even greater. In fact, as reported by Rebecca Vallas and Sharon Dietrich, 87 percent of employers now conduct criminal background checks on their applicants (as do approximately 80 percent of landlords and 66 percent of colleges).[51] There is also an important financial incentive for employers to avoid hiring people with criminal records, as doing so can be treated as a tort of negligent hiring.[52] For example, in *Tallahassee Furniture Co. v. Harrison,* an employer did not appraise himself of his employee's prior criminal history, and he was held liable to an injured plaintiff for compensatory damages of $1,900,000 and punitive damages of $600,000.[53]

Ultimately the issue boils down to the *stigma* of a criminal record, which makes employers both uncomfortable and fearful. The extent of this stigma was captured by an ingenious experimental study in Milwaukee conducted by Devah Pager (and later extended to New York in collaboration with Bruce Western and Bart Bonikowski[54]) that created matched pairs of putative job seekers who were assigned different characteristics, including both race and criminal record. Pager found that applicants with a criminal record are less than half as likely to be considered by employers, which "suggests that a criminal record indeed presents a major barrier to employment." As she points out, "With over 2 million people currently behind bars and over 12 million people with prior felony convictions, the consequences for labor market inequalities are potentially profound."[55] These effects are further compounded by the interaction with race, as blacks with no criminal record were considered less desirable by employers than whites *with* felony convictions.[56] And blacks with criminal records were considered by far the least desirable of all applicants. These studies demonstrate clearly the damaging impact of the carceral

state on the potential employment prospects of people stigmatized by a criminal record, long after their "debt to society" has been paid. This reality has
substantial ripple effects on families and communities, who also suffer from
the inability of former felons to acquire gainful employment.[57]

As with voting rights, there has been some pushback in recent years to
the discrimination against employees with criminal convictions, in the
form of "ban the box" campaigns that seek to remove the standard question on employment application forms that ask about a prospective applicant's criminal record. Twenty-four states and Washington, DC, have now
"banned the box" from public employment applications, and nine of them
have also removed the criminal background question from applications for
private employers.[58] Over 100 cities and counties have removed some of
these barriers as well. And on the federal level, the U.S. Equal Employment
Opportunity Commission (EEOC) has endorsed the removal of this question as well.[59] Despite this progress, those who seek to encourage genuine
employment opportunities for the formerly incarcerated face an uphill battle. It is important to realize that "ban the box" only removes the first level
of potential discrimination—albeit a very important one, where employers
sometimes impose automatic blanket policies that exclude applicants without
even looking at their qualifications or interviewing them—since employers
can still make easy use of background checks to remove potential applicants
from consideration at a later stage in the hiring process. And early research on
existing "ban the box" policies in New York City and New Jersey suggests the
unintended consequence that employers are now discriminating against even
more African Americans, by excluding them regardless of whether they have
a criminal history (which employers no longer know from reading the initial
job application).[60] Overall, it is clear that the stigma and lack of opportunity
of a criminal record remain very powerful and detrimental for ex-felons seeking productive employment.[61]

Restrictions on Housing

The third major restriction that former felons in the U.S. face after their
release from prison (or if their conviction leads to a sentence of probation
without prison time) involves housing. While there are no data available
on the number of people excluded from housing on account of a criminal record, under current federal policy, every individual convicted of a
felony is automatically ineligible for public housing for a minimum of five
years.[62] Moreover, people convicted of misdemeanors, or arrested but never

convicted of an offense, can be and often are excluded from public housing or federally assisted ("Section 8") housing as well.[63]

This exclusion—sometimes referred to as the "one strike" policy—was developed in the 1990s in response to the War on Drugs and was connected to President Bill Clinton's effort to "end welfare as we know it." In his 1996 State of the Union speech, Clinton firmly stated, "The rule in public housing should be one strike and you're out,"[64] and Congress later incorporated this policy into federal housing law. As a result, federal law requires that Public Housing Authorities (PHAs) deny housing to individuals with certain types of criminal records, and it grants a great deal of discretion to officials to further exclude other classes of former criminals.[65] Clinton's 1996 welfare law also imposed a lifetime ban—which some states have modified or eliminated, though most still abide by it—from welfare assistance (the Temporary Assistance for Needy Families, or TANF) and food stamps (the Supplemental Nutrition Assistance Program, or SNAP) for people convicted of a felony drug offense, thus pushing many poor people deeper into poverty.[66]

U.S. federal law bans three categories of former felons from admission to public housing: people convicted of methamphetamine production on the premises of federally funded housing, those required to register as sex offenders, and individuals currently using illegal substances, regardless of whether they have been convicted of a drug-related offense.[67] PHAs are also given the discretion to deny admission to an additional three categories of applicants: those evicted from public housing because of drug-related criminal activity (this applies for three years after the earlier eviction), those who have engaged in a pattern of disruptive alcohol consumption or illegal drug use (regardless of how long ago this behavior occurred), and a "catch-all" category, which includes any person who has been part of drug-related criminal activity, any type of violent criminal activity, or any other criminal activity deemed a safety risk by the PHA. According to Human Rights Watch, "These discretionary categories are used to exclude a wide swath of people with criminal records without any reasonable basis to believe they may actually pose a risk."[68] Most PHAs automatically deny public housing to applicants with a criminal record, without considering rehabilitation or mitigating factors. Successful appeals usually require a lawyer, but unsurprisingly most applicants cannot afford representation.[69]

What do these policies mean in practice? Since the vast majority of returning citizens are poor and therefore do not own property to which they can simply return, and since most do not have any income base that would allow them to rent on the private market (and even if they did, they might well be excluded by landlords who ask about their criminal record or conduct a background check), they have few options. One possibility is to stay with family members or friends, but if these people are themselves in public housing, they risk losing that right by allowing a returning citizen someone with a criminal record to stay in their home. As a result, many returning citizens face either precarious and/or illegal situations or have no choice but homelessness.[70] Another option is to stay in homeless shelters, but former prisoners are not always welcome there, and space is often not available. In short, while being released from prison may liberate a person from the confines of a cell and the associated struggles of prison life, finding a safe, warm, and welcoming place to sleep in society is not easy.

Putting these three categories together, we see that a criminal record in the U.S. leaves people in a position where they often lose the right to vote, face an uphill battle trying to find gainful employment, and are typically excluded from many types of housing. Moreover, for those who have been conditionally released on parole, the requirements of parole can be onerous and at times nonsensical, which explains why a majority of parole revocations result from technical violations, rather than new crimes.[71]

An additional dimension to the ongoing struggles of people with past criminal convictions involves the tremendous amount of revenue that courts and municipalities generate by charging fees and fines to those people—most of whom are already among society's most poor and disadvantaged—who encounter the criminal justice system.[72] Many states continue to require fathers' child support obligations while they are in prison, which virtually guarantees their failure to pay.[73] In some cases, the non-payment of debts can constitute violations of parole and probation, thus sending people back to prison.[74] And unpaid debt can lead to people having their driver's licenses suspended or revoked—which of course further hampers their chances of gainful employment, while also increasing the likelihood of a new criminal conviction if they choose to drive anyway.[75] Overall, this system of fees and fines has now become part of the "deeply institutionalized debt collection regime" of American law enforcement, and "a new punishment regime is becoming quietly embedded in the organizational structures and normative tenets of the American state."[76]

In the aftermath of the August 2014 shooting death of Michael Brown in Ferguson, Missouri, the U.S. Department of Justice's investigation of the Ferguson police department yielded numerous findings. In addition to the pattern of widespread and systematic racial bias, the report highlighted the everyday practices of collecting fines and fees from the city's least-privileged residents, writing that "Ferguson has allowed its focus on revenue generation to fundamentally compromise the role of Ferguson's municipal court. The municipal court does not act as a neutral arbiter of the law or a check on unlawful police conduct. Instead, the court primarily uses its judicial authority as the means to compel the payment of fines and fees that advance the City's financial interests."[77] The report presented numerous detailed examples of practices that it concluded were both racially discriminatory and unconstitutional. And subsequent research and analysis by the *New York Times* indicate that the practices in Ferguson are by no means exceptional—in fact they are quite typical for other municipalities across Missouri and America.[78] In fact, Mary Katzenstein and Maureen Waller refer to this widespread practice as a "new form of taxation" that "constitutes the very inversion of welfare for the poor."[79]

In short, in a country that supposedly believes in "second chances"—and in his 2004 State of the Union address, President George W. Bush stated, "America is the land of the second chance, and when the gates of the prison open, the path ahead should lead to a better life"[80]—it is extraordinarily difficult to start on a new path as a productive citizen. It is perhaps therefore not surprising that so many people fail—facing only obstacles, and provided no resources, support, or even opportunity—returning to a life of crime as a means of subsistence and survival.

Societal Reentry in Comparative Perspective: A Fresh Start

As with most of the issues covered in previous chapters, a comparative perspective helps to show just how anomalous, egregious, and harshly punitive the American model of societal reentry has become. Not only do the European countries not seek to add extra punishment to former prisoners beyond the term of their sentence, but many actually help them to reintegrate into society as productive and contributing citizens. And the existence of strong welfare states that support the poor allows former prisoners to be absorbed into their social safety nets for employment and housing, rather than being rejected by them.

The following subsections provide overviews of the societal reentry processes in France, Germany, and the U.K. Once again, the latter case lies somewhere in between its continental and Anglo-American allies, but British practices are arguably much more European than they are American.

France

As explained in Chapter 5, the French model emphasizes rehabilitation as the primary purpose of prison. Even as prisoners approach the end of their sentence, they receive assistance with searching for employment and can receive regular furloughs as they begin working before their official release. It is therefore not surprising that the French system provides considerable support for most former prisoners after their release.

In terms of voting, since almost all prisoners in France are allowed to vote while they are incarcerated, this right obviously continues unabated once they return home. There are only very exceptional cases where prisoners are stripped of their voting rights, and in such cases the ban can last up to 10 years after the end of the sentence.[81] These few exceptions aside, the notion of "felon disenfranchisement" is anathema and nonsensical in the French context. Moreover, people who have previously been sentenced have the right to run for office after their release. However, people convicted of serious crimes are unable to serve on juries—though it should be noted that jury trials are relatively rare in France—unless their records have been cleared.[82]

In terms of employment, French law does not impose nearly the same level of restrictions on job applicants with criminal records. Moreover, France "strongly limits access to criminal records," since "such access could be seriously detrimental to employment and consequently to distance/resocialization."[83] In other words, in most circumstances, the French system goes a step beyond even "ban the box," in that it actually prevents most employers from having access to the criminal records of job applicants—not just at the initial application, but throughout the process. That said, there are key exceptions, and the procedure is somewhat complicated.

French law provides for three different criminal "bulletins": Bulletin 1 provides full and complete information about all convictions, sentences, and proceedings; Bulletin 2 contains all convictions except for suspended sentences, juvenile records, or the equivalent of misdemeanors; and Bulletin 3 includes only prison sentences of more than two years as well as any sentences that a judge thought should prohibit specific professional activities, but it does not state the exact nature of the crime.[84] Given these three very different types of files, the key question is who gets to access which bulletin, and under what circumstances. Bulletin 1 is only available to judges and courts, so it does not come into play in the employment application process. Bulletin 2 can be consulted with regard to applicants for public service positions, and the state can access the file directly. Bulletin 3 can only be released directly to the applicant, but potential employers may ask for a copy. In practice, this occurs rarely, only when the job involves "a high degree of trust (bank, private security companies, positions involving regular contact with children, etc.) or for positons where specific legal rules actually exclude people with a criminal record (solicitor, banks, firms)."[85] Job applicants are under no obligation to reveal their criminal records unless asked, and probation officers actually recommend that they avoid the issue, and they even help former prisoners write " 'ameliorated' versions of their curriculum vitae, in order to try and explain why a person has not worked for several months or years."[86] This practice has actually received the imprimatur of France's highest court, the Cour de Cassation, which "ruled in 1990 that an employee had a right not to divulge his criminal past and that his being made redundant [i.e., fired] based on his lying was null and void."[87]

In addition to these wide-ranging safeguards on the privacy of people's criminal records, former prisoners in France have the right to a variety of processes whereby their records can be expunged, either based on "desistance" (to expunge specific parts of the file that may hurt a person's job chances) or "judicial rehabilitation" (to delete the entire criminal record, as if it had never existed). Within each category, there exist a variety of procedures and options, but the guiding principle is to create an incentive structure to leave the criminal world behind, and to reward those who have done so successfully.[88]

The one exception to this supportive approach to former prisoners involves sex offenders. Yet even here, the procedures differ tremendously from the American practice of demonization and mass hysteria. As of recently, sex offenders must register on the National Record for Sexual and Violent Offenders, report regularly to the police, and notify the police and courts of any changes of address. But these records, and the sex offender status, can only be accessed by the courts and the police, which means that they cannot serve to limit employment possibilities (unless the job involves sensitive work, or the care of children, of course), and employers do not get access to them. In other words, in comparison to the U.S., even sex offenders receive much more privacy and support in the employment process than Americans who were convicted of minor property or drug crimes.[89]

As a result of these extensive privacy protections, former prisoners in France do not face nearly the same level of hostility and discrimination on the job market. This is not to suggest that finding and acquiring a productive and satisfying job is easy—particularly in an economy that has long been plagued by high structural unemployment levels hovering around 10 percent for decades. And of course many former prisoners have low education levels and job skills that do not make them highly competitive applicants for high-status jobs. But the point remains that the state does not add on any additional procedural legal hurdles that expressly prohibit returning citizens from becoming gainfully employed, and parole and probation officials actually try to help them reach their potential, since unemployment is so strongly linked to recidivism.

Finally, with regards to housing, the French state does not discriminate against former prisoners in any respect. They are eligible for public housing and state-funded housing benefits and subsidies just like anybody else, based on their income status. And they can move in with relatives who live in public or private housing. Once again, the goal is to help these returning citizens acquire stability and safety in their lives, and the notion of denying them the right to public housing would be considered counterproductive and downright harmful.

Germany

The German model of societal reentry is very similar to the French version, but perhaps even more supportive to individual inmates given the lack of overcrowding in German prisons. As explained in Chapter 5, the primary purpose of prison in Germany is to prepare inmates for "resocialization" and reintegration. While confined, prisoners have many opportunities for educational and professional development, which are meant to improve their chances of leading productive lives after their release.

Unlike the U.S., Germany does not limit the rights of former prisoners after their release. This was not always the case, as "Germany, like the United States, allowed for restrictions on a vast array of an offender's civil rights until the late 1960s."[90] But a reform of the Criminal Code in 1969 resulted in the elimination of collateral consequences.[91] As a result, very few German prisoners lose their right to vote while they are incarcerated, and of course this right continues after their release from prison.

Ex-prisoners in Germany also benefit from strong privacy and legal protections. There are two types of criminal files in Germany, the first being the full criminal "register," the second a more abbreviated "certificate of conduct." The full register contains detailed and comprehensive information about a person's criminal history, but it is only accessible to courts, prosecutors, investigative units of the police and tax authorities, or state agencies that supervise highly sensitive areas such as radiation protection and flight safety.[92] Public and private employers have no access to a job applicant's criminal register, which thus prevents discrimination against people with prior criminal convictions. The certificate of conduct is a document that is released directly to the individual. It contains limited information, with no mention of minor crimes that were assessed small day fines or a prison sentence shorter than three months—and this applies to 77 percent of all sentences, so the vast majority of infractions do not appear on the certificate of conduct.[93] For those crimes that do appear on the document, the ex-offender is entitled to have entries removed after a certain period of time without reoffending (and also to have them removed from the full register after a longer period).[94]

In the German context, the protections for job applicants are so strong that "a person applying for a job is legally entitled to say 'no' when a future employer asks him whether he has a criminal record."[95] But an employer may ask for the certificate of conduct as proof, and in that case it can serve as an impediment to the applicant receiving the job. That said, such requests are not common practice, with the exception of employers in the area of childcare and youth organizations, which are particularly concerned with preventing sex offenders from becoming employed there. This process, along with a generally harsher approach to sex offenders, was facilitated in a 1998 reform, and then again in a 2009 reform that developed an "extended certificate of conduct" specifically geared to listing all sex-related offenses.[96]

Finally, in terms of housing, like France, Germany imposes no restrictions on former prisoners, allowing them to live as they choose, and with the same opportunities to benefit from welfare state benefits—whether concerning unemployment compensation or housing support—as other citizens. On balance, the German system clearly follows through on its stated aim of rehabilitation and reintegration after the prison sentence.

The United Kingdom

As with other issues, collateral consequences in the United Kingdom (England and Wales) lie somewhat in between the continental European countries and the U.S. On paper, they share numerous features with the U.S., even if in practice former prisoners in the U.K. face fewer restrictions and can benefit from the much more generous British welfare state.

Although the roots of prisoner disenfranchisement in American law stem from prior British traditions, these practices have evolved in the U.K. Unlike in numerous U.S. states, the moment British prisoners are released, these returning citizens immediately regain the right to vote.[97] For now, however, the U.K. remains one of the only European countries that does not allow prisoners to vote while they are incarcerated. This position has represented a long-standing defiance of an EU-level ruling on prisoner voting, a stance that will probably not change given the "Brexit" path chosen in 2016.[98]

The British collateral consequences for employment are more severe than in other European countries. As in the U.S., English law allows for many professional and trade associations to make their own determinations about excluding individuals with criminal records from the licensing process, and therefore precluding them from even applying for certain jobs.[99] Yet Michael Pinard argues that the "vast majority of employment-related barriers for formerly incarcerated individuals in England are tied to the availability of resources, the lack of employment-related qualifications among these individuals, or to the informal stigma that these individuals confront when seeking employment."[100] Although the challenges involved with seeking and obtaining employment are great, the U.K. does have "various reentry-related service providers" who "focus specifically on trying to secure employment for these individuals." And former prisoners are eligible upon release for a Job Seekers Allowance and Crisis Loans.[101] In other words, while it is still an uphill battle, and many restrictions make it difficult, the state does attempt to support former prisoners in their professional endeavors.

In terms of privacy protection, British former prisoners do not receive nearly the same level of safeguards as in France or Germany. First off, criminal court decisions remain in the public domain, and can thereby be easily accessed by anybody.[102] Potential employers in "a huge variety of jobs and appointments" can also access criminal records.[103] Former prisoners do have certain rights stemming from the Rehabilitation of Offenders Act of 1974, which rewards those who have not reoffended, while penalizing the "unauthorized disclosure of their previous convictions."[104] Yet there are a large and growing number of exceptions to this law, as the balance has gradually shifted since the 1970s from "the rights of the offender" to "the protection of the public."[105] As a result, the reality is that most former prisoners wind up being "forced to disclose their convictions before they can obtain a job."[106] And in the U.K. there is no process by which former offenders can wipe their record clean and become "judicially rehabilitated."[107]

As with the other countries, the terms are harsher with sex offenders. According to the 1997 Sex Offenders Act, former prisoners get listed on a Sex

Offenders Register, and they have to notify the police of their current address (and those who had been sentenced to over 30 months in prison must continue this notification process for the rest of their lives).[108]

The housing prospects of former prisoners in the U.K. can be negatively affected as a collateral consequence of prior convictions. The British government provides a housing benefit to poor people who need extra financial assistance for their lodging. But anyone who is sentenced to a prison term of more than 13 weeks will lose that benefit while in prison.[109] As a result, many incarcerated people lose their prior housing and have difficulty obtaining lodging after their release. Nonetheless, the state does not add any additional obstacles, and former inmates are not prohibited from any form of public or private housing options. The same applies for general welfare benefits, where the only excluded group of ex-offenders are those who were convicted of welfare fraud, and this is only for a four-week period after the conviction—which is very different from the U.S., where people are disqualified for drug and other offenses, and often for very long periods of time.[110]

Overall, it is fair to say that even though the collateral consequences in the U.K. are significantly more restrictive than in France or Germany, "England has richer and more sustained traditions of providing reentry services than the United States."[111] Although the U.K. does still impose some consequences in terms of employment and housing, these are much less severe and long-lasting than in the U.S.

Conclusion

This examination of the process of societal reentry following a person's release after a period of incarceration brings us to the end of the "life cycle" of the punishment of crime. This chapter has shown that in comparative perspective, the American system imposes more severe punishment not only in terms of lengthy sentences and brutal prison conditions, but also by inflicting additional, lasting (and in some cases permanent) obstacles to rebuilding a new life. This reality makes it hard to take seriously any rhetoric about the U.S. being a land of "second chances" after paying one's "debt to society," particularly when we see that other countries genuinely stop the punishment at the exit gates to the prison.

Indeed, the comparative references shown in this chapter—as in the others—shows that the U.S. has a long way to go in order to catch up with more humane policies. Moreover, the strategies for societal reentry applied

in France, Germany, and the U.K. provide clear and practical models for a
better way to organize the American criminal justice and prison systems. In
other words, it is not a pipe dream to imagine a better and more equitable way to support people who are reforming their lives and trying to get a
fresh start.

8

Explaining American Punitiveness

RACE, RELIGION, POLITICS, AND BUSINESS

CHAPTERS 2–7 OF THIS book have described in great detail the numerous ways in which the American criminal justice and prison systems are unusually cruel—both in absolute terms and in comparison to a similar set of European countries. The chapters have shown that in the United States, defendants' fates are typically determined by a system in which coercive plea bargaining substitutes for a fair trial, prison sentences are considerably longer, conditions within prisons are much more violent and unhealthy, rehabilitation has essentially disappeared as a goal or function of prison, the chances for discretionary parole have dwindled, and the obstacles to reintegration into society after release from prison are tremendous. In comparative perspective, the U.S. stands alone, "off the charts" on *each and every one* of these elements of the "life cycle" of crime and punishment. What explains this latest version of the (in)famous American exceptionalism?

This chapter moves from description to explanation as it seeks to account for the harsh reality of American punitiveness—and in particular the drastic change that occurred starting in the 1970s when mass incarceration began its steep climb. It develops an argument based on both the existence and transformation of four main causal factors that have a distinctively American form within the context of criminal justice and prisons: race, religion, politics, and business.

The concept of *change* is particularly important, since the crucial question in comparative terms is how and why the U.S. departed the realm of advanced industrialized countries starting in the 1970s, when incarceration rates—and other aspects of punitiveness discussed in previous chapters—began to shoot up. In this sense, my argument departs from that of James Whitman, whose book *Harsh Justice* constitutes the most important account of the long-standing criminal justice differences between the U.S. and Europe.[1] By focusing on historical class patterns and social mores surrounding them, Whitman makes a cultural argument about "traditions of social hierarchy" in different societies. He starts by showing that French and German cultures are more tolerant of both social hierarchy and state power. He then argues that this historical distinction between high-status and low-status groups transformed after the eighteenth century into the abolition of low-status treatment for *all people*, leaving them today with "a deep commitment to the proposition that criminal offenders must not be degraded—that they must be accorded *respect* and *dignity*."[2] In contrast, Whitman shows that American culture has strong norms of "egalitarian social status" and "resistance to state power." And even though these principles led Alexis de Tocqueville to marvel at what he viewed as America's "most benign criminal justice system," over time the lack of an "aristocratic element" in the U.S. paradoxically led to a culture of harsh punishment and the degradation of prisoners.[3]

Although Whitman's argument does point to an important cultural dynamic and sheds light on historically rooted social distinctions between the U.S. and Europe, it is less well-equipped to account for the dramatic changes that occurred in the U.S. starting in the 1970s. Indeed, it is worth taking another look again at a figure presented in the Introduction—and reproduced below as Figure 8.1—which shows American incarceration levels alongside those of other advanced democracies. The figure highlights two important phenomena: first, looking back historically, incarceration rates in the U.S. were only somewhat higher than those in Europe; second, starting in the 1970s, the gap increased significantly, such that it became 5–12 times higher in the U.S. than in the European countries. Whitman's historical argument can explain the first phenomenon, but a static cultural approach cannot account for the dramatic increase since the 1970s. This does not necessarily contradict or disprove Whitman's argument—and in fact, it may well be that these cultural features, and the slightly higher starting point that already existed in 1971, helped to enable the changes that took place since then. But in order to account for the post-1970s shifts we need to look to more proximate factors from that era. And it is precisely this more recent change—which occurred in a very short order of time—that my argument attempts to explain.

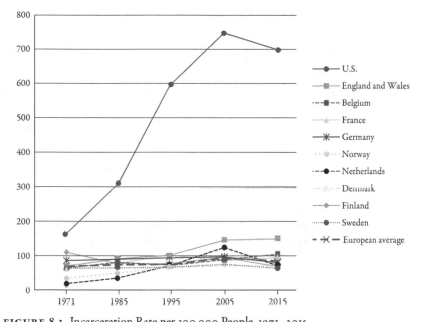

FIGURE 8.1 Incarceration Rate per 100,000 People, 1971–2015

Sources: All U.S. figures from Bureau of Justice Statistics (BJS) and U.S. Census Bureau; 1971 European figures from Lappi-Seppälä 2001, p. 106; 1985 and 1995 European figures from Tak 2001, p. 152; 2005 and 2015 figures from International Centre for Prison Studies 2005 and Institute for Criminal Policy Research 2016

My Argument:
Race, Religion, Politics, and Business

My explanation for the exceptionally high level of contemporary American punitiveness emphasizes four overarching factors: (1) *Race*, which has been a defining characteristic of criminal justice disparities, inequities, and outright discrimination throughout American history, extending from slavery to convict leasing to Jim Crow laws to the latest variant that followed the opening created by the civil rights movement, namely mass incarceration; (2) *Religion*, in particular the Christian fundamentalist fervor of many Americans—ordinary citizens and politicians alike—that often emphasizes a retributive "eye for an eye" perspective on punishment, and that emerged as an organized and strategic political force in the 1970s; (3) *Politics*, specifically the politicization of judicial decisions and criminal punishment, whereby American politicians—including virtually all prosecutors and most judges—compete in elections that have become driven both by fundraising and "tough on crime" rhetoric; and (4) *Business*, since one of the driving forces behind the rise of the "prison industrial complex" has been profit-motivated, including not only the private prison industry and prison unions, but also the vast array of businesses that generate huge profits from mass incarceration, and who structure their political lobbying and donations accordingly.

The following subsections address these four factors in turn, highlighting not only the existence or persistence of each, but also the way in which they have *changed* over the time period when mass incarceration expanded in the U.S. To be clear, I am not suggesting that static demographic factors such as race or religion are new or recent phenomena, but rather that their political manifestations and consequences have differed and changed over time. In other words, race, religion, politics, and business are long-standing American features that have been reinterpreted or refocused in a new context, thereby contributing to the expansion of mass incarceration in the U.S.

Race

The topics of race and racial discrimination are intricately woven into the national history of crime and punishment in America. As Glenn Loury writes, "Race helps to explain why the United States is exceptional among the democratic industrial societies in the severity and extent of its punitive policy."[4] The origins of American racial inequality go back to slavery, of course, but in terms of criminal justice, the more pivotal—but much less known or appreciated—period occurred during the era of "convict leasing" that followed emancipation and extended well into the twentieth century. In fact, the reality of convict leasing contradicts the simplistic and sanitized version of American history that glosses over the century in between the end of slavery and the beginning of the civil rights movement, either overlooking the post-emancipation period or implicitly portraying it as a gradual transition from slavery to full freedom and equality.

Pioneering recent research by historians such as David Oshinsky and Douglas Blackmon has shown that not only was there little improvement in the living conditions of African Americans following emancipation in 1865, but in many ways their situation actually *worsened*—something that is hard to imagine at first.[5] Oshinsky demonstrates that the system of convict leasing and the development of the Parchman Farm prison in Mississippi resulted in conditions that were genuinely "worse than slavery." And Blackmon tells a horrific story of "re-enslavement" through convict leasing in Alabama that amounted to "slavery by another name." Individually and collectively, these two excellent books—each of which focuses on a particular state, though the same story applies to most of the post–Civil War South—show that "emancipation" did not bring about the freedom, happiness, and prosperity that the term would suggest. Even more important, they demonstrate that the continuation (and even worsening) of African American suffering after slavery was the result of a conscious, concrete, and organized strategy by Southern whites to perpetuate racial domination. And this new social order served similar purposes to slavery, but with even less accountability. The identification of this strategy raises important and provocative questions about more recent tactics to use the penal system as a means for continued racial subjugation and control.

Here is how convict leasing worked, according to Oshinsky's account. Following the Civil War, there were almost no state penitentiaries in Mississippi—a state that had a strong and cherished tradition of people taking justice into their own hands, via lynchings, duels, and other vigilante means. Once Mississippi's slaves were freed—and they constituted a majority of the state's population—there were few existing means or structures of confinement. Mississippi's whites were petrified by the lawlessness that they thought would result from coexistence with impoverished, uneducated, but now-free former slaves. These whites held a deeply rooted cultural belief in racial hierarchy, and their goal was to separate the races. They also had economic motivations, namely the pursuit of cheap (or free) labor that would create profit for local entrepreneurs and create economic development statewide. So they developed a new system, convict leasing, based on a combination of judicial abuse and forced labor.

The system became extraordinarily effective and profitable. Blacks were arrested and convicted in massive numbers, usually on charges such as petty theft or disorderly conduct.[6] In some cases, when the "convict recruiters" needed a greater supply of labor, the local sheriff would get paid to round up more convicts, on petty or trumped-up charges, and send them over. The result was to perpetuate black captivity, this time legitimated not by slavery but by the veneer of a criminal justice system that imposed supposedly fair verdicts and sentences after careful consideration by judges and juries. And once they entered the penal system, convicts could be made to do any work, no matter how hard, long, or dangerous. In fact, it was easy to replace the lives lost to exhaustion, disease, or fatal injuries, which thus made convict leasing more "efficient" than slavery.[7] With convict leasing, the motto was simply, "One dies, get another."[8] And death rates approached 50 percent in some cases, as the "convicts" toiled in absolutely horrific and dangerous conditions.[9]

Economically, convict leasing was hugely profitable—though obviously not to the convicts themselves, nor to the "free labor" that suffered lower wages as a result. Those involved in the business of convict leasing enjoyed a virtually limitless supply of labor, which cost them almost nothing. For example, in Mississippi the lessee would pay the state $1.10 per convict per month, and then sublease each convict for $9 per month to plantation and business owners who would then have the work done at 20 percent of the cost of "free labor."[10] This arrangement was obviously very beneficial for the lessees and sublessees personally, but it also had wider ramifications for the state of Mississippi, and indeed the entire South. It is not an exaggeration to say that convict leasing—just like slavery before it—played a critical role in the economic development of the American South. Whether the work involved picking cotton, building railroads, or digging tunnels, most of it was a product of convict labor.

Convict leasing in Mississippi was abolished in the early 1890s, but its replacement was hardly less brutal. Parchman Farm was the creation of Governor James Vardaman, known as the "White Chief" for his rabid support of lynching and his pledge to protect white people from black "barbarians."[11] Parchman sought to recreate a plantation-like experience, simultaneously disciplining convicts and providing great profits to the state based on "free" prison labor. Vardaman created an intricate system of supervision and control, with a superintendent (playing the role of plantation master), sergeants, "trusty shooters" (the most feared and violent convicts), and "Black Annie" (the much-feared leather whip). Parchman Farm continued to subjugate blacks while generating considerable revenue to the state. Remarkably, Parchman lasted, virtually unchanged, until the civil rights movement of the 1960s—and even then, it took tremendous courage, some violence, and federal judicial intervention to end it.

In other words, contrary to the conventional version of history that suggests a gradual improvement of conditions for African Americans from the end of slavery to the civil rights movement, in reality convict leasing and plantation prisons essentially served similar means and goals to slavery. And both institutions coexisted closely with the criminal justice system, which arrested and convicted large numbers of African Americans on petty or false charges, and sentenced them to long years of brutal labor in filthy conditions, while rarely sentencing whites—and only for much more serious crimes, for much shorter sentences, and under much better conditions. In short, the judicial system was an integral part of the construction of post-emancipation equivalents to slavery.

Although at first glance this account of convict leasing may sound like "ancient history," the connection to contemporary mass incarceration is very strong and direct. Even though convict leasing had been discredited and abandoned in the South by the time mass incarceration began to expand in the 1970s, it represented the crucial link to mass incarceration because it established a lasting tradition of using the judiciary and prisons to achieve a long-standing societal goal of racial separation and oppression—albeit in a different form.

As discussed in earlier chapters, the racial disparities in today's criminal justice and prison systems are undeniable and overwhelming. They certainly help to explain the continuing high levels of mistrust that most African Americans have toward the police and criminal justice institutions.[12] And many scholars—most notably David Cole, Marc Mauer, and Loïc Wacquant—have analyzed and discussed these racial differences in their work, highlighting the historical parallels and continuity.[13] Yet in 2010 the debate reached a new level of public prominence after the publication of Michelle Alexander's bestselling and award-winning book, *The New Jim Crow: Mass Incarceration in the Age of Colorblindness*.[14]

According to Alexander's bold argument, not only is racial injustice *not* in the past, but mass incarceration represents the logical and practical modern extension of prior forms of racial domination (she calls them "racial caste systems"—referring to slavery, convict leasing, and Jim Crow laws) that died out but then readapted and re-emerged in different forms.[15] The opening paragraph to Alexander's book evocatively captures the overarching argument:

> Jarvious Cotton cannot vote. Like his father, grandfather, great-grandfather, and great-great-grandfather, he has been denied the right to participate in our electoral democracy. Cotton's family tree tells the story of several generations of black men who were born in the United States but who were denied the most basic freedom that democracy promises—the freedom to vote for those who will make the rules and laws that govern one's life. Cotton's great-great-grandfather could not vote as a slave. His great-grandfather was beaten to death by the Ku Klux Klan for attempting to vote. His grandfather was prevented from voting by Klan intimidation. His father was barred from voting by poll taxes and literacy tests. Today, Jarvious Cotton cannot vote because he, like many black men in the United States, has been labeled a felon and is currently on parole.[16]

In other words, Alexander draws a direct causal connection from one system of exclusion to the other.[17] And she goes on to identify a common pattern across each transition, based on explicit and implicit appeals to lower-class whites' vulnerabilities and racism.

The obvious retort to Alexander's argument is that while slavery, convict leasing, and Jim Crow were essentially state-sponsored systems that explicitly targeted people solely based on their race, today's mass incarceration results from people's own choices and actions—namely the commission of crimes in a now-colorblind society. Jarvious Cotton was convicted of murder, after all. Yet Alexander's analysis shows that even though today's laws have to be formally race neutral, in practice police and prosecutors enjoy tremendous *discretion* in terms of who gets stopped, frisked, searched, arrested, prosecuted, charged/plea bargained, and sentenced. And in the context of the "War on Drugs," within a country where approximately the same proportion of people within each racial/ethnic group consumes illegal drugs, this vast discretion in policing and prosecution has yielded enormous racial disparities.[18] For example, African Americans are 3.7 times more likely than whites to be arrested for marijuana possession, even though they consume it only at 1.3 times the rate of whites.[19]

Although *The New Jim Crow* has clearly struck a chord and galvanized a new and growing movement against mass incarceration, friendly critics such as Marie Gottschalk and James Forman have also claimed that the analogy is overstated—particularly in terms of its focus on drug crimes and race. Gottschalk points out that about half of all incarcerated people were convicted of *violent* crimes, and she adds that "even if we could release all drug offenders today, without other major changes in U.S. laws and penal practices, the United States would continue to be the world's warden."[20] She adds that despite the staggering racial disparities in the American criminal justice system, the mass incarceration crisis is also more than just about race: "Even if you released every African American from US prisons and jails today, we'd still have a mass incarceration crisis in this country."[21] Forman also makes these two critiques, while adding that the "New Jim Crow" metaphor "presents an incomplete account of mass incarceration,"[22] downplays black support for punitive measures when crime rates were high,[23] and ultimately "diminishes our understanding of the particular harms associated with the Old Jim Crow."[24] On balance, while the aggregate racial disparities and inequities in contemporary mass incarceration are indisputable, they seem less likely to result from an intentional racist plan (along the lines of slavery, convict leasing, and Jim Crow) than as a byproduct of legislation—motivated by a complexity of forces—to punish crime.

Either way, recent events have highlighted even further the importance of race in American debates about crime and policing. A discussion that was launched after the 2012 killing of Trayvon Martin in Florida reached a new level of outrage and protest after the 2014 death of Michael Brown in Ferguson, Missouri—along with a series of other African Americans who were killed by police officers around that same time, including Eric Garner, Tamir Rice, Akai Gurley, Walter Scott, Freddie Gray, Samuel Dubose, Laquan McDonald, Alton Sterling, Philando Castile, and Terrence Crutcher. The 2015 release of a Department of Justice report on the Ferguson Police Department revealed a shocking pattern of constitutional violations by the police, describing "a city that used its police and courts as moneymaking ventures, a place where officers stopped and handcuffed people without probable cause, hurled racial slurs, used stun guns without provocation, and treated anyone as suspicious merely for questioning police tactics."[25] Perhaps even more disturbing, it appears that Ferguson's methods are by no means exceptional, reflecting the norm in policing of minority cities and neighborhoods.[26] Moreover, a 2016 Justice Department investigation of Baltimore's police practices found that the police department "for years has hounded black residents [. . .], systematically stopping, searching and arresting them, often with little provocation or rationale."[27] These events and investigations have opened an ongoing national debate about race and policing, with direct implications for the current status of mass incarceration.

This renewed attention to racially disparate outcomes raises important questions about the root causes of these inequalities. Whereas the eras of slavery and Jim Crow were characterized by overt racial bias and discrimination, today such openly racist views have largely disappeared.[28] The election of an African American president in 2008 was supposed to herald a new "post-racial" era, or at least to signal the ongoing transformation of a "different racial America."[29] Yet the 2016 election of President Donald Trump on a "law and order" platform that included racially polarizing codes and rhetoric shows how far the country remains from such an achievement. Indeed, recent psychological research on *implicit* racial discrimination has revealed an important, striking, and troubling set of findings about how Americans relate to race and racial differences and stereotypes. As recounted by Mahzarin Banaji and Anthony Greenwald, a series of unobtrusive social science measures show that:

- Whites give less assistance to Blacks than to other Whites
- Blacks are less likely to obtain mortgage loans

- Blacks are less likely to be approved for apartment rentals
- Blacks are less likely to be hired (even compared to Whites with a criminal record)
- Blacks are less likely to receive quality health care and treatment
- Blacks are more likely to be ticketed or searched after a car stop
- Black taxi drivers and waiters receive lower tips (even from Black customers)[30]

And while some of these may be considered "minor" acts of discrimination, even small effects can add up and multiply in terms of their overall impact on education, employment, and performance raises.[31] Moreover, the cumulative personal consequences of being subjected to occasional offenses and slights—such as being mistaken for a low-level staff member, being stopped and frisked by the police, or seeing other people clutch their purses when walking by on the street—can be very hurtful and damaging.

Recent psychological studies know as Implicit Association Tests (IATs) provide a particularly revealing way to approach hidden or unconscious racism in a society that officially disavows it. The principle behind IATs is that survey research on racism[32] is of limited value since most people no longer hold explicitly racist views (and those who do may give socially acceptable answers anyway). Instead, IATs require respondents to choose quickly between alternatives and to make rapid connections between faces, labels, and concepts, thus tapping into people's *unconscious* attitudes and associations. The results of this powerful research show that 75 percent of Americans have implicit preference for whites, even if they are not necessarily overtly prejudiced.[33] And given that "White Americans are more punitive than people of color," "Whites misjudge how much crime is committed by African Americans and Latinos," and "Whites who more strongly associate crime with racial minorities are more supportive of punitive policies,"[34] it seems very likely that these implicit preferences play a major role in the current disadvantaged status of African Americans—probably even more so than overt racism.[35]

Overall, though it is hard to disentangle the specific elements and especially the question of intent, it is undeniable that race plays a central role in American society and in the American criminal justice and prison systems today. In comparative perspective, the factor of race—given the wide racial disparities on virtually every relevant measure, along with the history of slavery and its aftermath—is distinctively American. This is not to say, however, that race does not play an important role in criminal justice in European countries. On the contrary, there are racial and ethnic imbalances throughout the prison systems in France, Germany, and the U.K.[36] Each of these countries has experienced challenges with integrating immigrant populations, who typically have lower levels of education, higher rates of unemployment and poverty, and greater involvement in criminal activities.[37] Moreover, the police in these countries are probably just as biased as American police in terms of their attempts to control certain groups[38]—even if they are much less deadly in terms of their use of force. Yet despite the fact that European criminal justice is also very racially discriminatory, previous chapters have shown that the extent and level of punishment remains considerably lower there.

Indeed, although racism and racial disparities seem to exist virtually everywhere in some form, the issue of race in the U.S. is particularly pronounced, due to the enduring legacy of slavery and subsequent attempts to subjugate African American men over centuries. And given how instrumentally the stereotypical media-driven image of the "Black criminal" was perpetuated to galvanize public and political support for the "tough on crime" movement of the 1970s, 1980s, and 1990s, it is undeniable that American punitiveness was strongly shaped by the—sometimes explicit, now much more often implicit—issue of race.[39] In short, although race is obviously not a "new" or even "recent" issue in American history, its post–civil rights transformation into the criminal justice sphere has constituted an essential factor that helps to explain the phenomenon of mass incarceration in America.

Religion

The second factor that takes on a distinctively American form involves the religious fervor of many American evangelicals, whose political influence has increased significantly since the 1970s. This factor tends to be relatively neglected among the list of direct causes of the rise in American punitiveness,[40] since the issue of crime control has not galvanized the evangelical movement to nearly the same degree as abortion or gay marriage. Yet evangelicals have demonstrated strong support for the harsh and punitive measures and policies that were the hallmark of the "tough on crime" era in American criminal justice. Moreover, this punitive development occurred in lockstep with the rising organization and unification of an evangelical voice that has transformed so many aspects of American politics over the past four decades.

It is widely known that the U.S. is a much more religious society than most other advanced democracies, and that religion plays a greater role in American politics than elsewhere. Even if many European countries do refer to their

Christian origins and identities, it would be unthinkable for European leaders to hold regular "prayer breakfasts" or to close speeches with "God bless [country name]" as American presidents and public officials routinely do. Looking at public opinion, according to the nationally representative U.S. "Citizenship, Involvement, Democracy" survey, which was conducted in 2005 and replicated a series of questions from the European Social Survey, Americans score much higher on measures of religiosity and religious participation.[41] Respondents were asked to place themselves on 0–10 scale, with higher scores indicating greater levels of religiosity, in response to the question "how religious would you say you are?" Americans scored a 6.16, well above the 3.78 in France, 4.23 in Germany, and 4.3 in the U.K. Another measure captures actual behavior and religious participation, asking, "Apart from special occasions such as weddings and funerals, about how often do you attend religious services nowadays?" The results show that 52 percent of Americans attend religious services once a month or more frequently, compared to only 14 percent of French, 20 percent of Germans, and 19 percent of Brits. These findings highlight that religion is one of the main areas where the U.S. and Europe have diverged considerably over the past few decades, with Americans maintaining high levels of religious activity, while Europeans have become increasingly secular and nonreligious.[42]

In addition to these overall higher American levels of religious identification and activity, a distinctive feature in the U.S. is the vast number of evangelicals and "born-again" Christians. Approximately 34 percent of Americans self-identify as belonging to this category of religious identification that hardly even exists in most European countries, which are now highly secular.[43]

The key question that concerns us here is the extent to which this religious—and particularly evangelical—orientation has contributed to the rise of mass incarceration. As mentioned above, criminal punishment was not the primary issue fueling the evangelical fervor, which suggests that any effect must be indirect, or perhaps even unintentional, at best. In order to make a convincing case for the impact of religion on mass incarceration one would have to show that (1) evangelicals achieved greater prominence and political influence over the time period where mass incarceration rose steeply, and (2) evangelicals have harsher and more punitive views of crime and how criminals should be treated and punished.

In terms of the rise to political prominence of the evangelical movement, Anna Grzymała-Busse has provided a powerful historical analysis, showing that "while the United States has long been a religiously vibrant society, the last forty years have been remarkable for the degree to which religious conviction entered politics and translated into policy." She adds that "Conservative Protestants, and especially conservative Evangelicals, entered the political sphere in the 1970s. Beginning in the 1980s, references to 'morality politics' such as abortion, gay rights, or the religious content of education skyrocketed in Republican, and to a lesser degree, Democratic Party platforms."[44] Grzymała-Busse goes on to tell the fascinating story of how a set of initially quite disparate and divided conservative evangelicals came to power *within* the Republican Party, as "partisan activists, authors of party platforms, and vetters of political candidates."[45] This development in the 1970s represented a major change from prior practice, when "Evangelical Christians insulated themselves from formal politics as corrupt and too removed from the sacred."[46]

The unification and politicization of the evangelical movement took place gradually, in fits and starts, spurred by key events such as the Supreme Court's decision in 1971 to rescind the tax-exempt status of segregationist institutions such as Bob Jones University, and of course *Roe v. Wade* in 1973. At the same time as many evangelicals were becoming wealthier and eager to exert more influence, the ascendant post-Watergate Democratic Party chose a more secular message that alienated many evangelicals. As a result, Republicans managed to convince "evangelical and conservative Protestant leaders such as Jerry Falwell, Pat Robertson, and Ed McAteer to enter politics."[47] This led these three religious leaders to establish their highly politicized organizations— Moral Majority, Christian Voice, and Religious Round Table, respectively. And the next step was to "engage in a full range of political activities, ranging from newsletters and seminars to voter registration to lobbying."[48] They undertook indirect lobbying efforts as well, such as "rallying preachers around moral issues and counting on clergy to mobilize their flocks to flood congressional offices with letters and phone calls."[49]

This newly unified evangelical movement then found another ally in the Catholic Church, which "launched a right-to-life movement that vetted political candidates starting with the 1976 campaign and then entered the electoral fray" in the mid-1980s.[50] Over the next few decades, these forces solidified their message and perfected their political strategy.[51] By the turn of the century, it was fair to say that these "two nested alliances, an interdenominational partnership of conservative Christians and a coalition of these Christians and the Republican Party, were the critical element of religious influence on policy in the United States in the late twentieth century."[52] And while the political impact of this religious alliance sometimes occurred on the state or local level, more important was its influence on the national level, by contributing to a striking change in the broader conversation and proposed solutions.

Although the core of this movement was focused on "moral" issues, criminal justice became swept up in the evangelical fervor and religious impact on policymaking. The timing of these two phenomena—the political rise of the evangelical movement and the explosion in mass incarceration—could hardly be matched up more closely, as both began in the 1970s and then really took off in the 1980s and 1990s. While this correlation does not obviously prove that evangelicals *caused* mass incarceration—and it would be an overstatement to assert such a direct link in any case, especially since other causal factors played a crucial role as well—it does suggest some connection between these two major transformations in American politics and society.

But were evangelicals even concerned with criminal punishment during the relevant time period, and if so, what was their position? These questions tie into a distinguished lineage in the field of sociology, going back to Emile Durkheim's argument that—in both traditional and modern societies—punishment serves the retributive purpose of avenging an "outrage to morality."[53] David Garland updated this approach in his 1990 book, in which he claimed that "throughout the history of penal practice religion has been a major force in shaping the ways in which offenders are dealt with."[54] In the American context, Andrew Koch and Paul Gates emphasize the power of biblical doctrine on American society, which affects people's views on crime and punishment: "The nexus of retributive justice, and the characterization of human beings as sinners in need of atonement, generates a practical outcome in the criminal justice system that stresses incarceration and even death for those who commit crimes."[55]

Scholars began to explore these questions empirically in the early 1990s, when Harold Grasmick and his co-authors opened up a research paradigm focusing on the impact of religion on support for criminal punishment. Based on a survey conducted in Oklahoma City, Grasmick et al. found that people with "fundamentalist religious beliefs" supported significantly more retributivist positions.[56] A subsequent article reached the same conclusion in terms of people's support for the death penalty, as well as their opinions about the harshness of courts and severity of punishment.[57] The key argument running through Grasmick's work was that Protestant fundamentalism emphasized a "Biblical literalness" and "salvation status" that "promotes a dispositional rather than a situational causal attribution of crime, leading its adherents to view crime as an outcome of weak or sinful character rather than of unfortunate or unjust situations."[58] In other words, Grasmick argues that Christian evangelicals tend to blame the individual perpetrator for his or her illegal actions and therefore support harsh punishment for criminals.

Grasmick's findings and arguments spurred further research on the connection between evangelicals and punitiveness, and a number of other scholars conducted research that complemented or challenged those earlier findings. Applegate et al. broke down the Christian religious category into two groupings: a "fundamentalist" core that holds retributive and punitive views but also a "compassionate" group that supports rehabilitation and opposes capital punishment.[59] Similarly, Unnever, Cullen, and Applegate stressed the diversity of views within the evangelical population, whereby those holding "angry and judgmental images of God" are more punitive than those with "loving images of God," who are more "compassionate" toward criminals.[60]

These results are sometimes difficult to disentangle, particularly since many studies mix in capital punishment with other assessments of punitiveness—and some focus primarily on the death penalty as the main measure of punitive views.[61] Yet, as the Supreme Court has long stated, "death is different," and in this case it makes sense that the "compassionate" side of some religious evangelicals would be especially touched by the possibility of a person's execution, which is quite different from supporting long prison sentences and harsh conditions for "sinners" who have broken the laws of both society and the Bible.[62] In other words, in the more "normal" (non-death-penalty) situations of criminal punishment, the empirical studies do seem to demonstrate the existence of strong and clear differences between evangelicals—albeit not necessarily as a single, coherent, unified group—and non-evangelicals, whereby the former advocate for and support harsher punitive measures.

Other scholars have explored the link between religion and mass incarceration with county-level data. Looking at Pennsylvania courts, Ulmer, Bader, and Gault found that greater levels of Christian homogeneity in a particular county was associated with a higher chance of incarceration. They concluded that "Christian homogeneity affects sentencing practices primarily through local political processes that shape the election of judges and prosecutors."[63]

Overall, while the available evidence is complex and not always clear in terms of direct causality, there is an unmistakable connection between evangelicals and harsh views on criminal punishment (even if this is mitigated somewhat by a looser relationship on the issue of the death penalty). The group of Americans known as evangelicals—who hardly exist and do not have real equivalents in our comparative European countries—do seem to represent a distinct and coherent category of people who have particularly severe and unforgiving assessments of how crime and criminals should be punished.

And given the synchronous rise of evangelical political power alongside the upsurge in mass incarceration, this religious element appears to have played an important part in the creation of today's distinctively American punitiveness.

Politics

The third factor that helps to explain American punitiveness has to do with the role of politics in the punishment of crime. Although the connection between politics and criminal justice is a long-standing feature in American history, it underwent a sharp transformation in the 1970s—and, importantly, this change was driven by key contributions from actors in both major political parties. Starting in the 1970s and accelerating into the 1980s and 1990s, a highly politicized "tough on crime" climate came to influence virtually all American politicians—from small-town mayors to governors and members of Congress—and led them to pass ever-"tougher" legislation.[64] As discussed in prior chapters, the public opinion and legislative contexts were quite different in the U.S. than in our comparative cases, thus resulting in harsh federal and state legislation that punished crime much more severely.[65]

The starting point of this shift emerged with Richard Nixon and the Republican Party's "Southern strategy," which sought to make inroads in the historically Democratic South by appealing to white racism in reaction to the accomplishments of the civil rights movement, namely the dismantling of the Jim Crow system of explicit racial segregation and discrimination. The strategy also tapped into white resentment of the climate created by progressive Supreme Court decisions on criminal procedure, abortion, school integration, voting rights, and the death penalty from the 1950s through the early 1970s, along with the stoked-up fear of crime and urban riots. According to historian Dan Carter, "The trick [of the Southern strategy] lay in sympathizing with and appealing to the fears of angry whites without appearing to become an extremist and driving away moderates—or, as Ehrlichman described the process, to present a position on crime, education, or public housing in such a way that a voter could 'avoid admitting to himself that he was attracted by a racist appeal.'"[66] In the words of Kevin Phillips, one of the architects of Nixon's Southern strategy who is credited with popularizing the term:

> From now on, the Republicans are never going to get more than 10 to 20 percent of the Negro vote and they don't need any more than that ... but Republicans would be shortsighted if they weakened enforcement of the Voting Rights Act. The more Negroes who register

as Democrats in the South, the sooner the Negrophobe whites will quit the Democrats and become Republicans. That's where the votes are. Without that prodding from the blacks, the whites will backslide into their old comfortable arrangement with the local Democrats.[67]

Phillips's analysis proved prophetic, and the unspoken "dog whistle" nature of the Southern strategy slowly but surely led to a complete political realignment of the South, which has now been staunchly Republican for several decades.

Although the story of the Southern strategy is well-established and familiar, a new revelation in 2016 demonstrated a crucial link to the criminal justice system and the current mass incarceration crisis. John Ehrlichman, President Nixon's former domestic policy chief advisor, had given an interview in 1994 to journalist Dan Baum, as part of Baum's research for a book on the failure of the War on Drugs.[68] For some reason, Baum chose not to use a key portion of that interview, and 22 years later—long after Ehrlichman's death in 1999—Baum revealed these quotes for an article in *Harper's Magazine*. According to Ehrlichman:

> The Nixon campaign in 1968, and the Nixon White House after that, had two enemies: the antiwar left and black people. You understand what I'm saying? We knew we couldn't make it illegal to be either against the war or black, but by getting the public to associate the hippies with marijuana and blacks with heroin, and then criminalizing both heavily, we could disrupt those communities. We could arrest their leaders, raid their homes, break up their meetings, and vilify them night after night on the evening news. Did we know we were lying about the drugs? Of course we did.[69]

Although this information is not necessarily new or shocking to readers of Michelle Alexander or other critics of the War on Drugs, it demonstrates conclusively that the origins of mass incarceration derived from a conscious strategy that was historically rooted in American politics.

The Republican Party's manipulation of the links between African Americans and crime continued through the Reagan administration's expansion of the War on Drugs in the 1980s, reaching its culmination in 1988 with George H.W. Bush's powerful and effective "Willie Horton ad" (discussed in detail in Chapter 6). The message learned "the hard way" by Michael Dukakis was that being labeled "soft on crime" is politically deadly.[70] As Nicola Lacey has shown, only in the U.S. do local, state, and federal office holders have the power to influence criminal justice—but also to have their careers influenced (or even defined) by it. Political candidates at all levels therefore attempt to prove their mettle by pushing for "tough on crime" policies. Multiple campaigns at multiple levels multiply the severity of punishment.

Although the Republicans' Southern strategy was a crucial element, Democrats have also played a major role in the tough-on-crime movement and mass incarceration. Employing a longer historical perspective, Naomi Murakawa shows that the expansion and strengthening of the federal justice system—largely pushed by Democrat presidents, especially Truman—ironically enabled the eventual development of mass incarceration. She writes that "liberals established a law-and-order mandate: build a better carceral state, one strong enough to control racial violence in the streets and regimented enough to control racial bias in criminal justice administration."[71] The result was a "fortified criminal justice system," even if it was procedurally "race neutral."[72] Murakawa concludes that "liberal law-and-order was especially powerful in entrenching notions of black criminality."[73] Although the political and ideological elements of Murakawa's argument have become controversial due to her counterintuitive blaming of liberals for mass incarceration,[74] the institutional part of her argument echoes William Stuntz, who contends that the sharp rise in punishment across the U.S. occurred only after criminal justice became a national issue.[75] Moreover, Michael Javen Fortner has recently demonstrated that many of the punitive Rockefeller drug laws from 1970s New York were actively supported by what he calls the "black silent majority" that wanted to rid their neighborhoods of drug abuse and associated crime.[76]

By the 1990s, Bill Clinton and fellow members of the Democratic Leadership Council (DLC) showed that they had learned very quickly from the Horton-Dukakis debacle, and they took decisive measures to move the Democratic Party to the right on crime. Clinton himself famously returned to Arkansas from the 1992 campaign trail in New Hampshire to oversee the execution of Rickey Ray Rector, a man who had become so mentally disabled (after a self-inflicted gunshot wound resulted in a frontal lobotomy) that he left behind the pecan pie from his last meal because he was saving it "for later."[77] As president, Bill Clinton went on to strongly support—alongside Joe Biden, the lead Senate sponsor of the bill—the Violent Crime Control and Law Enforcement Act of 1994, which led to a massive increase in the incarceration rate in the U.S., particularly among African Americans. And fearmongering rhetoric by then-first lady Hillary Clinton about "super-predators" who should be "brought to heel" only intensified the tough-on-crime climate in a Democratic administration. In fact, the number of people incarcerated in the U.S. increased from 1.3 million when President Clinton took office in January 1993 to 1.95 million when he left in January 2001. The additional 650,000 people incarcerated over the eight years of the Clinton presidency represents an even greater increase in raw numbers than the additional 447,000 people who were incarcerated over the 1980–1988 term of President Reagan (though it also expanded by 345,000 during the four-year presidency of George H.W. Bush).[78]

In short, although I would still maintain that the initial impetus for the tough-on-crime movement came more from the Right than from the Left, both parties bear responsibility for the mass incarceration that developed and accelerated over several decades. In a sense, one could say that it represented a bipartisan consensus—and as I argue in Chapter 9, it will take a similar bipartisan consensus in the other direction to undo the damage caused by these punitive policies.

In addition to the extremely prominent role of crime and punishment in U.S. politics, another distinctively American feature involves the realm of judicial politics, namely the election of the prosecutors and judges who made most of the individual decisions in the courthouses that actually determine the fate of the people accused and convicted of crimes. On this front, the contrast between the U.S. and European countries—or really the rest of the world—could not be more clear-cut.

Simply put, the U.S. is the only country in the world that elects its lead prosecutors (which occurs in 47 of the 50 U.S. states), and it is one of the few that primarily elects its judges (which occurs in 39 states).[79] In other words, whereas prosecutors and judges in most comparable countries are neutral and nonpartisan civil servants, in most American jurisdictions they are effectively politicians, officially associated with a political party and running for office. Moreover, just like candidates for other elected positions, they often have to campaign in media-driven elections where their judicial decisions can result in being labeled "soft on crime," which is considered politically fatal in a populist climate. As a result, many American prosecutors and judges view harshness toward criminals as essential to their political survival and career advancement.

Prosecutors run for election[80] in all states except Alaska, Connecticut, and New Jersey, where they are appointed. This method of selection did not exist at the American founding, when prosecutors were appointed (as they still are at the federal level). The move to elections originated in Mississippi in 1832 and then quickly spread to almost three-quarters of the other states by 1861.[81] Although in principle the idea seems democratic—and therefore fitting for the American historical tradition and context where more decisions have been made at the local level by citizens[82]—in practice the shift to prosecutorial elections occurred because of concerns about excessive political patronage exercised when making appointments.[83] Yet "Not long after prosecutors became elected, however, [they] quickly became involved in and coopted by partisan politics."[84]

The selection process for judges is a bit more complicated, with several variants—and some states have different procedures for trial and appellate courts (which explains the range in the numbers that follow): judges can be (1) appointed, by either the state legislature or the governor, in four or five states; (2) elected in partisan elections in 10–14 states; (3) elected in nonpartisan elections in 13–16 states; or (4) elected in "merit" elections in 19–26 states.[85] In total, 87 percent of all state court judges face elections in some form.[86]

The simple fact that prosecutors and judges are elected in the U.S. does not necessarily or inherently suggest that they will be less principled or fair. On the contrary, there are good theoretical reasons to believe that prosecutors and judges who remain connected to the people in whose community they serve will better reflect the values and preferences of their constituency, without being beholden to a particular person who may have appointed them. Ultimately, it is an empirical question, but as shown below, the results are very striking: the election of American prosecutors and judges has created more punitive state actors and judicial outcomes.

The impact of elections on prosecutors is quite straightforward. Since prosecutors within the American adversarial system are typically evaluated based on whether they can win convictions—particularly in highly publicized cases that generate media and public attention—their incentive structure is clear.[87] Moreover, the internal motivations for career advancement require assistant prosecutors to win cases for their office, and the most successful ones will advance their careers. Particularly in the "tough on crime" era, this leads prosecutors to promote their "toughness" in their electoral campaigns. For example, in the advertisement reproduced below, Oklahoma prosecutor Bob Macy "stands on his record," which does not include any mention of his education or other qualifications, but he does highlight his main achievements in office, namely: "44 Murderers Put on Death Row," "30,000 Felons Sent to Prison," "15,000 Juvenile/Gang Crimes Prosecuted," and "85,000 Criminal Cases Prosecuted." In short, the combination of prosecutorial elections and a "tough on crime" political climate leads to prosecutors like Bob Macy.

FIGURE 8.2 Bob Macy Stands on His Record

Moreover, as a result of such "tough" campaign slogans, incumbent prosecutors rarely lose, mainly because "challengers do not come forward very
often, far less often than challengers in state legislative elections."[88] And when
competitive elections actually do take place, the research of Ronald Wright
shows that "campaign statements dwell on outcomes in a few high visibility
cases, such as botched murder trials and public corruption investigations.
Incumbents and challengers have little to say about the overall pattern of outcomes that attorneys in the office produce or the priorities of the office. The
debates do not pick up genuine ideological differences among candidates; they
are misguided attempts to measure non-ideological competence."[89] In other
words, although perhaps born out of democratic aspirations, the election of
prosecutors hardly creates a more democratic process or enlightened citizenry.

If we turn to judges, empirical research has generated similarly powerful findings about the impact of elections on judicial decision making. One article published in 2002 showed that judges who face an impending re-election campaign impose significantly longer sentences on convicted defendants. Based on their analysis of 22,095 criminal cases in Pennsylvania in the 1990s, Gregory Huber and Sanford Gordon "attribute at least 1,818 to 2,705 years of additional prison time to this electoral dynamic."[90] Moreover, in a 2015 study produced by the Brennan Center for Justice, Kate Berry reviewed "10 recent, prominent, and widely cited empirical studies" of judicial elections and determined that "all found that the pressures of upcoming re-election and retention election campaigns make judges more punitive toward defendants in criminal cases."[91] In other words, in the heart of the "tough on crime" era, defendants who had the misfortune of randomly appearing before a certain judge who happened to be approaching an election campaign received considerably longer sentences than other defendants who appeared before different judges, or before the same judge when there was not an election looming.

The effect of elections on judges is even more pronounced—and, for the convicted criminal, literally fatal—in cases involving capital punishment. Stephen Bright and Patrick Keenan provide powerful evidence that the election of judges leads to more death sentences, showing that most death penalty states elect their judges, many judges reached their positions after having served as prosecutors in capital cases, and the death penalty is often a prominent campaign issue in judicial elections.[92] They also show that—especially when an election is approaching—judges are more likely than juries to impose the death penalty, and that when judges have the opportunity to override a jury sentence, they do so overwhelmingly in the direction of changing a verdict from life to death, and only rarely from death to life.[93]

Today there are three states that allow a judge to override a jury verdict in a capital case: Alabama, Delaware, and Florida. The practice seems to have stopped in Florida, with the last judge override for death taking place in 1999,[94] and in Delaware judges are appointed, and nobody is currently on death row because of a judicial override.[95] But it is in Alabama that the most egregious outcomes have taken place, which may lead to an upcoming Supreme Court case. As explained by the *New York Times'* Adam Liptak, "Alabama law allows judges to override jury recommendations in either direction: from life to death or from death to life. But Alabama judges mostly choose death." Moreover, "Since the Supreme Court reinstated the death penalty in 1976, judges in Alabama have overridden recommendations

of life 101 times and of death just 10 times." And it turns out that over 20 percent of Alabama's death row inmates were sentenced by judges who overrode
a jury's recommendation of life.[96]

This situation seems to have greatly troubled Justice Sonia Sotomayor,
who in a 2013 dissenting opinion on a denial of certiorari (joined by Justice
Stephen Breyer), wrote:

> What could explain Alabama judges' distinctive proclivity for impos-
> ing death sentences in cases where a jury has already rejected that pen-
> alty? There is no evidence that criminal activity is more heinous in
> Alabama than in other States, or that Alabama juries are particularly
> lenient in weighing aggravating and mitigating circumstances. The
> only answer that is supported by empirical evidence is one that, in my
> view, *casts a cloud of illegitimacy over the criminal justice system* [empha-
> sis added]: Alabama judges, who are elected in partisan proceedings,
> appear to have succumbed to electoral pressures. One Alabama judge,
> who has overridden jury verdicts to impose the death penalty on six
> occasions, campaigned by running several advertisements voicing his
> support for capital punishment. One of these ads boasted that he had
> "presided over more than 9,000 cases, including some of the most hei-
> nous murder trials in our history," and expressly named some of the
> defendants whom he had sentenced to death, in at least one case over
> a jury's contrary judgment. With admirable candor, another judge,
> who has overridden one jury verdict to impose death, admitted that
> voter reaction does "have some impact, especially in high-profile cases."
> "Let's face it," the judge said, "we're human beings. I'm sure it affects
> some more than others." Alabama judges, it seems, have "ben[t] to
> political pressures when pronouncing sentence in highly publicized
> capital cases." [. . .]
> 　　These results do not seem to square with our Eighth Amendment
> jurisprudence [. . .], and they raise important concerns that are worthy
> of this Court's review.[97]

In her dissent, Sotomayor seems to be asking for a better case for a challenge
to Alabama's judge override system, and apparently there are two possibilities
that are currently working their way up the appellate courts.[98]

Justice Sotomayor seems to agree strongly with one of her predecessors,
Sandra Day O'Connor, who retired in 2006, three years before Sotomayor
assumed her seat on the Court. Since stepping down, O'Connor has pushed

for an end to judicial elections, arguing that "elected judges are susceptible to influence by political or ideological constituencies."[99] The crux of O'Connor's argument involves the role and influence of money through campaign contributions and fundraising—a point that is only amplified by the Court's 2010 ruling in *Citizens United*. Recent evidence does seem to show increasing levels of money being spent on judicial elections. The *Economist* describes "judges increasingly resembling ordinary politicians in partisan mudfights," and it gives several examples:

> In 2010, after Iowa's Supreme Court unanimously struck down a ban on gay marriage, anti-gay-marriage groups targeted three judges with half a million dollars in spending. All three lost their seats. Results like this made national news, and inspired more spending than ever in this election cycle: $28m on television alone, according to the Brennan Centre for Justice at New York University. Much of the cash came from outside groups, mainly super-PACs and parties: $15.9m this year, against $10.4m in 2008.[100]

Like Sotomayor and O'Connor, the *Economist* concludes that this system is "contaminating" the judicial process.

In a well-reasoned defense of the election of judges, James L. Gibson claims that judicial elections remain "legitimate." He shows that ordinary Americans trust the court system to be impartial, and he therefore concludes that the election of judges helps to sustain the legitimacy of courts. While based on solid public opinion research, this conclusion nonetheless overlooks the unfortunate reality that judicial elections *have* created pernicious and discriminatory effects—regardless of how legitimate they may be in the eyes of the public.[101]

Does this increasingly large influx of money into judicial elections necessarily indicate higher levels of favoritism and possibly corruption? Based on their analysis of 186 cases before the Louisiana Supreme Court from 1992 to 2006, which controlled for the philosophical orientations of the justices and a host of other factors, Vernon Palmer and John Levendis show that "some of the justices have been significantly influenced—wittingly or unwittingly— by the campaign contributions they have received from litigants and lawyers appearing before these justices."[102] They conclude that "the very qualities needed in the highest court—independence, impartiality, and adherence to the rule of law—may have been eroded by the corrosive effect of judicial campaign money."[103] More analysis is needed in a broader set of states, but this evidence—along with common sense—does seem to indicate that just like politicians, judges (perhaps unintentionally or even unconsciously) will allow themselves to be influenced by campaign money. Meanwhile, the amount of money being spent on judicial elections—mainly by outside special interest groups—continues to rise, having reached a record $19.4 million in the 2016 elections.[104]

What is certain, however, is that in the political climate of recent decades, a "tough on crime" message from judges leads to electoral success. Similar to Bob Macy, the Oklahoma prosecutor shown above who campaigned based on his eagerness to prosecute, convict, and sentence harshly, elected judges often run on "law and order" messages. For example, Justice Cliff Young, who served for almost 20 years on the Nevada Supreme Court, ran for office with the slogan "Tough and Trustworthy." As shown in the advertisement below, Young's first endorsement was from the state governor, who called him "Tough on Crime," and his first self-descriptive selling point was that he "Supports the death penalty and voted to uphold it in 76 cases."

Just like his fellow traveler, prosecutor Bob Macy, Justice Cliff Young successfully exploited populist anti-crime sentiment to win elected office for positions that are supposedly about fairness, impartiality, and justice.

From a comparative European perspective, the role of politics in the punishment of crime is much less prominent and public. This is not to say that European politicians are not as calculating and callous as their American counterparts. Indeed, many European politicians still feel the pressure to create "wedge" issues that often isolate or target racial and ethnic minorities in order to seek electoral gains. And particularly gruesome or horrific crimes still lead to soul-searching and public debate about whether the criminal justice system works properly. Yet a similar revolution in cruelty did not occur in Europe because the criminal justice and prison systems in European countries are significantly more insulated from political pressures than in the U.S. Simply put, in European countries, judicial policymaking is (largely) left to the judiciary, whereas in the U.S. it is squarely within the realm of politics (whether at the national, state, or local level).

Moreover, in France, Germany, and the U.K., the major ideological cleavages have tended to be along more traditional left/right lines, without the type of underlying identity issues that defined the "Southern strategy" in the U.S. And while far-right parties have made significant and influential inroads throughout Europe in recent decades with an anti-immigrant message of exclusion—one that many mainstream parties have begun to incorporate as well, in an attempt to co-opt a populist approach that is often politically

Trust Justice Young

NEVADA LEADERS SAY:

"Tough on Crime" - *Governor Bob Miller*

"Women Can Trust Justice Young" - *Attorney General Frankie Sue Del Papa*

"Dedicated and Tireless in His Efforts" - *Senate Majority Leader Bill Raggio*

"Justice Young Has earned The Support of Nevada Women" - *Margot Pescovich* (*First women President Nevada Bar Association*)

Endorsed By Former Chief Justices: *Mowbray, Batjer and Manoukian*

Tough and Trustworthy

"Young does indeed deserve another turn. He has served Nevada well, and should continue serving it."
RENO GAZETTE·JOURNAL
Oct. 13, 1996

"Young is the best choice"
LAS VEGAS **SUN**
Oct. 25, 1996

"Cliff Young's commitment to change, openness and modernizing the Supreme Court should earn him another term. He is our choice in this race."
LAS VEGAS **REVIEW-JOURNAL**
Oct. 23, 1996

SUPPORTED BY LAW ENFORCEMENT:

- Nevada Conference of Police and Sheriffs
- Las Vegas Police Protective Association (Metro)
- Nevada Highway Patrol Association
- Henderson Police Officers Association
- Clark County School District Police Officers Association

SUPPORTED BY NEVADANS' FROM ALL WALKS OF LIFE:

- Culinary Workers Union, Local #226
- Professional Firefighters of Nevada
- Nevada State AFL-CIO
- Hispanics in Politics
- Nevada Voters League
- Citizens For A Responsible Government

JUSTICE YOUNG:

- Supports the death penalty and voted to uphold it 76 times
- Cracked down on abuses in death penalty and criminal appeals
- Reforms to fight domestic violence
- U.S. Army combat veteran
- Nevada Senator
- U.S. Congressman
- Harvard Law School Graduate

SUPPORTED BY SENIOR CITIZENS.
- National Council of Senior Citizens
- Seniors United
- Veterans in Politics

A Tough Law and Order Judge. Re-Elect Justice Cliff Young.
Nevada Supreme Court

FIGURE 8.3 Trust Justice Young

effective—there is no equivalent to a nationwide "tough on crime" movement that spanned virtually all parties and actors.

Moreover, the American practice of electing most prosecutors and judges appears bizarre and almost nonsensical to European eyes. As Ronald

Wright explains in the context of prosecutors, "In the various civil law systems in other countries, the idea of electing prosecutors is jarring." He adds that in other countries, "the public prosecutor's job, training and experience hold criminal prosecutors accountable to public values and legal standards." And prosecutors essentially "perform a ministerial function as they progress through a career-long bureaucratic journey."[105] In other words, although certainly internal professional pressures may put into question the objectivity and impartiality of European prosecutors, the job is primarily technocratic and based on knowledge, training, and expertise, rather than ideology or partisan politics—much less fundraising and influence peddling.

Similarly, the election of judges goes against the principles and practices of European judicial systems. In an evocative *New York Times* article on judicial elections and American exceptionalism, Adam Liptak opens with the tale of a Wisconsin judge who was unseated "after a bitter $5 million campaign in which a small-town trial judge with thin credentials ran a television advertisement falsely suggesting that the only black justice on the state Supreme Court had helped free a black rapist." He then contrasts this with "the path to the bench of Jean-Marc Baissus, a judge on the Tribunal de Grand Instance, a district court, in Toulouse, France. He still recalls the four-day written test he had to pass in 1984 to enter the 27-month training program at the École Nationale de la Magistrature, the elite academy in Bordeaux that trains judges in France."[106] The contrast could hardly be starker: In the U.S., someone can become a judge despite having very limited qualifications or credentials by raising and spending a lot of money on effective but misleading "tough on crime" television advertisements, whereas in France, someone has to undergo over two years of training and then pass a grueling four-day examination that evaluates one's knowledge and application of the law—one that 95 percent of applicants, all of whom already have law degrees, fail.

Germany follows a similar procedure to France, with "an intensive three year course of studies followed by two years of training," and potential judges receive both written and oral examinations after each of these two phases.[107] And in the U.K., judges "are recommended by judicial commissions with final appointment by the Secretary of State for Constitutional Affairs," a procedure that places value on the preparation, knowledge, and competence of judges.[108] As Trevor Jones and Tim Newburn write, "UK political processes enjoy greater protection from direct voter involvement and from politicized victim lobbying—and also, arguably, a stronger tradition of judicial independence."[109]

One should not be naïve or idealistic about the moral purity of European politicians, prosecutors, or judges, as even the more meritocratic European model does not necessarily prevent careerist pressures, partisan influencing, or outright corruption. But the key distinction is that European political and judicial systems allow for a much more restrained and limited influence of electoral politics on decisions and policies dealing with crime and punishment. This institutional insularity protects elected officials from having to pander to a populist and fear-based "tough on crime" message. And although the American system of electing prosecutors and judges may arguably embody greater democracy—in the narrow sense of reflecting the majority preference of citizens based on the information made available to them—one should not be naïve about the political and judicial consequences. Indeed, the effects of politics have been nothing short of draconian in the American context, and they have greatly contributed to the vast American exceptionalism and punitiveness demonstrated in previous chapters.

Business

The fourth and final major factor that has contributed to the distinctively American level of punitiveness of recent decades involves the vast web of economic interests that have converged around the criminal justice and prison systems. Although the pursuit of profit is a long-standing feature of American capitalism, the role of business and profit only entered the equation *after* the rise in incarceration rates began—yet once established, these interests have successfully pushed for the further expansion of incarceration and prisons. The role of business starts with the intricate system of "fees and fines" discussed in Chapter 7, and it continues with the process of receiving bail—another uniquely American institution with a bizarre history and tradition.[110] But it then reaches an entirely new level with prisons, as entrepreneurs and companies treat prisoners as business opportunities, and they manage to find ways to generate tremendous profit from incarceration. And in recent decades, private prison corporations have expanded in scope and especially influence on politicians and criminal justice policymaking.[111] As a result, these business interests are deeply entrenched in the everyday functioning of prisons, and—with their efficient political lobbying organizations and deep pockets—they often stand in firm opposition to meaningful criminal justice and prison reform.

The exploitative use of prison labor for economic profit builds directly on the earlier race-based system of convict leasing that replaced and substituted for slavery. After the demise of convict leasing in the 1920s, prisons entered a roughly 50-year period during which they were entirely state-run, with the

exception of some "ancillary services and secondary facilities."[112] During this
time, many prisons still used convict labor to produce food and materials,
which could be consumed within the prison or sold outside for a handsome
profit. For example, prison farms in Texas "produced eleven million pounds
of milk, ten million eggs, and two million pounds of beef." The real money-
maker, however, was cotton, which mainly African American inmates picked
all day long while generating $2 million a year for the Texas Department of
Corrections.[113]

The Juvenile and Delinquency Prevention Act of 1974 marked a turning
point nationwide that "created an incentive for private entrepreneurs and corporations" to work within juvenile facilities.[114] This process accelerated over
the rest of the 1970s, as federal courts took control of many state prisons,
ordering and imposing costly reforms. As explained by Joseph Hallinan,

> This surge in spending spawned a new era in American prisons. Private
> corporations got wind of the money being spent and sensed oppor-
> tunity. They saw inmates as a great untapped market that needed the
> same things free people did: not only staples like food and clothing but
> "amenities" like telephones and TV sets, weight-lifting equipment and
> basketball hoops, shampoo and soap and even hair food. There was
> almost no end to the things that prisons could be sold. And now, with
> court orders in their back pockets, prisons had the money to buy.[115]

This "prison gold rush" coincided with the abandonment of rehabilitation,
as prisoners were no longer viewed as people in need of help and reform to
prepare for a safe and productive return to society but as valuable units who
could provide labor for fixed and extremely low wages and consume products
sold at fixed and extremely high prices.

By the 1980s, several private prison companies—most notably the
Corrections Corporation of America (CCA, which was renamed CoreCivic
in October 2016) and Wackenhut (renamed the GEO Group in 2003)—took
these business endeavors to another level, pushing aggressively for contracts
to manage and run existing prisons and to build new ones. Even though under
10 percent of American prisoners reside in privately owned prisons, these corporations have transformed the economic landscape of prisons, helping to
create what some call the "Prison Industrial Complex" (PIC), which views
and treats inmates as opportunities for economic windfalls. According to Eric
Schlosser, the PIC refers to "a set of bureaucratic, political, and economic
interests that encourage increased spending on imprisonment, regardless of

the actual need. The prison-industrial complex is not a conspiracy, guiding the nation's criminal-justice policy behind closed doors. It is a confluence of special interests that has given prison construction in the United States a seemingly unstoppable momentum."[116] Patrice Fulcher adds that the PIC is "a profiteering system fueled by the economic interests of private corporations, federal and state correctional institutions, and politicians."[117] And it turns out that running prisons can be very profitable, as the CCA alone reported revenues of $1.675 billion in 2010.[118]

The impact of private prison corporations goes well beyond the approximately 133,000 prisoners who currently reside in privately owned prisons—corresponding to 6.8 and 19.1 percent of the state and federal prison populations, respectively, and constituting 8.4 percent of American prisoners overall.[119] More importantly, they have developed a political lobbying machinery that has pushed for harsher sentencing laws and other punitive policies that have fueled the current mass incarceration crisis. For example, the CCA's 2014 Annual Report makes clear how that company's interests are aligned with any potential policy changes in the area of criminal justice:

> The demand for our facilities and services could be adversely affected by the relaxation of enforcement efforts, leniency in conviction and sentencing practices or through the decriminalization of certain activities that are currently proscribed by our criminal laws. For instance, any changes with respect to drugs and controlled substances or illegal immigration could affect the number of persons arrested, convicted, and sentenced, thereby potentially reducing demand for correctional facilities to house them. Legislation has been proposed in numerous jurisdictions that could lower minimum sentences for some nonviolent crimes and make more inmates eligible for early release based on good behavior.[120]

According to a report by the Justice Policy Institute, "private prison companies have developed a three-pronged approach to influence incarceration policy and secure government contracts. Through campaign contributions, lobbying, and building relationships and associations, private prison companies engage in an aggressive political strategy to influence criminal justice policies in ways that lead to more people in prison and more money in their pockets."[121] In financial terms, these private corporations—through their Political Action Committees and employee contributions—have donated over $835,000 to federal candidates and more than $6 million to state-level politicians from 2000 to 2010.[122]

As a result of the policies that were facilitated by such effective campaign contributions and lobbying strategies, the soaring prison population necessitated the building and operating of more and more cells and beds, and this continual growth has thus generated continual profit.[123] And as the prison population skyrocketed, so too did the costs. According to Bureau of Justice Statistics reports, the annual costs of corrections was at $10.4 billion in 1983,[124] $24.5 billion in 1996,[125] $44.7 billion in 2003,[126] and over $80 billion in 2010.[127] This staggering increase (of almost 800 percent over a 27-year period) even dwarfs the massive surge in incarceration levels (of about 300 percent over that same time period).

The prison business model also worked in tandem with other types of profiteering within prisons, ranging from food provision, to product suppliers, to phone companies, most of which have exclusive contracts and monopoly control over an already-poor population that has no possibility of negotiating better market outcomes. The irony of this system is that it has been constructed in the name of "efficiency" and with the ostensible goal of saving money and resources for state and federal governments. But at the core it depends on an implicit continuation and expansion of mass incarceration—one that often becomes explicit in the form of "guarantees" for "occupancy rates" within contracts with the state.[128] In other words, the underlying premise and need of the private prison industry is for more and more inmates to fill prison beds and for recidivism to remain high (thus ensuring high occupancy rates). As Schlosser puts it, "The higher the occupancy rate, the higher the profit margin," and "the success or failure of a private prison is determined by the number of 'man-days' it can generate."[129]

The various labor unions of correctional officers constitute another powerful vested interest in maintaining and expanding high levels of incarceration. In fact, these unions played a critical role in the passage of the "three strikes" law in California in 1994 (which was only scaled back in 2012 after California voters supported Proposition 36). The California Correctional Peace Officers Association (CCPOA) "poured millions into the campaign coffers of politicians who pledged to put more people behind bars, and ran aggressive ads against those who dared to cross them."[130] Beyond that particular issue, the CCPOA became a formidable force in California politics, as its aggressive campaign contributions successfully pressured political actors in Sacramento to push in an ever-more punitive direction—one that the rest of the nation followed.

More recently, after seeming to back off from the punitive agenda in recent years, the CCPOA is once again supporting a plan to alleviate California's overcrowding problem by building even more prisons.[131] Meanwhile, prison unions elsewhere are also fighting back against proposed prison closings and most reform proposals, including the loosening of drug-related penalties and sentences.[132] "Otherwise progressive unions are taking reactionary positions when it comes to prisons, supporting addiction to mass incarceration. And when it comes to issues of prisoner rights in general, and solitary confinement in particular, they are seen as a major obstacle to reform."[133] In short, most of these prison guard unions have a clear, rational interest in the status quo, namely maintaining high levels of incarceration (or even expanding it further), and in many states they have the financial resources to have an impact on the debate and policy decisions.

The economic implications of prisons go well beyond the facilities and staff who work there. As Hallinan shows vividly, prisons can represent a tremendous boon to towns and communities where they are located, especially since many were built in poor, largely white areas deserted by oil companies and military bases, or "abandoned by traditional industries."[134] For example, the wages for correctional officers at a prison in Beeville, Texas, are about four times higher than the per capita income there, and these jobs and salaries help to boost local restaurants, bars, movie theaters, car insurance companies, and many other businesses.[135] And Rebecca Thorpe has shown that state legislators in rural communities with prisons supported harsher criminal punishments for non-violent offenses than their colleagues, even when controlling for political party and other political views.[136] In other words, those benefitting economically from prison construction have sought to increase the mass incarceration of citizens from other (predominantly urban) areas.

Within prisons, one of the main opportunities for profit has involved phone companies. According to the standard model, the prison chooses a single phone company provider for an exclusive contract with a monopoly on pricing, and the phone company then returns kickbacks to the prison.[137] As Hallinan puts it, "on a one-dollar phone call, the prison might make 40 to 50 cents. In no time, corrections departments became phone-call millionaires. In 1997, New York rang up $21.2 million from phone-call commissions. California made $17.6 million. Florida earned $13.8 million"[138] This revenue, of course, came from the families of the prisoners—in other words, from some of the poorest members of American society, who nonetheless paid these extremely high rates and fees for the opportunity to have some rare but precious contact with their loved ones locked away.[139] In short, according to

Kukorowski, Wagner, and Sakala, the prison phone business model is that the "prisons and jails get their commissions, the phone industry gets the fees, and the families get the hefty bills."[140]

The latest prison telecommunications venture involves video visitation, which began in 1995 and has expanded in recent years.[141] Again, prisons sign exclusive contracts with private companies such as Global Tel Link, VuGate, and Renevo, which—in the era of Skype and other virtually free and high-quality video services—provide grainy video connections that cost up to $1.50 per minute plus additional fees and charges. And while the companies and the prisons generate revenue from these systems, the inmates and their families have little recourse to complain about poor quality feeds, dropped calls, and high charges. Making matters worse, many of these same prisons have been working together with the companies to "shut down the traditional in-person visitation room."[142] In other words, not only does online video visitation "run the risk of becoming exploitative,"[143] but it comes at the expense of the "real" visits that are so important for prisoners' future societal reentry.

Health care constitutes another major business undertaking within many prisons. Since prisons are constitutionally obligated to provide health care for all inmates—the one population in the U.S. that "enjoys" such universal coverage—this represents a significant portion of prison budgets, often over 10 percent.[144] These costs have been increasing significantly as prisons have not only become more crowded, but they are also packed with ever-older inmates who have expensive health needs. What might be viewed as a crisis situation could also be treated as an opportunity to make money, as companies such as Prison Health Services and Correctional Medical Services have swooped in to provide what they call "cost-effective" care for prisoners.[145] In 2005, "32 states contracted with private companies for some or all of their prison health care services."[146] Of course, the quality of such care is suspect, at best.

Finally, many state prisons also generate tremendous revenue to state coffers by "employing" inmates in shops and factories that make products—whether license plates, highway signs, flags, furniture, or clothing. The advantage to these state enterprises is that they can pay extremely low wages, sometimes measured in just a few dollars per *day* of work, without any benefits, while saving on the cost it would take for "free" labor to make the same items and then selling certain manufactured products for lower prices than could be found on the open market.[147] Although these enterprises pay lip service to the rehabilitative notion that their workers benefit from job training that will reduce recidivism, the purpose is clearly profit-driven.

The opportunities for profit from the criminal justice and prison systems do not end when inmates leave prison. Just as with bail bondsmen on the front end of the criminal process, parole supervision on the back end has become increasingly privatized as well. Ten states now "contract with private agencies to provide supervision of an estimated 300,000 clients on court-ordered probation, typically for misdemeanor, low-risk offenses," and these operate with minimal regulation of the fees charged to parolees or the compensation provided to private parole officers.[148] The increasing use of electronic monitoring and GPS tracking devices present further opportunities for economic profit-making. And for the many people who are convicted of crimes but not sentenced to prison, private probation has become a huge and very profitable industry, making money off the fees and fines levied—over $40 million a year in Georgia alone.[149]

Overall, putting these various features together, we see that there are numerous vested interests in the continued existence of a system of mass incarceration that locks up the largest number of people for the longest possible time. It is of course difficult to specify the extent to which these business interests have expanded mass incarceration, as opposed to simply profiting from it.[150] But these companies are certainly well-connected politically, having built effective lobbying and campaign donation machines that have consistently brought them suitable criminal justice results for several decades. On the other side, inmates themselves have few resources (as most are poor and rely on mostly outmatched prisoner-rights organizations to defend their interests and rights) and virtually no voice (deprived of the right to vote, and with many restrictions on interactions with the media and outside world).

In comparative perspective, the extent of profit-making off of prisons is almost incomprehensible, and it bears a distinctively American orientation. While other countries certainly do allow for negotiated contracts with private companies for food and other provisions, and there are even some joint public-private prisons, the circumstances are radically different. In our comparison cases, prisons remain under the control of state institutions, and their primary purpose remains to rehabilitate prisoners and return them safely to society—rather than to view and treat inmates as moneymaking business ventures. This comparative distinction relates to broader differences between the European approach to the role of the state in society—which connects to Europe's more generous welfare state provisions, including health care, unemployment, retirement, and support for housing and living expenses—as opposed to the American faith that private enterprise will achieve cheaper, more efficient, and ultimately better outcomes.[151] The crucial role of business interests in creating the current mass incarceration crisis in America helps to show the limits of a naïve belief that private enterprise will work in every context and setting. And the devastating effects of so many aspects of business activities connected to prisons—both on the prisoners themselves and their families, as well as on society overall that is left to foot the bill and solve the mass incarceration problem—should put into question this distinctively American feature of criminal justice and prisons.

Conclusion

In an ideal statistical world, it would be possible to weigh competing explanations against one another, while controlling for other possible variables. But the question of what explains American punitiveness does not lend itself to multiple regression analysis or scientific hypothesis-testing. Moreover, common sense says that any explanation for such a complex and multifaceted phenomenon will involve a host of different and interrelated factors. This chapter has made the case that four distinctively American features of criminal justice help to explain the divergence that took place since the 1970s, when the U.S. and European countries were relatively closely aligned. First, following the second emancipation of African Americans after the end of Jim Crow, incarceration became a new—albeit less direct and overt—method for excluding blacks from the vote and full participation in society. Second, the newfound political organization and strategic success of Christian evangelicals pushed for a harsh, "eye for an eye," approach to criminal justice. Third, the distinctively American practice of politicizing crime and punishment, and also holding elections for most prosecutors and judges—within a political climate driven by money, fear, and negative campaigns—created a situation whereby the label "soft on crime" became the kiss of death for any elected official. Fourth, starting in the mid-1970s, prisons transformed from essentially state-run institutions aimed at rehabilitating inmates to profit-driven business ventures that combined political lobbying with an agenda that required ever-more prison beds and prisoners to fill them.

Putting them all together, we see that each of these factors is almost exclusively an American phenomenon—with little relevance or applicability in our comparison countries of France, Germany, and the United Kingdom—and also that each one was transformed in the mid-1970s, precisely when mass incarceration in America began its steep climb. In other words, all four factors involve not only long-standing (i.e., static) features of American history and society, but also—and more importantly—a similar temporal (i.e., dynamic) change that mirrored the rise in mass incarceration. For it was over the course of the 1970s, 1980s, and 1990s that: (1) racial discrimination moved from being "explicit" to "implicit," while being portrayed as a race-neutral criminal justice problem; (2) religious evangelicals, with their harsh views on criminal behavior and support for retribution and stern punishment, organized and mobilized as a political force; (3) crime and punishment became highly politicized, whereby political elections for all offices—including even prosecutors and judges—engaged in modern campaign tactics, with fundraising, lobbying, and negative attacks and smear campaigns against opponents; and (4) various business interests realized that they could capitalize on the growth in the prison industry to create windfall profits. Collectively, these four factors helped to reshape American criminal justice and prisons by creating the most extensive, widespread, and punitive carceral system in world history.

Having accounted for the rise in American punitiveness that explains the current status quo, the next—and final—chapter concludes this book by exploring the possibilities for reform and a reversal of the trend of the past four decades. It addresses the promising bipartisan proposals and opportunities that seem to have emerged only recently, while weighing the impact of the unexpected resurgence of "law and order" politics that contributed to the election of President Donald Trump. It also evaluates the potential for change in each of the four factors discussed in this chapter, showing some small steps toward improvement in terms of race, religion, politics, and business. And in a debate that all-too-frequently remains myopically focused on the U.S. alone, the Conclusion points to the importance of learning from other countries and models that have already worked. In short, it seeks to bring together the "lessons learned" from the comparative perspective of this book, in order to provide a menu of proven options that could help to transform and improve the quagmire of American criminal justice and prisons.

9

Conclusion

ALTHOUGH THE EFFECTS of the 2016 presidential election and the arrival of the Trump administration remain unclear, the outlook for the American criminal justice and prison systems is very different in 2017 than it was even a decade ago. The increases in all aspects of American punitiveness that continued relentlessly throughout the 1970s, 1980s, 1990s, and 2000s may have come to an end. After decades of ever-"tougher" political and judicial decisions, recent years seem to indicate the early stages of a genuine turnaround. This concluding chapter briefly reviews and evaluates the recent changes in both rhetoric and policy, providing grounds for a cautious optimism about the current "window" that has opened for criminal justice and prison reform. It then turns to the comparative perspective provided in this book to suggest lessons and models that could be applied successfully to the American context. And it closes with a normative argument about the moral obligation that society has toward its incarcerated citizens.

Reasons for Optimism

There are many reasons for optimism about a potential retrenchment of mass incarceration. For the first time in nearly four decades, the number of incarcerated people in the United States actually decreased slightly in 2009, and this has been followed by further (though still quite small) declines in the subsequent years as well. This reversal is extraordinary given that the number of prisoners had grown *each and every year* for the preceding 35 years.

Perhaps more important, a surprising bipartisan alliance emerged in support of criminal justice and prison reform, bringing together a previously unthinkable coalition consisting of such liberal forces as the NAACP, ACLU, and George Soros, on the one hand, and the conservative "Right on Crime" movement, the National Association of Evangelicals, and the Koch brothers, on the other. Within Congress, this alliance is best captured by the voices and legislation of such leaders as Mike Lee (R-UT), Rand Paul (R-KY), and Cory Booker (D-NJ), along with others in the Senate and House from both parties. Although Senate Majority Leader Mitch McConnell (R-KY) has largely stayed silent, House Speaker Paul Ryan (R-WI) has added his support to the reform efforts, stating, "I think we need to let more people earn a second chance at life. Instead of locking people up, why don't we unlock their potential?"[1] Oddly enough, criminal justice reform has been one of the only issues that has engendered bipartisan support and action in an era of unprecedented partisanship and political division.

Although the recent reform movement is certainly a bipartisan effort, the real impetus and starting point has come from conservatives. During the heyday of the "tough on crime" era, Democrats not only offered little resistance to the onslaught of increased incarceration and punitiveness, but they joined in and piled on. In fact, most Democrats vowed not to be "Willie Horton'ed"[2] and suffer the fate of Michael Dukakis, whose presidential campaign was doomed when he was accused of being soft on crime (among other things). They therefore avoided taking a stance that criticized mass incarceration or recognized the humanity of prisoners. As a result, in the words of Grover Norquist, a noted fiscal conservative who has been outspoken in criticizing the costs of maintaining such high incarceration rates, "Conservatives can have a conversation here that can actually move the ball. Only the Republicans can come forward and talk about saving resources at the same time that you fight crime because nobody believes the Democrats are actually going to punish crime." Benjamin Jealous, former president of the NAACP, essentially agreed that reform will come from Republicans, since "so many Democrats have become reflexively afraid of appearing soft on crime."[3]

In their engaging account of the recent transformation among conservatives on mass incarceration, David Dagan and Steven Teles show and explain how this change took place.[4] In 2011, one of the leaders of this nascent movement was none other than Newt Gingrich—who 25 years earlier had called for a "decisive, all-out effort to destroy the underground drug empire," and who supported and steered many of the policies and laws of the punitive era. This time, though, Gingrich spoke of "an urgent need to address the astronomical growth in the prison population, with its huge costs in dollars and lost human potential." He added, "The criminal-justice system is broken, and conservatives must lead the way in fixing it."[5] Norquist and Gingrich then joined forces with other notable conservatives, including Pat Nolan, a former rising star in California's Republican Party, who was convicted of bribery and sentenced to 33 months in a federal prison.[6] Nolan and his family became connected with Prison Fellowship, an evangelical organization—created by Charles Colson, a former aide to President Richard Nixon who served time for his role in the Watergate scandal—which seeks to support prisoners and their families.[7] Moreover, Julie Stewart, who founded Families Against Mandatory Minimums in 1991 after her brother Jeff was sentenced to five years in federal prison for growing marijuana, aligned with other libertarians to create a nationwide organization that has garnered tremendous attention and moral authority.[8]

These powerful advocates were without question "real" conservatives, and they thereby had an authenticity and influence that allowed them to avoid any accusations of being "soft" or "liberal." And by creating an institutional platform through groups such as Right on Crime, they were able to change the terms of the debate within the conservative movement, and gradually build a coalition of other influential conservative allies.[9] Most important, they carved out a safe space for both conservatives and liberals to begin a conversation within a new, supportive, and less politicized climate. In short, "The conservative evolution has enabled the United States to finally break the persistent upward trajectory of incarceration and put in play the prospect of seriously reducing the nation's bloated prison population."[10]

Meanwhile, around the same time period, the media coverage of criminal justice and prisons has not only increased in quantity, but the tone has shifted from emphasizing crime and criminality to highlighting institutional shortcomings, official violations and abuses, and stories of racism and human injustice. This has taken place within numerous individual newspapers and outlets—both in print and online—as well as by organizations such as The Marshall Project that collect, tabulate, and disseminate stories from around the country.[11] Prominent newspapers, especially the *Washington Post* and the *Guardian*, as well as other independent analysts, have been tracking and publicizing incidents of police violence.[12] And the protest activities of Black Lives Matter, along with the organized activism of groups such as Van Jones's "#cut50" movement, which seeks to reduce the prison population by 50 percent over the next 10 years,[13] have generated regular and steady attention from the mainstream media.

Several states are leading the way in criminal justice reform, and others are taking notice. In an "unprecedented experiment in mass forgiveness,"[14] California was forced to release thousands of prisoners (including lifers convicted of murder) following the 2011 *Plata* ruling by the Supreme Court. Despite this "astounding 17 percent reduction in the size of the California prison population," there has been "no effect on aggregate rates of violent or property crime."[15] Texas was facing an enormous budgetary challenge in 2007, with projections of new prison construction to contain the ever-increasing number of inmates. But rather than spend over $2 billion on new prisons, the state "invested $241 million in probation, parole, and reentry of non-violent offenders." Since that point, the "incarceration, recidivism, and crime rates have all decreased in Texas."[16] Similar findings emerge from studies in New Jersey and Kentucky, providing further support for early parole policies that includes supportive post-release supervision.[17]

Many other states have passed a host of bills that are making a positive impact on criminal justice and prisons. The Vera Institute of Justice has been tracking these reforms for several years. In a 2014 report that focuses on the changes that took place in 2013, the Vera Institute finds that "35 states passed at least 85 bills to change some aspect of how their criminal justice systems address sentencing and corrections. These bills largely eschew the tough-on-crime policies of the past, and reflect the gathering momentum for criminal justice reform in the United States."[18] In a 2016 report that addresses the reforms from 2014 and 2015, it affirms that "46 states enacted at least 201 bills, executive orders, and ballot initiatives to reform at least one aspect of their sentencing and corrections systems."[19] These include some of the following examples of state-level reforms: judges in New Jersey now have more power to release defendants who cannot afford bail, rather than forcing them to stay in jail while awaiting trial; Idaho has 24-hour crisis centers for mental health patients who would otherwise be locked up unnecessarily; Georgia and Louisiana now have special courts for military veterans who are charged with crimes; and Hawaii has established and supported programs that facilitate regular contact between children and their incarcerated parents.[20] In addition, many states have legalized marijuana, and some (including Utah) have made heroin or cocaine possession only a misdemeanor.[21] Even though many of these reforms were relatively minor and not necessarily "game-changing" given the scope of mass incarceration, the collective impact and momentum across states has been significant.

On the federal level, the Obama administration implemented a series of criminal justice reforms, including banning juvenile solitary confinement, phasing out the use of private federal prisons, and granting clemency to numerous non-violent drug offenders.[22] In fact, President Obama, who was the first president to visit a federal prison while in office, commuted the sentences of more prisoners than any other president since Calvin Coolidge.[23] Although federal reforms usually have limited direct impact and are largely symbolic given that over 90 percent of prisoners reside in state facilities, the signals are important and can influence similar movement within states.[24] Moreover, in 2015 the Federal Communications Commission (FCC) passed new caps on phone rates, thus lowering the exorbitant cost of phone calls from all prisons and jails (federal and state), and thereby reducing the tremendous burdens on the budgets of the (usually poor) families of incarcerated people.[25]

At the same time, American public opinion seems to be moving away from punitive positions, in favor of alternatives to incarceration, lighter sentences, and rehabilitation programs within prisons. Perhaps this reflects the changing tenor of the discussion, driven in part by the attention paid to Michelle Alexander's *The New Jim Crow*, coverage of Black Lives Matter protests, and video recordings of police violence and brutality that have been widely distributed on social media. The American public seems to agree that "enough is enough" and to support different solutions to incarceration and punishment. For example, a 2015 survey of Texas residents hardly a liberal bastion commissioned by the conservative Right on Crime organization showed, among other findings, that 57 percent of Texans "would support legislation that would reduce the time an inmate spends in prison, so that they could spend some of their sentence being monitored under community supervision."[26] Moreover, a 2016 nationwide survey conducted by the Pew Charitable Trusts found that 60 percent of Americans (70 percent of Democrats and 50 percent of Republicans) agree that too many drug criminals are in prison, 79 percent support eliminating mandatory minimums for drug cases, and 85 percent favor programming in prison to reduce recidivism.[27] And the important public opinion research conducted by Peter Enns demonstrates that American punitiveness has been declining on many fronts for the first time in several decades, with increasing support for less harsh terms and forms of punishment.[28]

For all of these reasons, and for the first time in nearly half a century, there are significant reasons for optimism about the possibility of significant change that could lead to a relative reduction in mass incarceration and this unusually cruel form of American exceptionalism.[29]

Reasons for Caution

That said, there are still many reasons to remain circumspect about the long-term prospects and outcomes of this reform effort. One is that the actual reductions in incarceration have been very marginal thus far. At the 1.8 percent rate of decline of 2012, Marc Mauer and Nazgol Ghandnoosh estimate that it would take 88 more years—until the year 2101—for the prison population to reach the 1980 level.[30] Moreover, the overall decline masks a great deal of unevenness across the country, as certain states (notably California, New York, and New Jersey) have reduced their prison populations by 15–20 percent over the past decade, whereas incarceration levels in other states have hardly changed.[31] In other words, it is far too early to celebrate the declines in incarceration of the past several years. Overall, the U.S. remains by far the overwhelming leader in mass incarceration, and despite incremental reductions, this shows no sign of changing significantly in the foreseeable future.

As mentioned above, the legislative proposals in the U.S. Congress have generated a great deal of attention to these issues nationwide, but they are mainly restricted to *federal* laws and procedures, which only impact the approximately 215,000 federal prisoners; the additional 1,360,000 inmates in state prisons and 700,000 in state jails would not be affected by most of these federal-level changes.[32] And on the state level, although many states have implemented some incremental reforms on various criminal justice issues, only a few have really taken major steps to reverse mass incarceration, and other states have not even addressed the issue.

Part of the reason for the wide legislative variation across states stems from a lack of direction from the courts, as the Supreme Court has largely deferred to Congress and state legislatures on most issues related to criminal justice and prison policy (with the notable exception of the *Plata* decision discussed in Chapter 4). As a result, legislators feel little pressure—whether from the courts or from voters, since people with criminal convictions hardly represent an organized or effective interest group or constituency—to make meaningful changes. Even if they realize that it is the "right" thing to do, there is not much of an electoral or political logic to supporting such reforms—and of course many still fear the potential backlash should something go wrong.

As for the unusual—and tenuous—bipartisan alliance that has recently emerged, the terms of the debate have been framed primarily as an *economic* question that calls for a renewed cost-benefit analysis in the calculation and evaluation of state and federal budgets. Yet, according to Marie Gottschalk,

> Recasting the problem of mass incarceration in econometric or cost-benefit language is problematic in many ways. It does little to challenge the excessively punitive rhetoric that has left such a pernicious mark on penal policy over the last half century. It also is no match for the considerable economic interests that are now deeply invested in the perpetuation of the carceral state. Furthermore, it constricts the political space to challenge penal policies and practices on social justice or human rights grounds. Among elite policy makers and the wider public, creating a safe, healthy, and humane penal system is generally not considered a credible and desirable public policy goal on its own. This goal has to be linked somehow to enhancing public safety and saving public money.[33]

In short, Gottschalk argues that not only does this approach ignore the larger human question about the effect of mass incarceration on people, families, communities, and society, but it actually legitimates the very neo-liberal economic framework that is partly responsible for the poverty and inequality that created this situation in the first place.[34]

One constant throughout the public debate has been the politically more "palatable" emphasis on drug convictions and "nonviolent offenders." Many of the arguments for prison reform highlight the examples of people serving extremely long sentences for "victimless" crimes such as drug possession or theft. In fact, virtually all of President Obama's record number of commutations (1,715 in total) were granted to long-serving prisoners who had committed non-violent drug offenses. Yet while "nonviolent drug convictions are a defining characteristic of the federal prison system, [they] play only a supporting role at the state and local levels."[35] In fact, about 53 percent of those incarcerated in state prisons were convicted of a violent crime (often in addition to drug crimes).[36] In order to genuinely take on the deep and difficult challenges of prison reform, proponents will have to address the issue of violent crime, rather than settle for the "low-hanging fruit" of non-violent drug offenders. In short, the conversation about criminal justice and prison reform needs to address the circumstances surrounding the sentences, prison conditions, and opportunities for rehabilitation and societal reentry of (formerly-) violent criminals as well.

In terms of partisan politics, the 2016 presidential election campaign pushed the limits of the reform consensus, and the election of President Donald Trump highlights the tremendous power of the old theme of "law and order," with racially coded messages of fear of crime. Moreover, Trump's stance and success has emboldened other critics of criminal justice reform, especially Senator Tom Cotton (R-AK), who actually stated that the U.S. has an "under-incarceration problem."[37] Although other conservative supporters of reducing mass incarceration remained steadfast during a presidential campaign that they (like most expert analysts from all sides) expected Trump to lose, the Republican Party is now Trump's party, and the momentum of the past few years—even on the state level—could easily be reversed.[38] It remains to be seen whether the tenuous pre-election bipartisan consensus—initiated and led by conservatives—will survive within the Trump administration, or whether it will prove to have been a small blip on the long road toward continuing, perpetuating, and expanding mass incarceration.

As for public opinion, while there has without question been a shift away from the punitive model, the change has been more tentative than decisive, and it could easily shift back if politicians and the media renew their focus on crime and particular horrific incidents. As Peter Enns writes, "An uptick in crime, followed by the standard media coverage of crime, could push the public back in a more punitive direction."[39] The examples from previous decades show that public opinion can be easily manipulated, particularly by reductionist messages based on fear.[40] For example, New York governor Andrew Cuomo's proposal to spend $1 million on prison education—corresponding to just 0.036 percent of the state's $2.8 billion budget for corrections—was defeated after a popular uproar about public support for prison education, despite strong evidence that such programs are very effective in transforming people, saving money, and preventing future victims.[41] Opponents of Cuomo's plan coined slogans such as "Hell No to Attica University," and three New York congressmen introduced a bill in the House called the Kids Before Cons Act. After this backlash, Cuomo quickly retreated.[42] The example shows that highly politicized and fearmongering opposition to reform proposals can be extremely effective, even if research, logic, economic rationality, and common sense support the changes.

Overall, while the terms and tone of the conversation have clearly shifted in recent years, the challenges to criminal justice and prison reform remain multifaceted, deeply rooted, and extremely difficult to overcome.

Synthesis: Cautious Optimism

While it remains too early to evaluate the extent of change on the horizon—particularly after the tumult of the 2016 presidential election—the current situation still represents a new opportunity for criminal justice and prison reform. For the first time in memory, there is a real conversation about—and movement in favor of—such issues as holding police and prosecutors accountable for violations, shortening prison sentences, improving prison conditions, developing and supporting rehabilitation programs, allowing for early release and parole, and helping former prisoners with societal reentry. But there is also strong resistance to reform on each of these issues, and proposals to reduce mass incarceration, to bolster the rights of people behind bars, and to support the formerly incarcerated with societal reentry rarely find smooth sailing to passage and implementation.

In short, the situation looks better than it has in many decades, but the support for change is extremely fragile. Under such challenging circumstances as a particularly gruesome crime situation, changing news coverage, or political exploitation by President Trump or other like-minded candidates on the federal or especially state level, it could fall apart very quickly.

The Role of Race, Religion, Politics, and Business in Lasting Reform

Chapter 8 identified four factors—race, religion, politics, and business—that have a distinctively American flavor and that together help explain the unusual cruelty of American criminal justice and prisons. Obviously none of these explanatory factors can be eliminated or drastically changed overnight, but to the extent that reform is taking place, it would make sense for there to be some countermovement on each of them.

In terms of race, American society remains extremely divided along racial lines, with very different views and assessments of the criminal justice consequences of racial distinctions. But certainly the proliferation of videos of police and other institutionalized discrimination or brutality, along with much greater coverage of the everyday indignities that many African Americans face on a regular basis, has helped change the landscape on race. Although there may still be strong resistance to the agenda of Black Lives Matter and other such movements, there is clearly much greater awareness of the issues that were previously unknown to many white Americans.

As for religion, there has certainly been a softening of the harsh "eye for an eye" retributive approach of so many evangelicals, along with a more humane attitude toward the new heroin crisis and addiction epidemic that has reached into middle-class white America. Organizations such as Prison Fellowship aim to use a religious message of restoration, hope, and redemption to transform incarcerated people and support their families. And support for capital punishment among highly religious people and organizations has been declining as well.

It is difficult to find a clear direction in terms of politics, since so much can vary across individual races, depending on the particular region, background, and context. Indeed, the 2016 presidential election showed that the old "law and order" scare tactics employed by Donald Trump remain very effective in many parts of the country. Yet, at the same time, under the political cover and support provided by bona fide conservative organizations such as Right on Crime, we have been seeing a greater number of Republican politicians, along with some prosecutors and judges, who are taking a moral or economic stand against mass incarceration. It remains to be seen whether future Republican candidates—as well as their Democratic opponents, who may well respond to the Trump phenomenon with a "tough on crime" message that echoes Bill Clinton's move in 1992—will make crime, and especially the *fear* of crime, a major political issue in the future.

Finally, the business interests surrounding the prison industrial complex find themselves backpedaling for the first time in recent memory. Until the 2016 election sent their stocks soaring, the private prison industry was reeling from the decision to close down private federal prisons. And the prison telephone companies are still coping with the FCC's decision to cut phone rates substantially. This may change, of course, if the Trump administration pursues policies to bolster private prisons once again. The situation will likely change, depending on the policies pursued by the Trump administration. Either way, these companies are savvy and will seek to make adjustments to find other areas and ways to profit from prisons (one example is with "video visitation"). Yet there seems to be genuine movement and pushback against these industries, which until recently had little oversight, supervision, or even attention paid to their activities and profiteering.

Overall, while obviously the racial, religious, political, and business character of the United States are not features that can change in a matter of years, the country's orientation in terms of the punitive policies, practices, and culture has been evolving very quickly in recent times. And since these are the key features that combine to define American exceptionalism, it is possible that changes on each of them may lead to a continuation of the recent decrease in the levels of punitiveness in the U.S.

Comparative Advantage: Lessons from France, Germany, and the United Kingdom

Although wide-ranging in substance and motivation, most of the discussions about American criminal justice and prison reform remain in a vacuum, focused almost exclusively on the situation in the U.S. But the chapters in this book have shown that other countries have experience with many of the very solutions that the U.S. is seeking to implement. Any reforms of the American model will obviously require careful application to the very particular and difficult American historical, societal, and political context, especially since most American courts and Supreme Court justices have famously rejected the relevance of foreign law and examples.[43] Yet all protagonists in this policy debate—and their supporters in academia and the general public—would be well-served to explore the positive examples that have a proven and successful track record elsewhere.

The previous chapters have made clear that there is not one simple, singular, or specific problem with the American model that, if fixed, would make the other deficiencies go away. In other words, plea bargaining, sentencing, prison conditions, rehabilitation, parole, and societal reentry all represent interlinked but largely distinct elements or layers of American cruelty. Reforming just one would not necessarily entail significant movement in the others. This suggests that genuine, overarching reform will require movement on multiple fronts, ideally in sync with one another. In other words, it will require a new vision and approach to criminal punishment and the treatment and rehabilitation of those who have committed crimes.

Fortunately, the comparative cases analyzed in this book suggest models on all fronts that work better and achieve results that are more efficacious and humane for both perpetrators and victims. Starting with plea bargaining, American reformers should reduce the disturbingly high level of plea bargaining that exists across the federal and state systems, where fewer than 5 percent of criminal defendants actually go to trial. They should also learn from the recent French and German experiments with plea bargaining, which limit the circumstances and types of cases in which it is possible. At the very least, if keeping the American structure—though ideally there would be some rethinking of the current procedures for electing prosecutors and judges—they should reconsider the balance of power between prosecution and defense, and also ensure the genuine neutrality and openness of the judge, while giving much greater scrutiny to the extent of actual "voluntariness" of guilty pleas.

In terms of sentencing, there needs to be a nationwide recalibrating of the length of prison sentences associated with specific crimes, along with a clearer sense of the motivation of the sentence itself—whether incapacitation, deterrence, retribution, or rehabilitation. If the main purpose is to protect society from criminals and crime, more consideration should be given to the fact that most criminals "age out" of their bad ways when they reach "criminal menopause" by around age 40 (and often much earlier). The comparison countries offer much to emulate in terms of sentences that are by no means lenient, but do not necessarily remove a person from society—and from his or her family—for excessively long periods of time either. In contrast, the French, German, and British sentencing structures are much more rational (by seeking to reduce crime and keep society safe) and humane (by taking seriously the punishment of removing people from their families and society for a sufficient but not exorbitant period of time). These suggestions are not unrealistic, even if they would require a recalibration of current practices. The Sentencing Project's Marc Mauer has recently proposed that "federal sentencing structures should establish an upper limit of no more than 20 years in prison, except for exceptional circumstances," a policy that would align the U.S. with comparable European democracies without endangering public safety.[44] And states and the federal government should capitalize on recent judicial momentum by banning life without parole (LWOP) for juveniles, and also potentially for many adult prisoners as well, which would align the U.S. more closely with the comparison countries that seldom or never apply LWOP sentences.

Turning to prison conditions, it is hard to imagine any significant changes without reducing the number of people being sentenced to prison, diminishing the amount of time spent there, and increasing the opportunities for earning conditional release or parole. Indeed, overcrowding is a regular feature of American prison life, one that fuels violence, disease, and despair. And few reformers would argue in favor of building even more prisons in order to continue to warehouse the existing population more comfortably. Yet even within the existing physical structures of American prisons, greater attention should be paid to the demeaning lack of privacy, autonomy, rights, or recourse that incarcerated people are subjected to. Most European prisons are by no means pleasant or enjoyable settings—and many are overcrowded as well—but they build on the value that being sentenced to prison is punishment enough, and there is no need for added humiliation or degradation. In short, "Treat people like dirt, and they will be dirt. Treat them like human beings, and they will act like human beings."[45]

Improving the conditions within prisons goes hand in hand with offering programs that prioritize rehabilitation as a societal goal. This requires a shift in orientation to viewing "inmates" as human beings who can improve and develop life and vocational skills. European prison systems have been much more in touch with scientific research about the benefits—both to incarcerated people and the society to which they will eventually return—of rehabilitation programs, addiction treatment, education, and job training. The goal should be to help people along a path to personal transformation such that their release will allow them to succeed and flourish on the outside, thereby reducing costs, crime, and victims, while also benefiting from the resources and ingenuity that truly committed and reformed people can bring to those around them.

Another crucial step for reform involves a reopening of discretionary parole, which has been stuck in a political vicious cycle since the Willie Horton ad of 1988, with devastating consequences to countless incarcerated people and their families. American politicians are stuck in a position of fear that one mistake will cost them their careers. Yet the European models show that when conditional release and parole decisions are made separately from the political realm, not only can demagoguery and fearmongering be avoided, but productive incentives and choices can be built and made based on rational evidence and assessments. Reforming parole in the U.S. will require either a dramatically different orientation by politicians (which is unlikely, at least in the short term) or the depoliticization of the entire process, such that parole decisions would be made by panels of counselors or experts, rather than elected officials. It would also require the adoption of the European approach illustrated by Germany's system that states that "the exclusion of all risk is not required— a 'justifiable' degree of risk is accepted."[46] This "risk tolerance" must be able to overcome the occasional mistake that will be painful and lead to headlines and accusations—because otherwise the political incentive is to keep everyone locked up indefinitely out of fear that one person will reoffend. Reformers should learn from the European countries and attempt to implement clear and attainable incentives and goals for tangible rewards in terms of sentence reduction, interaction outside of prison, personal visits (including conjugal visits), furloughs, and ultimately conditional release.[47] Overall, a more judicious application of parole would alleviate some of the tremendous overcrowding in American prisons, especially if used in conjunction with effective rehabilitation programs that would help to further reduce the risk of recidivism.

Finally, for those prisoners who are eventually released, the American system offers few genuine chances to embark on a "second chance" when they face severe and lasting restrictions on their citizenship (voting, running for office, or serving on juries), employment, and housing. The European models, in contrast, offer tremendous privacy protections (with exceptions for specifics crimes that have bearing on certain types of potential employment), and they are based on the notion that the punishment ends when the person leaves the prison. Implementing these types of reforms in the U.S. would be difficult given the vastly different welfare state traditions and support for the poor and disadvantaged, but it would require going well beyond "Ban the Box" campaigns in order to provide genuine support for former criminals and prisoners to develop a law-abiding and productive life after incarceration.

A New American Vision

As explained in the Introduction to this book, even though other scholars have studied, analyzed, and criticized the American criminal justice and prison systems, most have worked within an exclusively American perspective. And while many of these accounts have been powerful and revelatory—indeed, they have inspired the writing of this book and illuminated many of its contents—they remain limited by their singular focus on the U.S., which unintentionally forecloses other models and solutions. In contrast, what this book has attempted to show through the comparison to France, Germany, the U.K., and occasionally other countries, is that there *are* other, better, safer, more cost-effective, and more productive ways to handle the punishment of crime. In other words, rather than examining and debating specific issues on a one-dimensional American timeline of past and current practices, one should consider other dimensions, namely the traditions and procedures that have worked and do work in other countries.

It should be clear, I hope, that being caught in a criminal justice and prison system is not—and arguably should not be—a positive or pleasant experience anywhere. But there are degrees of suffering and degrees of cruelty, and the analysis contained in this book has shown that the U.S. is on a completely different level for all of the elements of the "life cycle" of criminal justice—literally off the charts on every single measure. For people who are familiar only with the modern American way, this may seem to be the "natural" state of affairs—simply reflecting "the way it is." But hopefully this book has helped to open their eyes to other ways, methods, practices, and ideals that are not only different, but clearly better. And why not strive to apply some of these approaches to the U.S., particularly in this new—and hopefully not short-lived—era of reform and potential "de-incarceration"?

It is not hard to anticipate the vitriolic attacks of the "tough on crime" true believers—particularly following the recent election of a "law and order" president—who condemn any reformist arguments as being "soft," "lenient," or "coddling criminals." They often find a particularly shocking example of a brutal crime and then generalize and distort it as if reformers want to let such a perpetrator go free, or as if the victim of a crime has been forgotten and should be avenged. Of course, it is important never to forget that many people in prison have done something bad, sometimes horrible, and that they deserve to be punished—both for what they did, and to prevent other crimes and victims. But do they deserve to be subjected to constant fear, frequent violence, and perhaps rape, for periods of time that are considerably longer than people convicted of similar offenses in other countries?

Ultimately, we as a society must leave politics and venom aside and ask ourselves how we treat our fellow citizens and human beings. How would we want our friends, family members, even ourselves to experience punishment for a terrible mistake? It is not surprising that some of today's influential conservative reformers "saw the light" after themselves serving time in prison—when they were able to experience firsthand the humanity and suffering that lies within prison walls, lost from and to society.

In the end, we must decide whether we have a moral obligation toward our fellow citizens who are incarcerated. Do we treat them as people who have made bad choices, but can still be redeemed and restored, thus making true on the otherwise empty promises of "second chances"? Or do we warehouse them, humiliate them, and punish them repeatedly on a regular basis—and feel self-righteous about it? The lessons learned from the comparative European cases certainly do not provide all the answers, but they open up new perspectives, suggest other possible routes and outcomes, and provide hope and inspiration that genuine and lasting reform to American unusual cruelty may in fact be possible.

Notes

PREFACE

1. Howard 2011b.
2. See the *Washington Post Magazine* feature story on this class. Zak 2016.

CHAPTER 1

1. Tocqueville 1966 [1835], Book III, Chapter 1.
2. Liptak 2008.
3. For some of the most prominent and enlightening books from the past decade on American mass incarceration, see Alexander 2010, Barker 2009, Bosworth 2009, Butler 2010, Clear and Frost 2014, Dagan and Teles 2016, Enns 2016, Ferguson 2014, Garland 2010, Gottschalk 2006, Gottschalk 2015a, Kleiman 2010, Lerman 2013, Lerman and Weaver 2014, Mauer 2006, Miller 2008, Miller 2016, Simon 2007, Simon 2014, Stevenson 2014, and Stuntz 2011.
4. Institute for Criminal Policy Research 2016.
5. Those scholars who have focused on the comparative dimension include Cavadino and Dignan 2006, Céré and Japiassú 2011, Dreisinger 2016, Garland 2001, Lacey 2008, Miethe and Lu 2005, Pakes 2004, Pratt and Eriksson 2013, Sieber 2004, Tonry 2007, Tonry 2009, Tonry and Farrington 2005, Tonry and Frase 2001, van Zyl Smit and Snacken 2011, and Whitman 2003.
6. See Ceaser 2012.
7. Tocqueville 1966 [1835].
8. Sombart 1976 [1906]. Also see Lipset and Marks 2000.
9. Hartz 1955.
10. See Friedman 2012.
11. Ceaser 2012, p. 8.
12. Jones 2010.
13. Note that prior to its merger with ICPR in November 2014, this organization was known as the International Centre for Prison Studies, and its publication was called the "World Prison Population List."

14. The best available measures along these lines come from the Council of Europe's SPACE 2 data on "community sanctions and measures." But no comparable data exist in the U.S. (or outside of Europe).

15. See Barker 2009.

16. Selke 1993, p. 18. Selke adds that "It is difficult [. . .] to collect even the most rudimentary statistics about the granting of 'good time' or the average length of time spent for various offenses."

17. Selke 1993, p. 97.

18. See Selke 1993, p. 97. Francis Pakes provides a related example, contrasting France, where 90 percent of defendants who appear before the courts are found guilty, with England and Wales, where the "comparable" figure is only 39 percent. In actuality, though, the difference comes from a key procedural distinction, namely that in France there is little opportunity for a plea bargain or other guilty plea. In other words, the 39 percent in England and Wales refers to those who have not already accepted a guilty plea, whereas in France the 90 percent is a proportion of all people charged with a crime. See Pakes 2004, p. 22.

19. See Fields and Moore 2005, pp. 4–10.

20. Tonry and Farrington 2005, pp. 11–12.

21. See Pakes 2004, p. 20.

22. Cavadino and Dignan 2006, p. 5

23. Selke 1993, p. 97

24. Tonry and Farrington 2005, p. 7.

25. Cavadino and Dignan 2006, p. 9.

26. Interestingly, the increase in the number of parolees has not been as steep as the number of prisoners or people on probation, despite the soaring numbers of prisoners. This is partly a result of the increased severity of sentencing (as shown in Chapter 3), as fewer people come up for parole when the minimum sentences are very long. Also, mandatory minimums effectively prohibit parole, since people have to serve the full measure of their sentence behind bars. Finally, parole boards have become extremely reluctant to take a "risk" by granting parole when they do have that discretion (as discussed in Chapter 6).

27. Chapter 7 addresses these and other challenges of societal reentry.

28. Sentencing Project 2015b; Swavola, Riley, and Subramanian 2016.

29. See Liptak 2008, p. A14.

30. Although the recent decline in U.S. incarceration figures (from the all-time high in 2008) is striking and important, it corresponds to a very slight change when compared to the increases of previous decades. As Marc Mauer and Nazgol Ghandnoosh have pointed out, at the current annual rate of decline (approximately 1.8 percent in 2012), it would take another 88 years—until the year 2101— for the incarceration rate to fall back to the (already high) level from 1980. Mauer and Ghandnoosh 2013.

31. Indeed, as Terance Miethe and Hong Lu argue, "When all forms of economic, incapacitative, and corporal punishments are considered, there is little question that the United States in the twenty first century is the most punitive country of the Western industrialized world." They add, "This statement is ironic given its global reputation as one of the most economically advanced and free societies of the modern world." Miethe and Lu 2005, p. 108.

32. For an enlightening recent discussion of the difficulty of tracking and comparing crime rates across different U.S. cities and jurisdictions, particularly in a politically-loaded electoral climate, see Dance and Meagher 2016.

33. Ruth and Weitz 2003, pp. 15–16.

34. Ruth and Weitz 2003, pp. 15–16.

35. Garland 2001.

36. Simon 2007.

37. Enns 2016. See also Miller 2016.

38. Fortner 2015.

39. Ruth and Weitz 2003, p. 17.

40. Chettiar 2015.

41. Wilson 1975.

42. See, for example, Lynch 1999, DeFina and Arvanites 2002, Tonry 2014, and Roeder, Eisen, and Bowling 2015 (a recent report by the Brennan Center for Justice).

43. Chettiar 2015.

44. See, for example, Frost 2006, Mauer and Ghandnoosh 2013, and Pew Charitable Trusts 2015.

45. Mauer and Ghandnoosh 2013.

46. See Zimring and Hawkins 1997.

47. See Cavadino and Dignan 2006, p. 56; Mauer 2006, p. 25; Tonry 2014, pp. 20–25.

48. Tonry 2014, p. 35. See also Lappi-Seppälä and Lehti 2014; Farrell, Tilley, and Tseloni 2014.

49. Tonry and Farrington 2005, pp. 1–2. Tonry and Farrington also provide an interesting comparison of four Scandinavian countries, showing that a major drop in Finland's prison population did not affect its crime rates. For more on these arguments, see Howard 2011a.

50. Tonry 2014, pp. 5–6.

51. See Apuzzo and Cohen 2015.

52. See, for example, Schulhofer, Tyler, and Huq 2011; Burke 2013; American Civil Liberties Union 2014.

53. See Ross 2007, 2008a, 2008b.

54. On Europe, see Open Society Institute 2009, European Union Agency for Fundamental Rights 2010, Human Rights Watch 2012. On the U.S., see the synthetic review provided by Meares 2014.

55. European Union Agency for Fundamental Rights 2010.

56. New York Civil Liberties Union 2015.

57. See also Geller and Fagan 2010.
58. See Schneider 2014.
59. *The Washington Post* 2015, 2016.
60. See Balko 2013.
61. Witte 2015.
62. *The Guardian* 2015, 2016.
63. *Frankfurter Allgemeine Zeitung* 2015; also see Stute 2014.
64. Lartey 2015.
65. Lartey 2015.
66. Hirschfield 2015.
67. For an important study of comparative criminal punishment that finds strong similarities between the U.S. and the U.K.—based on having "liberal market economies" (LME), as opposed to the coordinated market economies (CME) of continental Europe—see Lacey 2008.
68. Howard 2009.
69. Whitman 2005, p. 18.

CHAPTER 2

1. The 95 percent figure comes from Michael O'Hear, who has the most recent estimates. See O'Hear 2008, p. 409. Other analysts give figures around 90–95 percent, and older works mention the 80--90 percent range.
2. Black's Law Dictionary 1979, p. 1037.
3. Bibas 2004, p. 2466.
4. Ma 2002, p. 26.
5. U.S. Constitution, Article II, Section 2, Clause 3.
6. U.S. Constitution, Sixth Amendment.
7. Alschuler 1979, p. 6
8. *United States v. Jackson*, 390 U.S. 570 (1968).
9. *Brady v. United States*, 397 U.S. 742 (1970).
10. *Santobello v. New York*, 404 U.S. 260 (1971).
11. Ma 2002, p. 46.
12. Federal Rules of Criminal Procedure, Rule 11 ("Pleas").
13. *Bordenkircher v. Hayes*, 434 U.S. 357 (1978).
14. See Medwed 2012.
15. This point was impressed upon me by my students at the Jessup Correctional Institution, some of whom relayed very disturbing personal stories about the plea bargaining process in practice. Whereas at first I thought the application of the term "extortion" was overstated and inappropriate in this context, I've come to realize that it is not such a far stretch, since a key component of extortion involves "the verbal or written *instillation* of fear that something will happen to the victim if they do not comply with the extortionist's will," and it is precisely that fear (of

high charges, of a longer sentence, or of a punitive judge who resents the defendant for going to trial) that often makes defendants "voluntarily" agree to a plea that they might otherwise resist or contest. See the definition of extortion provided by *Lexbook*, available at http://lexbook.net/en/extortionist (accessed February 13, 2015). Moreover, I later discovered that the eminent late Harvard Law School criminal law scholar, William Stuntz, had referred to "guilty pleas produced by what amounts to legalized extortion." Stuntz 2005 (abstract).

16. Richer and Anderson 2016.
17. Bowers 2008, pp. 1173–1174.
18. Yant 1991, p. 172.
19. Lynch 2003, p. 24.
20. Lynch 2003, p. 26.
21. See also Dubber 1997.
22. Bibas 2004, p. 2466–2468.
23. Bibas 2004, p. 2468.
24. For an incisive and sobering analysis of inadequate defense counsel, see Amy Bach 2009.
25. Bibas 2004, p. 2467.
26. Schulhofer 1984, p. 1037.
27. Schulhofer 1984, p. 1037.
28. O'Hear 2008, p. 425. On the importance of prosecutorial power and discretion in plea bargaining decisions, see also Stuntz 2004.
29. Heumann 1978, p. 35 (quoted by O'Hear 2008, pp. 415–416).
30. O'Hear 2008, p. 418.
31. Ma 2002, p. 26.
32. Ashcroft 2003; Holder 2010.
33. O'Hear 2008, p. 419.
34. Several other countries have also incorporated jury trials in recent years, explicitly modeled after the U.S. For an analysis of the transplanting of American legal practices—including jury trials and plea bargaining—see Goldbach, Brake, and Katzenstein 2013.
35. Ma 2002, p. 31.
36. Frase 1995, p. 275.
37. Frase 1995, p. 275.
38. Ma 2002, p. 31.
39. Ma 2002, p. 31.
40. Ma 2002, p. 32.
41. Ma 2002, p. 33. With regard to confessions, Ma adds that "under French law a defendant's admission of guilt does not replace trial, and a confession is never irrevocable. Even after an admission of guilt, a defendant still has to go through a trial" (p. 33).
42. Ma 2002, p. 33. Moreover, Ma adds that since French sentencing law requires that convicted defendants serve only the one sentence (for the highest crime

committed), prosecutors are precluded from adding multiple charges, as commonly occurs with American prosecutors—as a tool for pressuring plea bargains (p. 34).

43. Ma 2002, p. 34.
44. Tagliabue 2003.
45. Bradley 2007, p. 277.
46. Cited in Tagliabue 2003.
47. French Ministry of Justice 2006.
48. Frase and Weigend 1995, p. 346.
49. Langbein 1979, p. 204.
50. Ma 2002, p. 36; Rauxloh 2011, pp. 297–306.
51. Deutsche Welle 2013.
52. Bundesverfassungsgericht 2013, p. 82.
53. See Schemmel, Corell, and Richter 2014; Weigend and Turner 2014.
54. Ma 2002, pp. 36–37; Frase and Weigend 1995, pp. 344–346.
55. Frase and Weigend 1995, p. 345.
56. Ma 2002, p. 38.
57. Ma 2002, p. 39.
58. Cited in Bundesverfassungsgericht 2013.
59. Frase and Weigend 1995, p. 353.
60. Schemmel, Corell, and Richter 2014, pp. 45, 56.
61. Ma 2002, p. 24.
62. Ma 2002, p. 42.
63. Marcus 1992, p. 1194.
64. Marcus 1992, p. 1193.
65. Merryman 1985, pp. 130–131.
66. See, for example, the debate between Abraham Goldstein and Martin Marcus, supporting the adversarial model, and John Langbein and Lloyd Weinreb, who prefer inquisitorial systems. Goldstein and Marcus 1977; Langbein and Weinreb 1978.
67. Marcus 1992, p. 1195.
68. Frase and Weigend 1995, p. 359.
69. Garoupa and Stephen 2008, p. 324. Note, however, that this figure does not necessarily mean that all of these cases yield formal plea agreements.
70. Flynn 2011, p. 371.
71. Flynn 2011, p. 371.
72. Waby 2005, p. 152.
73. Flynn 2011, p. 372.
74. Tague 2007, p. 295.
75. Davis 1975, p. 457.
76. Davis 1975, p. 459.
77. Waby 2005, p. 160.
78. Waby 2005, p. 160.

79. Tague 2007, p. 293.
80. Tague 2007, p. 288.
81. Flynn 2011, p. 362.
82. Flynn 2011, p. 372.
83. Flynn 2011, p. 374.
84. Indeed, although criminal trials yield convictions when the evidence is "beyond a reasonable doubt," probation violations are determined according to "the preponderance of the evidence," a much weaker standard.

CHAPTER 3

1. Tonry 2001, p. 4.
2. Tonry 2001, p. 17. Note that these figures do not include jail sentences, which are received by a portion of American criminals—estimates range from 2 to 27 percent of violent crimes, depending on the crime—and are typically of shorter duration. The overall average would therefore be somewhat lower, but still dramatically higher than in comparable countries.
3. Tonry 2001, p. 4.
4. Kurki 2001, p. 355.
5. Article 37 of the Convention states that "States Parties shall ensure that: (a) No child shall be subjected to torture or other cruel, inhuman or degrading treatment or punishment. Neither capital punishment nor life imprisonment without possibility of release shall be imposed for offences committed by persons below eighteen years of age." United Nations 1989.
6. Tonry 2001, p. 16.
7. Whitman 2016. Whitman adds that this "is true even of notorious offenders like Mehmet Ali Ağca, the attempted assassin of Pope John Paul II, who was sentenced nominally to life in prison but released in 1999 after only nineteen years." Whitman 2016, p. 990.
8. Tonry and Farrington 2005, p. 22.
9. Tonry and Farrington 2005, p. 32.
10. Mauer 2006, p. 35.
11. Mauer 2006, p. 35.
12. Mauer 2006, pp. 35–36.
13. Frase and Weigend 1995, p. 348.
14. Lynch 1995, p. 37.
15. Lynch et al. 1994, p. 7.
16. Lynch et al. 1994, p. 4.
17. Lynch et al. 1994, p. 9.
18. Van Zyl Smit 2002, p. 197.
19. Nellis 2013, p. 1.
20. U.K. Ministry of Justice 2015.

21. Albrecht 2013 and Institute for Criminal Policy Research 2016. Note that this percentage was calculated by dividing the total number of life sentences in Germany in 2010 (provided by Albrecht) by the total prison population in 2010 (provided by the Institute for Criminal Policy Research's "World Prison Brief" on Germany).

22. In other words, as shown in Chapter 6, in the U.S. a sentence of "life" often means "until death," whereas in the European countries, "life" typically signifies "for several decades."

23. Mauer et al. 2004, p. 28. Mauer et al. also point out that the prevalence of LWOP in the U.S. is largely driven by the existence of the death penalty, which "serves to exert upward pressure on the severity of the penalties imposed for all offenses" (p. 28).

24. Nellis 2013, p. 1. Moreover, Nellis points out that about 10,000 of the lifers were convicted of non-violent offenses, nearly half are African-American, over 10,000 were juveniles at the time of the crime, and over 5,300 (3.4 percent) are women.

25. Mauer et al. 2004, p. 9.

26. Liptak 2005.

27. Dolovich 2011, p. 96.

28. Jefferson and Head 2008, pp. 89–90.

29. Jefferson and Head 2008, p. 144.

30. De la Vega and Leighton 2008.

31. *Graham v. Florida*, 560 U.S. 48 (2010) .

32. *Miller v. Alabama*, 567 U.S. ____ (2012).

33. Liptak 2007, p. A1.

34. Binder 2008, p. 966.

35. For a comparison of the quite different uses of accomplice liability in the U.S. and Germany, see Dubber 2007.

36. Garland 2010, p. 114.

37. Garland 2010, pp. 121–122.

38. Garland 2010, p. 280.

39. The most recent state to ban capital punishment was Nebraska in May 2015, where a solidly Republican majority overrode a Republican governor's veto. But a 2016 referendum sponsored by the governor resulted in 61 percent support for suspending the legislature's repeal, which means that capital punishment has now returned to Nebraska.

40. Death Penalty Information Center 2015.

41. Jones and Newburn 2002; 2006.

42. Jones and Newburn 2006, p. 798.

43. Bagaric 2014, p. 363.

44. Roberts 2013, p. 5.

45. Gilpin 2012, p. 96.

46. Gilpin 2012, p. 91.

47. Gilpin 2012, p. 91.

48. U.K. Ministry of Justice 2012.

49. U.K. Ministry of Justice 2012.

50. Frase 1995a, p. 275.

51. Frase 1995a, p. 275.

52. Aharonson 2013, p. 174.

53. Roché 2007, p. 543.

54. Frase 2001, p. 18.

55. Subramanian and Shames 2013, p. 9.

56. Subramanian and Shames 2013, p. 10.

57. Frase 2001, p. 52. It should be mentioned, as discussed in Chapter 7 on societal reentry, that even when the U.S. does grant non-custodial sentences, these are still extremely punitive compared to those in France and Germany, since the "collateral consequences" of probation and community supervision are extremely strict and unforgiving.

58. Albrecht 2013, p. 211.

59. Albrecht 2013, p. 211.

60. Hornle 2013, p. 189.

61. Frost 2006, p. 13.

62. Stemen, Rengifo, and Wilson 2006, p. 17.

63. See Frase, 1995b, p. 431.

64. Martinson 1974, p. 25. For an overview of the controversy surrounding the report, see Hallinan 2001, pp. 33–38.

65. Garland 2001, p. 8.

66. Mauer 2001, p. 11.

67. See Reitz 2001, pp. 223–224.

68. Reitz and Reitz 1993, p. 169.

69. Lowenthal 1993, p. 63.

70. Frost 2006, p. 14.

71. Stemen, Rengifo, and Wilson 2006, p. 11.

72. Stemen, Rengifo, and Wilson 2006, p. 14.

73. Stemen, Rengifo, and Wilson 2006, p. 15.

74. Frost 2006, p. 16.

75. Frost 2006, p. 15.

76. Stemen, Rengifo, and Wilson 2006, p. 16.

77. Frase 2000, p. 432.

78. Tonry 1996, p. 17.

79. U.S. Sentencing Commission (no date).

80. Schanzenbach and Tiller 2007, p. 5.

81. Mauer 2006, p. 58.

82. *United States v. Booker*, 543 U.S. 220 (2005).

83. Frost 2006, p. 17.

84. Frase 2000, p. 426.

85. Frase gives the example of the guidelines commission in Minnesota, which has allowed for some flexibility in sentencing, while also keeping the state's imprisonment rate far below the national average. Also see Frost 2006, p. 17.

86. Stemen, Rengifo, and Wilson 2006, p. 26.

87. Reitz 2001, p. 229.

88. Frost 2006, p. 19.

89. Reitz 2001, p. 229,

90. Reitz 2001, p. 229.

91. Reitz 2001, p. 230.

92. *Rummel v. Estelle*, 445 U.S. 263 (1980).

93. Reitz 2001, p. 25.

94. Zimring, Hawkins, and Kamin 2001.

95. Zimring, Hawkins, and Kamin 2001, p. 4.

96. *Ewing v. California*, 538 U.S. 11 (2003).

97. Stanford Law School 2013, p. 1.

98. Stemen, Rengifo, and Wilson 2006, p. 19.

99. Stemen, Rengifo, and Wilson 2006, p. 20.

100. Mauer 2006, p. 62.

101. Musto 1999, p. 274.

102. Mauer 2006, p. 62.

103. Mauer 2006, p. 68

104. Mauer 2006, pp. 31–32.

105. Mauer 2006, p. 90.

106. Berman 2011, pp. 167–170.

107. Aharonson 2013, p. 162.

CHAPTER 4

1. Dolovich 2012.

2. Of course, this does not mean that American prisons are the worst in the entire world, as clearly those in many developing, poor, and authoritarian countries are even worse. It is important to remember that the relevant and appropriate point of comparison for the U.S. remains countries that are similarly wealthy, democratic, and free.

3. In those situations, violent and non-violent offenders are often mixed, as prisons claim not to have the resources to keep them separated.

4. For the sake of simplicity, this chapter uses the word "prisons" inclusively, thus capturing both jails and prisons. It should be noted that over 700,000 people reside in one of the great number of American local or county jails at any given time, and there are about 11–14 million annual admissions to an American jail (the figure was 13.6 million in 2008, 11.8 million in 2011, and 11.6 million in 2012). Minton 2013, p. 4.

5. Cavadino and Dignan 2006, pp. 54–55.
6. Cavadino and Dignan 2006, p. 57.
7. Dolovich 2009a, pp. 237–238 (references omitted).
8. Dolovich 2009a, pp. 240–241.
9. Dolovich 2009a, p. 241.
10. See Rhodes 2010.
11. Mumola and Karberg 2006, p. 6; Karberg and James 2002, pp. 1–2
12. See Wagner 2003.
13. It appears that many prisoners have found a way around the phone restrictions by having smuggled cell phones (often brought in by guards), which are now apparently rampant in many prisons. See Severson and Brown 2011.
14. See Braman 2002.
15. See Berkman 1995; McDonald 1999; Delgado 2009; Cloud 2014.
16. See Haney 2003.
17. Dolovich 2009a, pp. 251–252 (references omitted). See also Gilligan 1997; Kupers 2001; Donaldson 2001.
18. It should be noted that the passage of PREA did not lead to immediate or decisive change. In fact, only in 2012 did the Department of Justice produce its "National Standards to Prevent, Detect, and Respond to Prison Rape," and these have yet to be implemented systematically across American jails and prisons. See U.S. Department of Justice 2014.
19. Kupers 2001, p. 111.
20. See Feeley and Rubin 1998.
21. Feeley and Rubin 1998, p. 27.
22. 482 U.S. 78 (1987).
23. 482 U. S. 78, 84–85 (1987).
24. See Dolovich 2012, pp. 246–247.
25. 490 U.S. 401 (1989).
26. 468 U.S. 576 (1984).
27. 539 U.S. 126 (2003).
28. 511 U.S. 825 (1994).
29. 429 U.S. 97 (1976).
30. See Dolovich 2009b, pp. 889–890.
31. 452 U.S. 337 (1981).
32. 452 U.S. 337, Syllabus (1981).
33. See Dolovich 2009b, p. 948–949.
34. 501 U.S. 294 (1991).
35. 475 U.S. 312 (1986).
36. 503 U.S. 1 (1992).
37. 518 U.S. 343 (1996).
38. Lehmann 2011, p. 493.
39. Prison Litigation Reform Act (PLRA) 1996.

40. Bronstein and Gainsborough 2004, p. 813.
41. Jon O. Newman, chief judge of the U.S. Court of Appeals, effectively debunks these misleading and fabricated examples. See Newman 1996.
42. Bronstein and Gainsborough 2004, p. 813.
43. Bronstein and Gainsborough 2004, p. 814.
44. Prison Litigation Reform Act (PLRA) 1996.
45. See Schlanger 2003; Schlanger 2006; Schlanger 2015. According to a 2009 Human Rights Watch report, "If the effect of the PLRA were to selectively discourage the filing of frivolous or meritless lawsuits, as its sponsors predicted, then we would expect to find prisoners winning a larger percentage of their lawsuits after the law's enactment than they did before. But the most comprehensive study to date shows just the opposite: since passage of the PLRA, prisoners not only are filing fewer lawsuits, but also are succeeding in a smaller proportion of the cases they do file. This strongly suggests that rather than filtering out meritless lawsuits, the PLRA has simply tilted the playing field against prisoners across the board." Human Rights Watch 2009.
46. 563 U. S. _____ (2011) (p. 3 from Slip Opinion).
47. 563 U. S. _____ (2011) (p. 3 from Slip Opinion).
48. 563 U. S. _____ (2011) (p. 4 from Slip Opinion).
49. 563 U. S. _____ (2011) (p. 5 from Slip Opinion).
50. 563 U. S. _____ (2011) (p. 8 from Slip Opinion). Quoting from the District Court ruling in *Coleman* v. *Wilson*, 912 F. Supp. 1282, 1316 (E.D. Cal.).
51. 563 U. S. _____ (2011) (p. 6 from Slip Opinion).
52. 563 U. S. _____ (2011) (pp. 5–6 from Slip Opinion).
53. 563 U. S. _____ (2011) (pp. 9–10 from Slip Opinion).
54. 563 U. S. _____ (2011) (p. 11 from Slip Opinion).
55. The photographs come from pp. 51–52 of the Slip Opinion.
56. 563 U. S. _____ (2011) (p. 13 from Slip Opinion).
57. Dolovich 2012, p. 250.
58. For a positive and very optimistic assessment of the effect of *Plata* on California and the U.S. in general, see Simon 2014.
59. Simon 2014, especially pp. 145–154.
60. It is worth noting that Alito seems to have been wrong here, as the post-*Plata* drop in incarceration levels has not affected the continuing decline in crime rates. See Mauer and Ghandnoosh 2013.
61. Rubin 2015. Also see Schlanger 2013.
62. Liptak 2015c.
63. Some readers might prefer the word "lenient" to "humane." But since the term "lenient" can give the implication of being *excessively* soft—and thus provide easy ammunition to critics of the Scandinavian model—I prefer to use "humane," which highlights the role of compassion and benevolence in the treatment of other human beings. My thanks to Michael Tonry for pointing this out to me.

64. Pratt 2008, p. 120.
65. Ward et al. 2013, p. 2.
66. Ward et al. 2013, p. 2.
67. Pratt 2008, p. 120.
68. Pratt 2008, p. 120.
69. Pratt 2008, p. 120.
70. Ward et al. 2013, p. 2.
71. Pratt 2008, pp. 122–123.
72. Pratt 2008, p. 129.
73. Ward et al. 2013, pp. 3–4.
74. Tonry 2014, p. 13.
75. Pratt 2008, p. 133.
76. Crétenot and Liaras 2013, p. 19; Silvestri 2013, p. 23.
77. See, for example, Daguzan 2014; Morio 2015; Radio France Internationale 2015; Ouest France 2015.
78. Vasseur 2000. See also Vasseur and Mouesca 2011.
79. Pasteau 2014; Piel 2014.
80. Johannès 2012.
81. Selke 1993, pp. 58, 105.
82. Crétenot and Liaras 2013, p. 20; Roucaute 2014.
83. Johannès 2014; Clatot 2014.
84. Silvestri 2013, p. 24.
85. Terrill 1997, p. 72.
86. Snortum and Bødal 1985, p. 582. Of course, in the U.S., supermax facilities also have solid doors, but these are for the purpose of ensuring complete separation and sensory deprivation, not for providing comfortable enclosed rooms for incarcerated people.
87. Snortum and Bødal 1985, p. 585; Selke 1993, p. 58; Human Rights Watch 1995, p. 6.
88. Kaiser 1984, p. 102.
89. Weschler and Garro 1992, pp. 25–26; Kaiser 1984, p. 102.
90. Subramanian and Shames 2013, pp. 11–12.
91. Crétenot and Liaras 2013, p. 22.
92. Silvestri 2013, p. 26.
93. Cloud 2014, p. 13.
94. Yale Law School Liman Program 2015, p. 3.
95. Vera Institute of Justice 2015. See also Browne, Cambier, and Agha 2011.
96. Even the U.S. government has begun to recognize and address the problem of solitary confinement. In a report commissioned by President Obama and released in January 2016, the Department of Justice gathered available data concerning "the overuse of solitary confinement across American prisons" and recommended major reforms, stating that "as a matter of policy, we believe strongly this practice should be used rarely, applied fairly, and subjected to reasonable constraints."

This attention on the federal level is important, but since 90 percent of prisoners reside in state facilities, genuine nationwide reform will take a long time. U.S. Department of Justice 2016.

97. Silvestri 2013, p. 22.
98. Crétenot and Liaras 2013, p. 18.
99. Subramanian and Shames 2013, p. 12.
100. See the evocative and colorful depictions of various U.S. prison meals in Santo and Iaboni 2015.
101. Barclay 2014.
102. Silvestri 2013, p. 27.
103. Crétenot and Liaras 2013, p. 23.
104. Crétenot and Liaras 2013, p. 23. Note that in 2013 a French court ruled that prisons must accommodate Muslim prisoners by providing them with halal meals, but this policy was then overturned for cost and practicality reasons in 2014. See *Le Monde* 2014. This contrasts unfavorably with the American practice of serving kosher and halal meals within prisons—which is indicative of a greater respect for religious freedom and practice in the U.S. more generally.
105. Weschler and Garro 1992, pp. 22–23.
106. O'Mahony 2000, pp. 29, 51; Kaiser 1984, p. 83.
107. Terrill 1997, p. 72.
108. Terrill 1997, p. 156.
109. Subramanian and Shames 2013, p. 12. Subramanian and Shames add that "training spans two years with 12 months of theoretical education followed by 12 months of practical training. Courses include criminal law and self-defense as well as constitutional law, educational theory, psychology, social education, stress and conflict management, and communicating with prisoners."
110. According to Rule 51.2 of the European Prison Rules, which consist of nonbinding recommendations, "The security which is provided by physical barriers and other technical means shall be complemented by the dynamic security provided by an alert staff who know the prisoners who are under their control." Council of Europe 2006, p. 23.
111. *Overton v. Bazzetta*, 539 U.S. 126 (2003).
112. Terrill 1997, pp. 219–220.
113. Terrill 1997, pp. 69, 219–220.
114. Kaiser 1984, p. 69.
115. Weschler and Garro 1992, pp. 25–26. I was also able to visit one such "apartment" at the Centre Penitentiaire du Havre in the town of Le Havre, in Normandy.
116. Kaiser 1984, p. 72.
117. Terrill 1997, p. 72.
118. Crétenot and Liaras 2013, p. 25; Silvestri 2013, p. 29.
119. Weschler and Garro 1992, p. 14; Kaiser 1984, p. 63.

120. Mbodla 2002, p. 98; Sentencing Project 2013, p. 1.
121. Hurst 2015.
122. Subramanian and Shames 2013, p. 13; Demleitner 2000, p. 761.
123. Crétenot and Liaras 2013, p. 26.
124. Silvestri 2013, p. 30. Note that Canada actually allows prisoners to vote while they are incarcerated. See Reid 2012 (especially the chapter entitled "Tough Guys Do So Vote").
125. As Katzenstein, Ibrahim, and Rubin write, "Unlike most Western European nations, where the voting rights of those released from confinement are unquestioned and where the legal debates have concerned only the voting rights of the currently incarcerated, the entire spectrum of felony voting rights is intently contested in the United States." Katzenstein, Ibrahim, and Rubin 2010, p. 1036. Also see Manza and Uggen 2006.
126. Murphy 2005, p. 31.
127. Delgado 2009, p. 154.
128. Delgado 2009, p. 153.
129. Bretschneider, Elger, and Wangmo 2013, pp. 270–271.
130. Michel et al. 2008, p. 6.
131. Peterka-Benton and Masciadrelli 2013, p. 176; European Commission 2007, p. 62.
132. Kaiser 1984, p. 29.
133. Terrill 1997, p. 218.
134. Simon 2014.

CHAPTER 5

1. The book was finally published in 1975, well after the controversy over Martinson's 1974 article had erupted. See Lipton, Martinson, and Wilks 1975.
2. Martinson 1974, p. 25.
3. Martinson 1974, p. 49.
4. Cullen 2007, p. 2.
5. Cullen 2007, p. 2. Other restrictions intended to reduce the comfort and amenities in prisons included the removal of air conditioning, and the imposition of restrictions on television watching.
6. Samaha 2009, p. 28.
7. Wilson 1980, p. 7.
8. MacKenzie 2006, p. 55.
9. MacKenzie 2006, p. 56.
10. MacKenzie 2006, p. 56.
11. MacKenzie 2006, p. 56.
12. Martinson 1974, p. 36.
13. Martinson 1974, p. 36.
14. Martinson 1974, pp. 37–38.

15. Adamson and Dunham 1956, p.320.
16. Martinson 1974, p. 40.
17. Martinson 1974, pp. 31–32.
18. It is impossible to know why Martinson may have exaggerated his findings in this way, other than the perhaps all-too-human desire to make a bigger splash by presenting more bold and striking findings.
19. Palmer 1975.
20. Palmer 1975, p. 142.
21. Palmer 1975, p. 143.
22. Andrews et al. 1990, p. 374.
23. Palmer 1975, p. 150.
24. Gendreau and Ross 1987, pp. 350–351.
25. Gendreau and Ross 1979, pp. 465–466.
26. Gendreau and Ross 1979, p. 467.
27. Cullen and Gendreau 2000, p. 133.
28. Gendreau and Ross 1987, pp. 370–374.
29. Gendreau 1996, p. 118.
30. Cullen and Gendreau 2000, p. 145.
31. Andrews and Bonta 1988, pp. 224–225.
32. Andrews 1995, p. 37.
33. Cullen and Gendreau 2000, p. 145.
34. Andrews 1995, p. 56.
35. Andrews and Hoge 1995, p. 36.
36. MacKenzie 2006, p. 83. It should be noted that this same study, however, could not find such support for life training or vocational education programs.
37. Cullen and Gendreau 2000, p. 147.
38. Andrews and Bonta 1998, p. 243.
39. Cullen and Gendreau 2000, p. 147.
40. Andrews and Bonta 1998, p. 245. Cullen et al. offer an example of how offenders with low IQs should be dealt with, particularly how "they would perform more effectively than higher functioning offenders in an instructional format that requires less verbal and written fluency and less abstract conceptualizations." See Cullen, Gendreau, Jarjoura, and Wright 1997, p. 403.
41. Lipsey 1992, p. 124.
42. Cullen and Gendreau 2000, p. 155.
43. Andrews and Hoge 1995, p. 36.
44. Lin 2000, p. 6.
45. Martinson 1979, p. 244.
46. Martinson 1979, pp. 254–255.
47. Martinson 1979, p. 254.
48. Hallinan, p. 35.
49. Hallinan, p. 36.

50. Petersilia 2003, p. 65. See also Hallinan 2001.

51. See also Lerman 2013.

52. Note, however, that if the goal of prison is incapacitation rather than rehabilitation, a high recidivism rate arguably confirms that it was wise to keep the person locked up for so long, and it actually supports instituting even *longer* prison sentences. I am grateful to an anonymous reviewer for making this point. See Zimring and Hawkins 1995; Simon 2014.

53. See Fazel and Wolf 2015.

54. See Benko 2015 for a fascinating *New York Times Magazine* account of the efforts at rehabilitation in the Halden prison in Norway, which is known as "the world's most humane maximum-security prison." This contrasts starkly with the American "ADX" prison in Colorado, which Binelli (2015) describes vividly in the same magazine issue.

55. CBS News 2015.

56. Quoted in Crétenot and Liaras 2013, p. 14.

57. Crétenot and Liaras 2013, p. 19.

58. Crétenot and Liaras 2013, p. 26.

59. Crétenot and Liaras 2013, p. 43.

60. Crétenot and Liaras 2013, pp. 43–44.

61. Interview with Ludovic Fossey, French judge (juge de l'application des peines), February 20, 2015, Paris.

62. Genders 2014, p. 436.

63. Subramanian and Shames 2013, p. 7.

64. Subramanian and Shames 2013, p. 7.

65. Subramanian and Shames 2013, p. 9.

66. Subramanian and Shames 2013, p. 9.

67. Subramanian and Shames 2013, p. 12.

68. Nayeri 2013, p. 123.

69. Nayeri 2013, p. 123.

70. Nayeri 2013, pp. 123–124.

71. See also Chammah 2015.

72. Silvestri 2013, p. 57.

73. Silvestri 2013, p. 23.

74. Silvestri 2013, p. 30.

75. Genders 2014, p. 436.

76. Muffitt 2013.

77. Quoted in Muffitt 2013.

78. Muffitt 2013.

79. Prison Radio Association 2016. Also see Bedford 2015 and Wilkinson and Davidson 2010.

80. Petersilia 2003, p. iv.

81. See Gendreau and Ross 1987, especially pp. 370–374.

CHAPTER 6

1. Fellner and Price 2012.
2. Petersilia 2003, p. 56.
3. Petersilia 2003, p. 57.
4. Petersilia 2003, p. 57.
5. Petersilia 2003, p. 58.
6. Petersilia 2003, p. 58.
7. Hoffman 1997, p. 1.
8. Petersilia 2003, p. 58.
9. Petersilia 2003, pp. 61–62.
10. See Martinson 1974. As discussed on Chapter 5, this controversial "Martinson report" purported that "nothing works" in the realm of prison rehabilitation.
11. Petersilia 2003, p. 63.
12. Sabol et al. 2009, p. 3.
13. See also Travis and Lawrence 2002, p. 17.
14. Actually, Maine was the first state to abolish discretionary parole, in 1976, but it received far less attention and emulation than the changes in California.
15. Stith and Cabranes 1998, pp. 18–19.
16. Ditton and Wilson 1999, p. 3.
17. Ditton and Wilson 1999, p. 2.
18. *Swarthout v. Cooke*, 562 U.S. ___ (2011).
19. Hughes et al. 2001, p. 5.
20. Hughes et al. 2001, p. 7.
21. One little-noticed countervailing trend, however, has been the application of "supervised release" in federal prisons, in which "the court has discretion to adjust the length of a prison term after sentencing based on its evaluation of the post-judgment progress of the offender." According to Fiona Doherty, this "muddled and unprincipled form of indeterminate sentencing [...] that flouts the insights and vision of the nineteenth-century movement as well as the twentieth-century determinacy movement" has impacted over 100,000 people. Doherty 2013, p. 958.
22. Hughes et al. 2001, p. 1.
23. Hughes et al. 2001, p. 4.
24. U.S. Department of Justice 2003, p. 33.
25. U.S. Department of Justice 2006, pp. 9–10.
26. This factor applies only to the states that still maintain discretionary parole, of course.
27. Richardson 2011, p. 8. See California Penal Code 3041.5 (b).
28. Richardson 2011, p. 22.
29. Richardson 2011, p. 23.
30. Richardson 2011, p. 4.

31. Lee Atwater, Bush's campaign manager, famously stated, "By the time we're finished, they're going to wonder whether Willie Horton is Dukakis' running mate." Anderson 1995, p. 223.

32. For example: the ad changed Horton's first name from William to "Willie"; suggested that the crimes had been committed while Horton was on the furlough, rather than 10 months after he had gone missing; inserted a haunting picture of Horton that was actually taken after he had emerged from many months in solitary confinement; inserted blatantly racial codes into a message that terrified white voters of the stereotypical image of a black violent criminal; implied that Dukakis had personally approved Horton's furlough release, when it was actually approved by the prison bureaucracy, and the program itself had been instituted by a prior Republican governor; and suggested that Massachusetts was an outlier in terms of granting furloughs, even though similar programs existed in most states and the federal system, and such conservatives as Ronald Reagan had previously defended their purpose and utility. In other words, although it was crudely produced, the ad was carefully crafted to create a terrifying image of Horton, while misleading voters into personally blaming Dukakis for Horton's actions. See Anderson 1995; Schwartzapfel and Keller 2015.

33. See Mendelberg 2001. It is impossible to know, of course, if the Horton ad genuinely changed the outcome of the 1988 presidential election. Journalistic accounts tend to focus on particularly dramatic events and people (see, e.g., Simon 1990), whereas political scientists generally emphasize larger structural factors (see, e.g., Vavreck 2009, and Sides and Vavreck 2013).

34. Korte 2016.

35. Dolovich 2011, p. 112.

36. *Rummel v. Estelle*, 445 U.S. 263, 265–67, 280 (1980).

37. Weisberg et al. 2011, p. 13.

38. Liptak 2005.

39. Dolovich 2011, p. 13 (drawing on the work of Keith Wattley).

40. Weisberg et al. 2011, p. 13.

41. Liptak 2005.

42. Liptak 2005.

43. See, for example, AP/Huffington Post 2010.

44. AP/Huffington Post 2010.

45. Liptak 2005.

46. Nellis 2013, p. 1

47. Liptak 2005.

48. Mauer et al. 2004, p. 12.

49. Liptak 2005.

50. *Rhodes v. Chapman*, 452 U.S. 337, 372 (dissenting).

51. Western et al. 2002, p. 176.

52. Dolovich 2011, p. 9.

53. Richert 1977, p. 19.

54. Richert 1977, p. 19.

55. Blakesley 1978, p. 3.

56. Interview with Ludovic Fossey, French judge (juge de l'application des peines), February 20, 2015, Paris.

57. Reuflet 2010, p. 170.

58. I was able to observe such proceedings myself at the Fresnes prison (the second-largest prison in France) on February 21, 2013.

59. Interview with Ludovic Fossey, February 20, 2015, Paris.

60. Fellner and Price 2012.

61. Richert 1977, pp. 20–21.

62. Interview with Ludovic Fossey, February 20, 2015, Paris.

63. Dünkel and Pruin 2010, p. 185. And of course one should recall that German sentences are already considerably shorter than those imposed in the U.S. for similar crimes.

64. Pruin 2012, p. 63.

65. Dünkel and Pruin 2010, p. 187.

66. Dünkel and Pruin 2010, p. 191.

67. Dünkel and Pruin 2010, p. 193.

68. Dünkel and Pruin 2010, p. 193.

69. Pruin 2012, pp. 64, 67–68.

70. Hallett 2014.

71. Padfield 2010, p. 104.

72. Hallett 2014.

73. Maguire and Raynor 1997, pp. 1–2.

74. Hallett 2014. Also see BBC News 2013. Approximately 600 prisoners a year would be affected by the new restriction, which would not necessarily prevent their release, but just make it non-automatic, and instead require them to prove to the Parole Board the lack of risk in being released.

75. Bottomley 1990, pp. 331–332.

76. For more on Thompson's story, see Liptak 2005.

77. Liptak 2005.

78. Mauer et al. 2004, p. 2.

79. Mauer et al. 2004, p. 7.

80. Liptak 2005.

81. Mauer et al. 2004, p. 3.

82. Weisberg et al. 2011, p. 4.

83. Lomax and Kumar 2014, pp. 5, 23.

84. Mauer et al. 2004, p. 3.

85. Liptak 2005. See also Fellner 2012.

86. Howard 2004. Note that as mayor of Oakland (before becoming governor again in 2011), Brown added that "the determinate sentence means you treat different

people equally, those who should be locked up for a short time and others who should be locked up for a long time. When you don't distinguish between the two cases, you eventually increase the sentences to keep them longer. That's the fatal flaw of determinate sentencing. You keep people who could return to society too long, and you don't incarcerate long enough the people who are entirely unsuitable for society." Howard 2004.

87. Liptak 2005.
88. Liptak 2005.

CHAPTER 7

1. Jacobs and Larrauri 2012, p. 3.
2. Jacobs 2015; Ewald 2012.
3. This applies to 48 of the 50 states and the District of Columbia, with the two exceptions being Maine and Vermont.
4. Katzenstein, Ibrahim, and Rubin 2010.
5. American Civil Liberties Union 2006, p. 6.
6. Fellner and Mauer 1998, p. 1. Also see Mauer 2000.
7. American Civil Liberties Union 2006, p. 6.
8. American Civil Liberties Union 2006, p. 6.
9. Mauer 2004, p. 16.
10. *Richardson v. Ramirez*, 418 U.S. 24, 56 (1974).
11. Mauer 2004, p. 16.
12. These 14 states consist of Hawaii, Illinois, Indiana, Maryland (since 2016) Massachusetts, Michigan, Montana, New Hampshire, North Dakota, Ohio, Oregon, Pennsylvania, Rhode Island, and Utah.
13. California, Colorado, Connecticut, and New York.
14. Alaska, Arkansas, Georgia, Idaho, Kansas, Louisiana, Minnesota, Missouri, New Jersey, New Mexico, North Carolina, Oklahoma, South Carolina, South Dakota, Texas, Washington, West Virginia, and Wisconsin.
15. Alabama, Arizona, Delaware, Florida, Iowa, Kentucky, Mississippi, Nebraska, Nevada, Tennessee, Virginia, and Wyoming.
16. Sentencing Project 2016, p. 1. See also Brennan Center for Justice 2016; Ewald 2012.
17. Sentencing Project 2016, p. 3; Uggen, Larson, and Shannon 2016.
18. Ramirez 2008, p. 372.
19. Munn 2011, p. 223.
20. See Mondesire 2001; Stiber 2006; Taylor 2012; Witherspoon 2007; Alexander 2010.
21. Durose and Langan 2003.
22. Mitchell 2006, p. 855.
23. Sentencing Project 2013, p. 5.
24. Uggen and Manza 2002. See also Manza and Uggen 2006.
25. Note that this figure now stands at 1.5 million people. Bouie 2013.

26. Bouie 2013.

27. Sentencing Project 2013, p. 4.

28. Sentencing Project 2013, p. 4.

29. Nirappil and Portnoy 2016.

30. Wines 2016.

31. Brennan Center for Justice 2014.

32. Steinacker 2003, p. 806. These states include Maine, Arizona, Alaska, California, Colorado, Connecticut, Maryland, Michigan, Minnesota, Missouri, Nebraska, Nevada, New Jersey, New Mexico, Virginia, Washington, and Wyoming.

33. Georgia, Louisiana, Oklahoma, Rhode Island and South Carolina.

34. Steinacker 2003, p. 807.

35. Binnall 2014, p. 1. Note that Binnall adds that "while felon jury exclusion does not offend applicable constitutional standards, it is an imprecise and perhaps unnecessary practice that may come at substantial costs."

36. Kalt 2003, p. 1.

37. Mitchell 2006, p. 849.

38. Western 2006, p. 112.

39. Clark 2004, p. 193.

40. *Ellestad v. Swayze*, 130 P.2d 349, 353 (Wash. 1942). Cited in Clark 2004, p. 194.

41. *Hawker v. New York*, 170 U.S. 189, 197 (1898). Cited in Clark 2004, p. 195.

42. Clark 2004, p. 195.

43. Cited by Clark 2004, p. 195.

44. Clark 2004, p. 195.

45. Travis, Solomon, and Waul 2001, p. 31.

46. Clark 2004, p. 196.

47. Clark 2004, p. 196.

48. Hebenton and Thomas 1993.

49. Petersilia 2003, p. 115.

50. See Holzer 1996. Cited by Travis, Solomon, and Waul 2001, p. 31.

51. Vallas and Dietrich 2014, pp. 9, 19, and 28.

52. Clark 2004, p. 197.

53. *Tallahassee Furniture Co. v. Harrison.* 583 So. 2d 744 (Florida District Court of Appeals 1991).

54. Pager, Western, and Bonikowski 2009.

55. Pager 2003, p. 960.

56. Pager 2003, p. 960.

57. In this vein, see Hagan and Dinovitzer 1999.

58. Rodriguez and Avery 2016. Also see National Employment Law Project 2015, p. 4.

59. National Employment Law Project 2015, p. 4.

60. Agan and Starr 2016; Mullainathan 2016.

61. Jacobs 2015, pp. 275–300.

62. Human Rights Watch 2004, p. 1.

63. Travis, Solomon, and Waul 2001, p. 35.

64. Clinton 1996.

65. Human Rights Watch 2004, p. 2.

66. The Sentencing Project estimates that in 2013 the TANF ban affected over 180,000 women in the 12 most punitive states. Mauer and McCalmont 2013, p. 3; see also Vallas and Dietrich 2014, p. 22.

67. Human Rights Watch 2004, p. 3.

68. Human Rights Watch 2004, p. 3.

69. Human Rights Watch 2004, p. 4.

70. According to the California Department of Corrections, about 10 percent of parolees in the state are homeless, and the figure reaches the 30–50 percent range in Los Angeles and San Francisco. Cited in Travis, Solomon, and Waul 2001, p. 35.

71. Kaeble, Maruschak, and Bonczar 2015, p. 6.

72. Beckett and Harris 2011.

73. Comfort et al. 2011, p. 845.

74. Gottschalk, 2011, p. 490.

75. Dewan 2015.

76. Katzenstein and Nagrecha 2011, pp. 555, 557.

77. U.S. Department of Justice 2015.

78. Robertson, Dewan, and Apuzzo 2015.

79. Katzenstein and Waller 2015, p. 638.

80. Bush 2004.

81. Herzog-Evans 2011, p. 16.

82. Herzog-Evans 2011, p. 17.

83. Herzog-Evans 2011, p. 8.

84. Herzog-Evans 2011, pp. 7–8.

85. Herzog-Evans 2011, p. 8.

86. Herzog-Evans 2011, p. 8.

87. Herzog-Evans 2011, p. 8.

88. Herzog-Evans 2011, pp. 9–17.

89. Jacobs and Larrauri 2012.

90. Demleitner 2000, p. 757.

91. This reform did, however, leave room for exceptions on the issue of the right to vote in extreme situations involving crimes such as "preparation of a war of aggression, treason, use of insignia of a prohibited political organization, sabotage, espionage, election fraud, bribery of voters, and similar crimes." Demleitner 2000, p. 761.

92. Morgenstern 2011, p. 25.

93. Morgenstern 2011, p. 26.

94. Morgenstern 2011, p. 22.

95. Morgenstern 2011, pp. 26–27. Again, there are some exceptions in cases of highly sensitive lines of work.

96. Morgenstern 2011, pp. 24, 27.
97. Pinard 2010, p. 497.
98. Nayeri 2014, p. 125.
99. Pinard 2010, p. 495.
100. Pinard 2010, p. 495.
101. Pinard 2010, pp. 496–497.
102. Padfield 2011, p. 39.
103. Padfield 2011, p. 40.
104. Padfield 2011, p. 41.
105. Padfield 2011, p. 41.
106. Padfield 2011, p. 45.
107. Padfield 2011, p. 36.
108. Padfield 2011, p. 39.
109. Pinard 2010, p. 496.
110. Pinard 2010, p. 496.
111. Pinard 2010, p. 482.

CHAPTER 8

1. Whitman 2003.
2. Whitman 2003, pp. 8–9.
3. Whitman 2003, pp. 7, 9–10.
4. Loury 2007.
5. Oshinksy 1996; Blackmon 2008.
6. More serious charges such as rape, attempted rape, or looking at a white woman in the wrong way, would often result in extrajudicial consequences, namely lynching.
7. Under slavery, a master once had to pay for dental or medical care for his slaves. This "need" to provide care disappeared under convict leasing.
8. Mancini 1996.
9. Oshinsky 1996, pp. 50, 60.
10. Oshinsky 1996, p. 81.
11. Oshinsky 1996, p. 92.
12. According to a Gallup survey conducted in 1993, 2008, and 2013, the percentage of African Americans who "think the American justice system is biased against black people" has remained steady at 67 or 68 percent, whereas the percentage of whites agreeing with that statement has dropped from 33 to 32 to 25 percent over that time period. Cited by Ghandnoosh 2014, p. 29.
13. See especially Cole 1999, Mauer 2006, and Wacquant 1999 and 2000.
14. Alexander 2010.
15. Also see Wacquant 2000 for an analysis of what he views as the continuities of the American criminal justice system in terms of its maintenance of racial domination

of blacks, from slavery to Jim Crow to ghettos and housing discrimination to mass incarceration.

16. Alexander 2010, p. 1.

17. In a similar vein, Vesla Weaver shows how the success of the civil rights movement led opponents of racial equality to regroup and focus their efforts on fusing the issues of race and crime. She writes, "The same actors who had fought vociferously against civil rights legislation, defeated, shifted the 'locus of attack' by injecting crime onto the agenda. Fusing crime to anxiety about ghetto revolts, racial disorder—initially defined as a problem of minority disenfranchisement—was redefined as a crime problem, which helped shift debate from social reform to punishment." Weaver 2007, p. 230.

18. Alexander 2010, p. 7.

19. Cited by Ghandnoosh 2015, p. 15. This important report, issued by the Sentencing Project, also lays out numerous additional racial disparities in Ferguson, New York City, and nationwide.

20. Gottschalk 2015a, p. 5.

21. Gottschalk 2015b.

22. Forman 2012, p. 113.

23. Forman 2012, p. 103. See also Fortner 2015.

24. Forman 2012, p. 103.

25. Apuzzo and Eligon 2015.

26. Robertson, Dewan, and Apuzzo 2015.

27. Oppel Jr., Stolberg, and Apuzzo 2016.

28. Banaji and Greenwald 2013, pp. 175–187.

29. Hochschild, Weaver, and Burch 2011, 2012.

30. The empirical studies behind these findings are nicely summarized in Banaji and Greenwald 2013, pp. 193–201.

31. Banaji and Greenwald 2013, pp. 203–205.

32. Note that IATs have been conducted on many other topics as well, including gender, religion, disability, weight, age, and sexuality.

33. Banaji and Greenwald 2013, p. 47.

34. These three findings come from Ghandnoosh 2014, p. 3.

35. This, indeed, is the final conclusion reached by Banaji and Greenwald, who write, "given the relatively small proportion of people who are overtly prejudiced and how clearly it is established that automatic race preference predicts discrimination, it is reasonable to conclude not only that implicit bias is a cause of Black disadvantage but also that it plausibly plays a greater role than does explicit bias in explaining the discrimination that contributes to Black disadvantage." Banaji and Greenwald 2013, p. 209.

36. Precise statistics do not exist, and the categories vary, but in Germany, where about 9 percent of the population is foreign (with the largest group being Turkish), just over 20 percent of criminal convictions involve foreigners (Statistiches Bundesamt

2011, p. 14); in the U.K., where 2.9 percent of the general population is black and 4.2 percent Muslim, the prison population consists of 13.1 and 13.4 percent of each group, respectively (The Young Review 2014, p. 10); France does not officially track race or ethnicity, but the disparities are massive, with some estimates stating that over 60 percent of the prison population is Muslim, much higher than the 12 percent of the population (Moore 2008).

37. Howard 2009.

38. Schneider 2014, p. 7.

39. See Ghandnoosh 2014, pp. 22–24; Mendelberg 2001.

40. One important exception, however, would be Michael Tonry, who argues that "Moralistic crusades against drugs and crime in our time enabled fundamentalist Protestants and social conservatives to express disapproval of people unlike themselves and to assert their moral superiority," thus resulting in harsh views of good and evil that are viewed in absolutist terms. See Tonry 2009, p. 383.

41. Howard, Gibson, and Stolle 2005; Howard 2007.

42. Howard 2007, pp. 13–15, 25.

43. Howard, Gibson, and Stolle 2005.

44. Grzymała-Busse 2015, pp. 229–230.

45. Grzymała-Busse 2015, p. 239.

46. Grzymała-Busse 2015, p. 239.

47. Grzymała-Busse 2015, p. 243.

48. Grzymała-Busse 2015, p. 244.

49. Grzymała-Busse 2015, p. 244.

50. Grzymała-Busse 2015, p. 245.

51. Jerry Falwell famously stated that his goal was to "Get them saved, baptized, and registered." See Grzymała-Busse 2015, p. 251.

52. Grzymała-Busse 2015, p. 248.

53. Durkheim 1997 [1893], p. 47.

54. Garland 1990, p. 203.

55. Koch and Gates 2012, p. 74

56. Grasmick et al. 1992.

57. Grasmick et al. 1993.

58. Grasmick and McGill 1994, p. 23.

59. Applegate et al. 2000.

60. Unnever et al. 2005; also see Bader et al. 2010.

61. Grasmick et al. 1993; Young 2000; Unnever and Cullen 2006.

62. In fact, although a March 2015 Pew Research Center survey shows that 71 percent of white evangelicals still favor capital punishment, the National Association of Evangelicals (NAE)—which had explicitly supported the death penalty in a 1973 resolution—has softened its approach. In October 2015 the NAE adopted a new resolution that recognized the variety of evangelical views on this issue, stating that "Evangelical Christians differ in their beliefs about capital punishment,

often citing strong biblical and theological reasons either for the just character of the death penalty in extreme cases or for the sacredness of all life, including the lives of those who perpetrate serious crimes and yet have the potential for repentance and reformation. We affirm the conscientious commitment of both streams of Christian ethical thought." See Bailey 2015 and National Association of Evangelicals 2015.

63. Ulmer, Bader and Gault 2008, p. 737.
64. See Lacey 2008.
65. See Enns 2016.
66. Carter 1999, p. 30.
67. Boyd 1970, p. 215. See also Phillips 1969.
68. Baum 1997.
69. Baum 2016.
70. The ghost of "Willie Horton" continues to haunt the politics of criminal justice. Recall President Obama's comment that "everybody remembers the Willie Horton ad." Korte 2016.
71. Murakawa 2014, p. 3.
72. Murakawa 2014, p. 71.
73. Murakawa 2014, p. 151.
74. See, for example, Goldstein 2015a; Schlanger 2015.
75. For centuries, according to Stuntz, only local juries, local judges, and local police made decisions on crime and punishment. Local officials and juries were less likely to impose harsh punishment, especially in the North. Even in the South, Stuntz writes, extrajudicial forms of punishment, such as lynching, were more commonly used against blacks than lengthy prison terms. With the passage of national- and state-level mandatory sentencing schemes (following the politicization of crime control nationally) voters least likely to be either victims of crime or incarcerated were those most likely to support punitive measures. Stuntz thereby provides a dynamic institutional explanation of how American criminal justice policy became exceptional. See Stuntz 2011, pp. 13–62.
76. Fortner 2015, p. 9.
77. See Frady 1993.
78. Bureau of Justice Statistics.
79. Tonry 2007, p. 35.
80. Note that the elections are only for the position of lead prosecutor, usually called district attorney or state's attorney. The many assistant prosecutors in each jurisdiction are subsequently appointed by the winner of the election.
81. Ellis 2012, p. 1530.
82. Tocqueville 1966 [1835].
83. This appears to represent yet another case of "progressive" and "anti-political" reforms that have unintended consequences on criminal justice and prisons.
84. Ellis 2012, pp. 1551, 1565.

85. American Judicature Society 2015.

86. Liptak 2008b.

87. Gordon and Huber 2002.

88. Wright 2009, p. 582.

89. Wright 2009, pp. 582–583.

90. Huber and Gordon 2004, p. 247.

91. Berry 2015, p. 1.

92. Bright and Keenan 1995, pp. 776–792.

93. Bright and Keenan 1995, pp. 792–795. Note that juries are not exactly "soft" on the death penalty, as all juries in capital cases must be "death qualified," meaning that jurors who express any reservation about the death penalty are automatically excluded from the jury pool. Such "death qualification" of juries makes the propensity for judges to override and impose the death penalty against the jury's wishes even more striking.

94. Radelet 2011, p. 795.

95. That said, the authors of a comprehensive study of capital punishment in Delaware—which "shifted responsibility for death penalty sentencing from the jury to the judge" in 1991—found that even when controlling for a host of other factors, "the shift to judge sentencing significantly increased the number of death sentences." Hans et al. 2015, p. 70.

96. Liptak 2015a. See also Equal Justice Initiative 2011.

97. *Woodward v. Alabama*, 571 U. S. _____ (2013).

98. Liptak 2015a. For an informed speculation about the possibility of a majority of Supreme Court justices finding that the election and re-election of judges violates the due process clause of the Constitution, see Freeman 2012.

99. O'Connor 2010.

100. *Economist* 2012.

101. Gibson 2012.

102. Palmer and Levendis 2008, p. 1292.

103. Palmer and Levendis 2008, p. 1292.

104. Brennan Center for Justice 2016.

105. Wright 2009, p. 581.

106. Liptak 2008b.

107. Varsho 2007, p. 503.

108. Varsho 2007, p. 517.

109. Jones and Newburn 2006, p. 796.

110. Liptak 2008a.

111. See Dolovich 2005.

112. Mulch 2009, p. 72.

113. Hallinan 2001, p. 22

114. Mulch 2009, p. 73.

115. Hallinan 2001, p. 144.

116. Schlosser 1998, p. 54.
117. Fulcher 2012, p. 589.
118. Brickner and Diaz 2011, p. 13.
119. Carson 2014, p. 14. In August 2016, the Obama administration announced that it would "begin to phase out the use of private for-profit prisons to house federal inmates." Savage 2016. But the Trump administration seems likely to reverse this order and reinvigorate the use of private federal prisons.
120. Corrections Corporation of America 2014, p. 22.
121. Justice Policy Institute 2011, p. 15.
122. Justice Policy Institute 2011, pp. 15–16.
123. See Mason 2012.
124. Bureau of Justice Statistics 1986.
125. Stephan 1999.
126. Hughes 2006.
127. U.S. Department of Justice 2013.
128. According to a report by In the Public Interest, 65 percent of private prison contracts include such minimum occupancy guarantees, usually in the range of 80–100 percent. Three private prisons in Arizona require 100 percent occupancy, whereby the state "is contractually obligated to keep these prisons filled to 100 percent capacity, or pay the private company for any unused beds." In the Public Interest 2013, pp. 1–3.
129. Schlosser 1998, pp. 64–65.
130. Knafo 2013.
131. Knafo 2013.
132. Boettke, Coyne, and Hall 2013, p. 1091.
133. Ridgeway and Casella 2013.
134. Hallinan 2001, pp. xii–xiii, 83.
135. Hallinan 2001, p. 7.
136. Thorpe 2015.
137. Hallinan 2001, p. xiv.
138. Hallinan 2001, p. xiv. In Baldwin County, Alabama, calls cost $3.95 for the connection charge, plus $0.89 per minute. From those charges, the phone company chosen, ICSolutions, pays 84.1 percent back to the county and actually guarantees an average commission of "$55.00 per inmate per month." See Kukorowski, Wagner, and Sakala 2013, p. 5.
139. Williams 2015.
140. Kukorowski, Wagner, and Sakala 2013, p. iii. More recently, the FCC has intervened to lower costs by imposing caps for interstate calls and reclassifying commissions, but the prison phone companies have consequently increased their credit card fees, while refusing to send back the portion of their profits to the prisons—and in 2014 the company Securus generated windfall profits, based on a 51 percent gross profit margin. See Wagner 2015.

141. Fulcher 2013, p. 83.
142. Rabuy and Wagner 2015, p. i.
143. Fulcher 2013, p. 108.
144. Hallinan 2001, p. 49.
145. Hallinan 2001, p. 49.
146. Hartney and Glesmann 2012, p. 17.
147. Note that they are usually restricted from selling products directly on the open market, and can only sell to state agencies and nonprofit organizations—including universities, as the head of Maryland Correctional Enterprises (MCE) always reminds me when I take my Georgetown students to visit the Jessup Correctional Institution, while he provides me with several copies of MCE's thick, snazzy, and colorful catalogue filled with the latest products and prices.
148. Hartney and Glesmann 2012, p. 18.
149. Rosenberg 2015.
150. I thank Marc Mauer for urging me to articulate this distinction.
151. This point connects to the compelling argument made by Cavadino and Dignan, who claim that neo-liberal countries—a group that includes Australia, England and Wales, New Zealand, and South Africa, along with the U.S.—have a "highly individualistic social ethos" that leads to the "exclusion both of those who fail in the economic marketplace and of those who fail to abide by the law." In other words, without a social safety net, many people fall through the cracks, into poverty and/or into prison. Cavadino and Dignan 2006, p. 23.

CHAPTER 9

1. Hohmann 2016.
2. Dolovich 2011, p. 112.
3. Ali 2011.
4. Dagan and Teles 2016.
5. Dagan and Teles 2016, pp. ix–xi.
6. See Gingrich and Nolan 2011.
7. Dagan and Teles 2016, pp. 44–45.
8. Dagan and Teles 2016, pp. 31–32.
9. Dagan and Teles 2016, p. 45.
10. Dagan and Teles 2016, p. 159.
11. The daily coverage provided by The Marshall Project, available at https://www.themarshallproject.org, is fantastic.
12. See *The Washington Post* 2015; *The Washington Post* 2016; Burghart 2014.
13. Goldstein 2015b.
14. Kuznia 2016.
15. Sundt, Salisbury, and Harmon 2016.

16. Glod 2015.
17. Glod 2015.
18. Subramanian, Moreno, and Broomhead 2014.
19. Silber, Subramanian, and Spotts 2016.
20. *New York Times* Editorial Board 2016.
21. Goldstein and Goodman 2016.
22. See Dunne 2016.
23. Baker 2015; Reilly 2016.
24. Davidson 2016.
25. Schwartzapfel 2015.
26. Glod 2015.
27. Arkin 2016.
28. Enns 2016.
29. See Clear and Frost 2013.
30. Mauer and Ghandnoosh 2013.
31. Sentencing Project 2013; 2015a. See also Prison Policy Initiative's very enlightening "States of Incarceration" charts and data. Wagner and Walsh 2016.
32. Carson 2014.
33. Gottschalk 2015, p. 17.
34. See Gottschalk 2015, pp. 7–19.
35. Wagner and Rabuy 2016.
36. Wagner and Rabuy 2016.
37. Schwartz 2016.
38. Keller 2016.
39. Enns 2016, p. 164.
40. A quick perusal of the anonymous "comments" section following news coverage of criminal justice and prison reform reveals numerous angry and venomous statements about "coddling criminals," opposition to any amenities or rights in prisons by contrasting them to "country clubs," and reductionist platitudes such as "don't do the crime if you can't do the time." Even if public opinion has shifted against punitiveness in recent years, one should recognize that the hostility to that change lies just below the surface—aided by the cloak of anonymity.
41. Davis et al. 2013.
42. Kaplan 2014. Also see Enns 2016, p. 163.
43. Liptak 2015b.
44. Mauer 2015.
45. This phrase comes from the "governor" of Norway's Bastoy Prison, as reported by Baz Dreisinger in her engaging account of prisons and justice in eight very different countries. The full quote is as follows: "There's a perception that, 'Oh, this is the lightweight prison; you just take the nice guys for the summer-camp prison.' But in fact, no. Our guys are into, pardon my French, some heavy shit. Drugs and violence. And the truth is, some have been problematic in other

prisons but then they come here, and we find them easy. We say, 'Is that the same guy you called difficult?' It's really very simple: Treat people like dirt, and they will be dirt. Treat them like human beings, and they will act like human beings." Dreisinger 2016, p. 277.

46. Pruin 2012, p. 63.
47. See also Kleiman 2010.

References

Adamson, LeMay, and H. Warren Dunham. 1956. "Clinical Treatment of Male Delinquents: A Case Study in Effort and Result." In *American Sociological Review*, Vol. 21, No. 3, pp. 312–320.

Agan, Amanda Y, and Sonja B. Starr. 2016. "Ban the Box, Criminal Records, and Statistical Discrimination: A Field Experiment." University of Michigan Law & Economics Research Paper No. 16-012.

Aharonson, Ely. 2013. "Determinate Sentencing and American Exceptionalism: The Underpinnings and Effects of Cross-National Differences in the Regulation of Sentencing Discretion." In *Law and Contemporary Problems*, Vol. 76, No. 1, pp. 161–187.

Albrecht, Hans-Jörg. 2013. "Sentencing in Germany: Explaining Long-Term Stability in the Structure of Criminal Sanctions and Sentencing." In *Law and Contemporary Problems*, Vol. 76, No. 1, pp. 211–236.

Alexander, Michelle. 2010. *The New Jim Crow: Mass Incarceration in the Age of Colorblindness*. New York: The New Press.

Ali, Ambreen. 2011. "Norquist Sees Savings in Prison Reform." In *Roll Call*. April 6.

Alschuler, Albert. 1979. "Plea Bargaining and Its History." In *Columbia Law Review*, Vol. 79, No. 1, pp. 1–43.

American Civil Liberties Union. 2006. "Out of Step with the World: An Analysis of Felony Disfranchisement in the U.S. and Other Democracies." Available at https://www.aclu.org/sites/default/files/field_document/asset_upload_file825_25663.pdf (accessed January 31, 2017).

American Civil Liberties Union. 2014. *War Comes Home: Excessive Militarization of American Policing*. Available at https://www.aclu.org/report/war-comes-home-excessive-militarization-american-police (accessed January 31, 2017).

American Judicature Society. 2015. "Judicial Selection in the States." Available at http://www.judicialselection.us/ (accessed January 31, 2017).

Anderson, David C. 1995. *Crime and the Politics of Hysteria: How the Willie Horton Story Changed American Justice*. New York: Random House.

Andrews, D.A. 1995. "The Psychology of Criminal Conduct and Effective Treatment." In *What Works: Reducing Reoffending*, edited by James McGuire. West Sussex, England: John Wiley & Sons.

Andrews, D.A., Ivan Zinger, Robert D. Hoge, James Bonta, Paul Gendreau, and Francis T. Cullen. 1990. "Does Correctional Treatment Work? A Clinically Relevant and Psychologically Informed Meta-Analysis." In *Criminology*, Vol. 28, No. 3, pp. 369–404.

Andrews, D.A., and James Bonta. 1998. *The Psychology of Criminal Conduct.* 2nd ed. Cincinnati, OH: Anderson Publishing Company.

Andrews, D.A., and R.D. Hoge. 1995. "The Psychology of Criminal Conduct and Principles of Effective Prevention and Rehabilitation." In *Forum on Corrections Research*, Vol. 7, No. 1, pp. 34–36.

AP/Huffington Post. 2010. "Huckabee Granted Clemency to Maurice Clemmons, Person of Interest, In Ambush That Killed 4 Cops." March 18. Available at http://www.huffingtonpost.com/2009/11/29/multiple-police-officers-_n_373119.html (accessed January 31, 2017).

Applegate, Brandon K., Francis T. Cullen, Bonnie S. Fisher, Thomas Vander Ven. 2000. "Forgiveness and Fundamentalism: Reconsidering the Relationship between Correctional Attitudes and Religion." In *Criminology*, Vol. 38, No. 3, pp. 719–754.

Apuzzo, Matt, and John Eligon. 2015. "Ferguson Police Tainted by Bias, Justice Department Says." In *The New York Times*. March 4, p. A1.

Apuzzo, Matt, and Sarah Cohen. 2015. "Data on Use of Force by Police across U.S. Proves Almost Useless." In *The New York Times*. August 11.

Arkin, James. 2016. "Poll: Majority Supports Prison and Justice Reforms." RealClearPolitics. Available at http://www.realclearpolitics.com/articles/2016/02/11/poll_majority_supports_prison_and_justice_reforms_129635.html (accessed January 31, 2017).

Ashcroft, John. 2003. "Department Policy concerning Charging Criminal Offenses, Disposition of Charges, and Sentencings." Department of Justice. September 22. Available at http://www.justice.gov/archive/opa/pr/2003/September/03_ag_516.htm (accessed January 31, 2017).

Bach, Amy. 2009. *Ordinary Injustice: How America Holds Court.* New York: Metropolitan Books.

Bader, Christopher D., Scott A. Desmond, F. Carson Mencken, and Byron R. Johnson. 2010. "Divine Justice: The Relationship between Images of God and Attitudes toward Criminal Punishment." In *Criminal Justice Review*, Vol. 35, No. 1, pp. 90–106.

Bagaric, Mirko. 2014. "Punishment Should Fit the Crime—Not the Prior Convictions of the Person That Committed the Crime: An Argument for Less Impact Being Accorded to Previous Convictions in Sentencing." In *San Diego Law Review*, Vol. 51, No. 2, pp. 343–418.

Bailey, Sarah Pulliam. 2015. "The National Association of Evangelicals Has Changed Its Position on the Death Penalty." In *The Washington Post*. October 19.

Baker, Peter. 2015. "Obama, in Oklahoma, Takes Reform Message to the Prison Cell Block." In *The New York Times*. July 16.

Balko, Radley. 2013. *Rise of the Warrior Cop: The Militarization of America's Police Forces*. New York: PublicAffairs.

Banaji, Mahzarin R., and Anthony G. Greenwald. 2013. *Blind Spot: Hidden Biases of Good People*. New York: Delacorte Press.

Barclay, Eliza. 2014. "Food as Punishment: Giving U.S. Inmates 'The Loaf' Persists." National Public Radio. January 2.

Barker, Vanessa. 2009. *The Politics of Imprisonment: How the Democratic Process Shapes the Way American Punishes Offenders*. New York: Oxford University Press.

Baum, Dan. 1997. *Smoke and Mirrors: The War on Drugs and the Politics of Failure*. New York: Back Bay Books.

Baum, Dan. 2016. "Legalize It All: How to Win the War on Drugs." In *Harper's Magazine*. April.

BBC News. 2013. "Early Jail Release to Be Curtailed under Government Plans." October 3. Available at http://www.bbc.com/news/uk-24384154 (accessed January 31, 2017).

Beckett, Katherine, and Alexes Harris. 2011. "On Cash and Conviction: Monetary Sanctions as Misguided Policy." In *Criminology & Public Policy*, Vol. 10, No. 3, pp. 509–537.

Bedford, Charlotte. 2015. "Making Waves behind Bars: The Story of the Prison Radio Association." Doctoral Dissertation, University of Adelaide. Available at https://digital.library.adelaide.edu.au/dspace/bitstream/2440/96911/3/02whole.pdf (accessed January 31, 2017).

Benko, Jessica. 2015. "The Radical Humaneness of Norway's Halden Prison." In *The New York Times Magazine*. March 26.

Berkman, Alan. 1995. "Prison Health: The Breaking Point." In *The American Journal of Public Health*, Vol. 85, No. 12, pp. 1616–1618.

Berman, Douglas A. 2011. "The Many (Opaque) Echoes of Compromise Crack Sentencing Reform." In *Federal Sentencing Reporter*, Vol. 23, No. 3, pp. 167–170.

Berry, Kate. 2015. "How Judicial Elections Impact Criminal Cases." Brennan Center for Justice. Available at https://www.brennancenter.org/sites/default/files/publications/How_Judicial_Elections_Impact_Criminal_Cases.pdf (accessed January 31, 2017).

Bibas, Stephanos. 2004. "Plea Bargaining outside the Shadow of Trial." *Harvard Law Review*, Vol. 117, No. 8, pp. 2463–2547.

Binder, Guyora. 2008. "The Culpability of Felony Murder." In *Notre Dame Law Review*, Vol. 83, No. 3, pp. 965–1060.

Binelli, Mark. 2015. "Inside America's Toughest Federal Prison." In *The New York Times Magazine*. March 26.

Binnall, James M. 2014. "A Field Study of the Presumptively Biased: Is There Empirical Support for Excluding Convicted Felons from Jury Service?" In *Law & Policy*, Vol. 36, No. 1, pp. 1–34.

Blackmon, Douglas A. 2008. *Slavery by Another Name: The Re-enslavement of Black Americans from the Civil War to World War II*. New York: Anchor Books.

Black's Law Dictionary, 5th ed. 1979. St. Paul, MN: West.

Blakesley, Christopher L. 1978. "Conditional Liberation (Parole) in France." In *Louisiana Law Review*, Vol. 39, pp. 1–41.

Block v. Rutherford, 468 U.S. 576 (1984).

Boettke, Peter J., Christopher J. Coyne, and Abigail R. Hall. 2013. "Keep Off the Grass: The Economics of Prohibition and U.S. Drug Policy." In *Oregon Law Review*, Vol. 91, No. 4, pp. 1069–1096.

Bordenkircher v. Hayes. 434 U.S. 357 (1978).

Bosworth, Mary F. 2009. *Explaining U.S. Imprisonment*. Los Angeles: Sage.

Bottomley, A. Keith. 1990. "Parole in Transition: A Comparative Study of Origins, Developments, and Prospects for the 1990s." In *Crime and Justice: A Review of Research*, Vol. 12, pp. 319–374.

Bouie, Jamelle. 2013. "The Ex-Con Factor." In *The American Prospect*. August 20. Available at http://prospect.org/article/ex-con-factor (accessed January 31, 2017).

Bowers, Josh. 2008. "Punishing the Innocent." University of Pennsylvania Law Review, Vol. 156, No. 5, pp. 1117–1179.

Boyd, James. 1970. "Nixon's Southern Strategy: 'It's All in the Charts.' " In *The New York Times*. May 17.

Bradley, Craig M., ed. 2007. *Criminal Procedure: A World Wide Study*, 2nd ed. Durham, NC: Carolina Academic Press.

Brady v. United States, 397 U.S. 742 (1970).

Braman, Donald. 2002. "Families and Incarceration." In *Invisible Punishment: The Collateral Consequences of Mass Imprisonment*, edited by Marc Mauer and Medea Chesney-Lind. New York: The New Press.

Brennan Center for Justice. 2016. "Criminal Disenfranchisement Laws across the United States." Available at http://www.brennancenter.org/criminal-disenfranchisement-laws-across-united-states (accessed January 31, 2017).

Brennan Center for Justice. 2014. "Democracy Restoration Act." Available at https://www.brennancenter.org/legislation/democracy-restoration-act (accessed January 31, 2017).

Brennan Center for Justice. 2016. "Spending by Outside Groups in Judicial Races Hits Record High, Secret Money Dominates." Available at https://www.brennancenter.org/press-release/spending-outside-groups-judicial-races-hits-record-high-secret-money-dominates (accessed January 31, 2017).

Bretschneider, Wiebke, Bernice Elger, and Tenzin Wangmo. 2013. "Ageing Prisoners' Health Care: Analysing the Legal Settings in Europe and the United States." In *Gerontology*, Vol. 59, No. 3, pp. 267–275.

Brickner, Michael, and Shankyra Diaz. 2011. "Prisons for Profit: Incarceration for Sale." In *Human Rights*, Vol. 38, No. 3, pp. 13–16.

Bright, Stephen B., and Patrick J. Keenan. 1995. "Judges and the Politics of Death: Deciding between the Bill of Rights and the next Election in Capital Cases." In *Boston University Law Review*, Vol. 73, pp. 759–835.

Bronstein, Alvin and Jenni Gainsborough. 2004. "Using International Human Rights Laws and Standards for U.S. Prison Reform." In *Pace Law Review*, Vol. 24, pp. 811–824.

Brown, Governor of California, et al. *v. Plata* et al., 563 U. S. ____ (2011).

Browne, Angela, Alissa Cambier, and Suzanne Agha. 2011. "Sentencing within Sentencing." In *Federal Sentencing Reporter*, Vol. 24, No. 1, pp. 46–49.

Bundesverfassungsgericht [Federal Constitutional Court]. 2013. Case No. 2 BvR 2628/10. 2 BvR 2883/10, 2 BvR 2155/11. In *Neue Juristische Wochenschrift*.

Bureau of Justice Statistics. 1986. "Justice Expenditure and Employment, 1983." A Bureau of Justice Statistics Bulletin. Available at http://www.bjs.gov/content/pub/pdf/jcc83.pdf (accessed January 31, 2017).

Burghart, D. Brian. 2014. "What I've Learned from Two Years Collecting Data on Police Killings." Gawker. Available at http://gawker.com/what-ive-learned-from-two-years-collecting-data-on-poli-1625472836 (accessed January 31, 2017).

Burke, Alafair. 2013. "Policing, Protestors, and Discretion." In *Fordham Urban Law Journal*, Vol. 40, No. 3, pp. 999–1022.

Bush, George W. 2004. "State of the Union Address." January 20. Available at http://www.washingtonpost.com/wp-srv/politics/transcripts/bushtext_012004.html (accessed January 31, 2017).

Butler, Paul. 2010. *Let's Get Free: A Hip-Hop Theory of Justice.* New York: The New Press.

Carson, E. Ann. 2014. "Prisoners in 2013." U.S. Department of Justice, Office of Justice Programs, Bureau of Justice Statistics. Available at http://www.bjs.gov/content/pub/pdf/p13.pdf (accessed January 31, 2017).

Carter, Dan C. 1999. *From George Wallace to Newt Gingrich: Race in the Conservative Counterrevolution, 1963–1994.* Baton Rouge: Louisiana State University Press.

Cavadino, Michael, and James Dignan. 2006. *Penal Systems: A Comparative Approach.* London: Sage.

CBS News. 2015. "EU Anti-Terror Chief Urges Rehab, Not Prison, for Jihadis." Available at http://www.cbsnews.com/news/eu-anti-terror-chief-urges-rehab-not-prison-for-jihadis/ (accessed January 31, 2017).

Ceaser, James W. 2012. "The Origins and Character of American Exceptionalism." In *American Political Thought: A Journal of Ideas, Institutions, and Culture,* Vol. 1, No. 1, pp. 3–28.

Céré, Jean-Paul, and Carlos Eduardo A. Japiassú, eds. 2011. *Les Systèmes Pénitentiaires Dans Le Monde*, 2nd ed. Paris: Dalloz.

Chammah, Maurice. 2015. "Can German Prisons Teach America How to Handle Its Most Violent Criminals?" The Marshall Project. Available at https://www.themarshallproject.org/2015/06/18/can-german-prisons-teach-america-how-to-handle-its-most-violent-criminals (accessed January 31, 2017).

Chettiar, Inimai M. 2015. "The Many Causes of America's Decline in Crime." In *The Atlantic*. February 11.

Clark, Leroy D. 2004. "A Civil Rights Task: Removing Barriers to Employment of Ex-Convicts." In *University of Southern Florida Law Review*, Vol. 38, pp. 193–212.

Clatot, Jean-Pierre. 2014. "Pas de cellules individuelles pour tous dans les prisons avant 2019 voire 2022." In *Le Monde*. December 4.

Clear, Todd R., and Natasha A. Frost. 2014. *The Punishment Imperative: The Rise and Failure of Mass Incarceration in America*. New York: New York University Press.

Clinton, Bill. 1996. "State of the Union Address." January 23. Available at http://clinton2.nara.gov/WH/New/other/sotu.html (accessed January 31, 2017).

Cloud, David. 2014. "On Life Support: Public Health in the Age of Mass Incarceration." New York: Vera Institute of Justice.

Cole, David. 1999. *No Equal Justice: Race and Class in the American Criminal Justice System*. New York: The New Press.

Coleman v. *Wilson*, 912 F. Supp. 1282, 1316 (E.D. Cal.).

Comfort, Megan, Anne M. Nurse, Tasseli McKay, and Katie Kramer. 2011. "Taking Children into Account: Addressing the Intergenerational Effects of Parental Incarceration." In *Criminology & Public Policy*, Vol. 10, No. 3, pp. 839–850.

Corrections Corporation of America. 2014. "2014 Annual Report on Form 10-K." Available at http://www.sec.gov/Archives/edgar/data/1070985/000095014406001892/g99938e10vk.htm (accessed January 31, 2017).

Council of Europe. 2006. *European Prison Rules*. Council of Europe Publishing. Available at www.coe.int/t/dgi/criminallawcoop/Presentation/Documents/European-Prison-Rules_978-92-871-5982-3.pdf (accessed January 31, 2017).

Crétenot, Marie, and Barbara Liaras. 2013. "Prison Conditions in France." European Prison Observatory. Rome: Antigone Edizioni.

Cullen, Francis T. 2007. "Make Rehabilitation Corrections' Guiding Paradigm." In *Criminology & Public Policy*, Vol. 6, No. 4, pp. 717–728.

Cullen, Francis T., and Paul Gendreau. 2000. "Assessing Correctional Rehabilitation: Policy, Practice, and Prospects." In *Policies, Processes, and Decisions of the Criminal Justice System*, Vol. 3, pp. 109–175.

Cullen, Francis T., Paul Gendreau, G. Roger Jarjoura, and John Paul Wright. 1997. "Crime and the Bell Curve: Lessons from Intelligent Criminology." In *Crime & Delinquency*, Vol. 43, No. 4, pp. 387–411.

Dagan, David, and Steven M. Teles. 2016. *Prison Break: Why Conservatives Turned Against Mass Incarceration*. New York: Oxford University Press.

Daguzan, Jean-François. 2014. "Les prisons, incubatrices du terrorisme." In *Le Monde*. June 2.

Dance, Gabriel, and Tom Meagher. 2016. "Crime in Context." The Marshall Project. Available at https://www.themarshallproject.org/2016/08/18/crime-in-context (accessed January 31, 2017).

Davidson, Joe. 2016. "Will States Follow DOJ's Private Prison Move? Some Are Ahead of the Feds." In *The Washington Post*. August 26.

Davis, Anthony. 1975. "Sentencing Procedures in England and America—American Bargains or English Justice?" In *Journal of Psychiatry and* Law, Vol. 3, No. 4, pp. 447–462.

Davis, Lois M., Robert Bozick, Jennifer L. Steele, Jessica Saunders, Jeremy N. V. Miles. 2013. "Evaluating the Effectiveness of Correctional Education: A Meta-analysis of Programs That Provide Education to Incarcerated Adults." A RAND Corporation report. Available at http://www.rand.org/pubs/research_reports/RR266.html (accessed January 31, 2017).

De la Vega, Connie, and Michelle Leighton. 2008. "Sentencing Our Children to Die in Prison: Global Law and Practice." In *University of San Francisco Law Review*, Vol. 42, No. 4, pp., 983–1044.

Death Penalty Information Center. 2015. "Facts about the Death Penalty" (updated May 13). Available at http://www.deathpenaltyinfo.org/documents/FactSheet.pdf (accessed January 31, 2017).

DeFina, Robert H., and Thomas M. Arvanites. 2002. "The Weak Effect of Imprisonment on Crime: 1971–1998." In *Social Science Quarterly*, Vol. 83, No. 3, pp. 635–653.

Delgado, Melvin. 2009. *Health and Healthcare in the Nation's Prisons*. Lanham, MD: Rowman and Littlefield.

Demleitner, Nora V. 2000. "Continuing Payment on One's Debt to Society: The German Model of Felon Disenfranchisement as an Alternative." In *Minnesota Law Review*, Vol. 84, No. 4, pp. 753–804.

Deutsche Welle. 2013. "German Court Upholds Plea Bargains." March 19.

Dewan, Shaila. 2015. "Driver's License Suspensions Create Cycle of Debt." In *The New York Times*. April 14.

Ditton, Paula M., and Doris James Wilson. 1999. "Truth in Sentencing in State Prisons," a Bureau of Justice Statistics Special Report. Available at http://bjs.ojp.usdoj.gov/content/pub/pdf/tssp.pdf (accessed January 31, 2017).

Doherty, Fiona. 2013. "Indeterminate Sentencing Returns: The Invention of Supervised Release." In *New York University Law Review*, Vol. 88, No. 3, pp. 958–1030.

Dolovich, Sharon. 2005. "State Punishment and Private Prisons." In *Duke Law Journal*, Vol. 55, No. 3, pp. 437–546.

Dolovich, Sharon. 2009a. "Incarceration American-Style." In *Harvard Law and Policy Review*, Vol. 3, pp. 237–259.

Dolovich, Sharon. 2009b. "Cruelty, Prison Conditions, and the Eighth Amendment." In *New York University Law Review*, Vol. 84, No. 4, pp. 881–979.

Dolovich, Sharon. 2011. "Creating the Permanent Prisoner." In *Life without Parole: America's New Death Penalty*, edited by Charles J. Ogletree Jr. and Austin Sarat. New York: NYU Press.

Dolovich, Sharon. 2012. "Forms of Deference in Prison Law." In *Federal Sentencing Reporter*, Vol. 24, No. 4, pp. 245–259.

Donaldson, Stephen. 2001. "A Million Jockers, Punks, and Queens." In *Prison Masculinities*, edited by Don Sabo et al. Philadelphia: Temple University Press.

Dreisinger, Baz. 2016. *Incarceration Nations: A Journey to Justice in Prisons around the World*. New York: Other Press.

Dubber, Markus Dirk. 1997. "American Plea Bargains, German Lay Judges, and the Crisis of Criminal Procedure." *Stanford Law Review*, Vol. 49, No. 3, pp. 547–605.

Dubber, Markus D. 2007. "Criminalizing Complicity: A Comparative Analysis." In *Journal of International Criminal Justice*, Vol. 5, pp. 977–1001.

Dünkel, Frieder, and Ineke Pruin. 2010. "Germany." In *Release from Prison: European Policy and Practice*, edited by Nicola Padfield, Dirk van Zyl Smit, and Frieder Dünkel. Devon, U.K.: Willan, pp. 185–212.

Dunne, Grainne. 2016. "Four Ways the Obama Administration Has Advanced Criminal Justice Reform." Brennan Center for Justice. Available at https://www.brennancenter.org/blog/four-ways-obama-administration-has-advanced-criminal-justice-reform (accessed January 31, 2017).

Durkheim, Emile. 1997 [1893]. *The Division of Labor in Society*. Translated by W.D. Halls. New York: Simon and Schuster.

Durose, Matthew R., Alexia D. Cooper, and Howard N. Snyder. 2014. "Recidivism of Prisoners Released in 30 States in 2005: Patterns from 2005 to 2010." A Bureau of Justice Statistics Special Report. Available at www.bjs.gov/content/pub/pdf/rprts05p0510.pdf (accessed January 31, 2017).

Durose, Matthew R., and Patrick A. Langan. 2003. "Felony Sentences in State Courts, 2000." A Bureau of Justice Statistics Special Report. Available at www.bjs.gov/content/pub/pdf/fsscoo.pdf (accessed January 31, 2017).

Economist. 2012. "Judging the Judges." November 24.

Ellestad v. Swayze, 130 P.2d 349 (Wash. 1942).

Ellis, Michael J. 2012. "The Origins of the Elected Prosecutor." In *Yale Law Journal*, Vol. 121, No. 6, pp. 1528–1569.

Enns, Peter K. 2016. *Incarceration Nation: How the United States Became the Most Punitive Democracy in the World*. New York: Cambridge University Press.

Equal Justice Initiative. 2011. "The Death Penalty in Alabama: Judge Override." Available at http://eji.org/sites/default/files/death-penalty-in-alabama-judge-override.pdf (accessed January 31, 2017).

Estelle v. Gamble, 429 U.S. 97 (1976).

European Commission. 2007. "Mentally Disordered Persons in European Prison Systems—Needs, Programmes and Outcome (EUPRIS)." In *The Central Institute of Mental Health*.

European Union Agency for Fundamental Rights. 2010. "Data in Focus Report: Police Stops and Minorities." Available at http://fra.europa.eu/en/publication/2010/eu-midis-data-focus-report-4-police-stops-and-minorities (accessed January 31, 2017).

Ewald, Alec C. 2012. "Collateral Consequences in the American States." In *Social Science Quarterly*, Vol. 93, No. 1, pp. 211–247.

Ewing v. California, 538 U.S. 11 (2003).

Farmer v. Brennan, 511 U.S. 825 (1994).

Farrell, Graham, Nick Tilley, and Andromachi Tseloni. 2014. "Why the Crime Drop?" In *Why Crime Rates Fall and Why They Don't. Crime and Justice*. Vol. 43, edited by Michael Tonry. Chicago: University of Chicago Press.

Fazel, Seena, and Achim Wolf. 2015. "A Systematic Review of Criminal Recidivism Rates Worldwide: Current Difficulties and Recommendations for Best Practice." In *PLoS One*, Vol. 10, No. 6.

Federal Rules of Criminal Procedure, Rule 11.

Feeley, Malcolm M., and Edward L. Rubin. 1998. *Judicial Policy Making and the Modern State: How the Courts Reformed America's Prisons*. New York: Cambridge University Press.

Fellner, Jamie. 2012. "Old Behind Bars: The Aging Prison Population in the United States." A Human Rights Watch report. Available at http://www.hrw.org/reports/2012/01/27/old-behind-bars-0 (accessed January 31, 2017).

Fellner, Jamie, and Marc Mauer. 1998. "Losing the Vote: The Impact of Felony Disenfranchisement Laws in the United States." A joint report of the Sentencing Project and Human Rights Watch. Available at http://www.hrw.org/legacy/reports/reports98/vote/usvot980.htm (accessed January 31, 2017).

Fellner, Jamie, and Mary Price. 2012. "The Answer Is No: Too Little Compassionate Release in US Federal Prisons." A joint report by Human Rights Watch and Families Against Mandatory Minimums. Available at http://www.hrw.org/reports/2012/11/30/answer-no (accessed January 31, 2017).

Ferguson, Robert A. 2014. *Inferno: An Anatomy of American Punishment*. Cambridge, MA: Harvard University Press.

Fields, Charles B., and Richter H. Moore. 2005. *Comparative and International Criminal Justice*, 2nd ed. Long Grove, IL: Waveland Press.

Flynn, Asher. 2011. "Fortunately We in Victoria Are Not in that UK Situation: Australian and United Kingdom Legal Perspectives on Plea Bargaining Reform." In *Deakin Law Review*, Vol. 16, No. 2, pp. 361–404.

Forman, James Jr. 2012. "Racial Critiques of Mass Incarceration: Beyond the New Jim Crow." In *New York University Law Review*, Vol. 87, No., 1, pp. 101–146.

Fortner, Michael Javen. 2015. *Black Silent Majority: The Rockefeller Drug Laws and the Politics of Punishment*. Cambridge, MA: Harvard University Press.

Frady, Marshall. 1993. "Death in Arkansas." In *The New Yorker*. February 22.

Frankfurter Allgemeine Zeitung. 2015. "Polizisten erschossen 2014 sieben Menschen." July 17.

Frase, Richard S. 1995a. "Sentencing Laws & Practices in France." *Federal Sentencing Reporter*, Vol. 7, No. 6, pp. 275–280.

Frase, Richard S. 1995b. "State Sentencing Guidelines: Still Going Strong." In *Judicature*, Vol. 78, pp. 173–179.

Frase, Richard S. 2000. "Is Guided Discretion Sufficient? Overview of State Sentencing Guidelines. *St. Louis University Law Journal*, Vol. 44, pp. 425–446.

Frase, Richard S. 2001. "Sentencing in Germany and the United States: Comparing Äpfel with Apples." Freiburg: Max Planck Institute for Foreign and International Criminal Law.

Frase Richard S., and Thomas Weigend. 1995. "German Criminal Justice as a Guide to American Law Reform: Similar Problems, Better Solutions?" *Boston College International and Comparative Law Review*, Vol. 18, No. 2, pp. 317–360.

Freeman, Monroe H. 2012. "The Unconstitutionality of Electing State Judges." In *Georgetown Journal of Legal Ethics*, Vol. 26, No. 1, pp. 75–80.

French Ministry of Justice. 2006. *Les Chiffres-Clefs de la Justice.*

Friedman, Uri. 2012. "'American Exceptionalism': A Short History." In *Foreign Policy*. June 18.

Frost, Natasha A. 2006. *The Punitive State: Crime, Punishment, and Imprisonment across the United States.* New York: LFB Scholarly.

Fulcher, Patrice A. 2013. "Double-Edged Sword of Prison Video Visitation: Claiming to Keep Families Together while Furthering the Aims of the Prison Industrial Complex." In *Florida A&M University Law Review*, Vol. 9, No. 1, pp. 83–112.

Fulcher, Patrice A. 2012. "Hustle and Flow: Prison Privatization Fueling the Prison Industrial Complex." In *Washburn Law Journal*, Vol. 51, No. 3, pp. 589–618.

Furman v. Georgia, 408 U.S. 238 (1972).

Garland, David. 1990. *Punishment and Modern Society.* Chicago: University of Chicago Press.

Garland, David. 2001. *The Culture of Control: Crime and Social Order in Contemporary Society.* Chicago: University of Chicago Press.

Garland, David. 2010. *Peculiar Institution: America's Death Penalty in an Age of Abolition.* Cambridge, MA: Harvard University Press.

Garoupa, Nuno, and Frank H. Stephen. 2008. "Why Plea Bargaining Fails to Achieve Results in So Many Criminal Justice Systems." In *Maastricht Journal of European and Comparative Law*, Vol. 15, No 3, pp. 323–358.

Geller, Amanda, and Jeffrey Fagan. 2010. "Pot as Pretext: Marijuana, Race and the New Disorder in New York City Street Policing." In *Journal of Empirical Legal Studies*, Vol. 7, No. 4, pp. 591–633.

Genders, Elaine. 2014. "Rehabilitation, Risk Management, and Prisoner's Rights." In *Criminal and Criminal Justice*, Vol. 14, No. 4, pp. 434–457.

Gendreau, Paul. 1996. "The Principles of Effective Intervention with Offenders." In *Choosing Correctional Options that Work: Defining the Demand and Evaluating the Supply*, edited by Alan T. Harland. Newbury Park, CA: Sage.

Gendreau, Paul, and Robert R. Ross. 1979. "Effective Correctional Treatment: Bibliotherapy for Cynics." In *Crime & Delinquency*, Vol. 25, No. 4, pp. 463–489.

Gendreau, Paul, and Robert R. Ross. 1987. "Revivification of Rehabilitation: Evidence from the 1980s." In *Justice Quarterly*, Vol. 4, No. 3, pp. 349–407.

Ghandnoosh, Nazgol. 2015. "Black Lives Matter: Eliminating Racial Inequity in the Criminal Justice System." A Sentencing Project report. Available at http://sentencingproject.org/doc/publications/rd_Black_Lives_Matter.pdf (accessed January 31, 2017).

Ghandnoosh, Nazgol. 2014. "Race and Punishment: Racial Perceptions of Crime and Support for Punitive Policies." A Sentencing Project report. Available at http://sentencingproject.org/doc/publications/rd_Race_and_Punishment.pdf (accessed January 31, 2017).

Gibson, James L. 2012. *Electing Judges: The Surprising Effects of Campaigning on Judicial Legitimacy*. Chicago: University of Chicago Press.

Gilligan, James. 1997. *Violence: Reflections on a National Epidemic*. New York: Vintage Books.

Gilpin, Ashley. 2012. "The Impact of Mandatory Minimum and Truth-in-Sentencing Laws and Their Relation to English Sentencing Policies." In *Arizona Journal of International and Comparative Law*, Vol. 29, No. 1, pp. 91–135.

Gingrich, Newt, and Pat Nolan. 2011. "Prison Reform: A Smart Way for States to Save Money and Lives." In *The Washington Post*. January 7.

Glod, Greg. 2015. "Strong Public Support for Expansion of Parole and Reentry Programs." *Townhall*. Available at http://townhall.com/columnists/gregglod/2015/03/24/strong-public-support-for-expansion-of-parole-and-reentry-programs-n1975690 (accessed January 31, 2017).

Goldbach, Toby S., Benjamin Brake, and Peter Katzenstein. 2013. "The Movement of U.S. Criminal and Administrative Law: Processes of Transplanting and Translating." In *Indiana Journal of Global Legal Studies*, Vol. 20, No. 1, pp. 141–184.

Goldstein, Abraham S., and Martin Marcus. 1977. "The Myth of Judicial Supervision in Three 'Inquisitorial' Systems: France, Italy, and Germany." In *Yale Law Journal*, Vol. 87, No. 2, pp. 240–283.

Goldstein, Dana. 2015a. "Blame Liberals." The Marshall Project. Available at https://www.themarshallproject.org/2015/01/15/blame-liberals (accessed January 31, 2017).

Goldstein, Dana. 2015b. "How to Cut the Prison Population by 50 Percent." The Marshall Project. Available at https://www.themarshallproject.org/2015/03/04/how-to-cut-the-prison-population-by-50-percent#.a2Gl8Bk1W (accessed January 31, 2017).

Goldstein, Joseph, and J. David Goodman. 2016. "Criminal Justice Reforms Stall in a Liberal Capital: New York." In *The New York Times*. August 21.

Gordon, Sanford C., and Gregory A. Huber. 2002. "Citizen Oversight and the Electoral Incentives of Criminal Prosecutors." In *American Journal of Political Science*, Vol. 46, No. 2, pp. 334–351.

Gottschalk, Marie. 2006. *The Prison and the Gallows: The Politics of Mass Incarceration in America*. New York: Cambridge University Press.

Gottschalk, Marie. 2011. "The Past, Present, and Future of Mass Incarceration in the United States." In *Criminology & Public Policy*, Vol. 10, No. 3, pp. 483–504.

Gottschalk, Marie. 2015a. *Caught: The Prison State and the Lockdown of American Politics*. Princeton, NJ: Princeton University Press.

Gottschalk, Marie. 2015b. "It's Not Just the Drug War." In *Jacobin Magazine*. March 5. Available at https://www.jacobinmag.com/2015/03/mass-incarceration-war-on-drugs/ (accessed January 31, 2017).

Graham v. Florida, 560 U.S. 48 (2010).

Grasmick, Harold G., Elizabeth Davenport, and Mitchell B. Chamlin. 1992. "Protestant Fundamentalism and the Retributive Doctrine of Punishment." In *Criminology*, Vol. 30, No. 1, pp. 21–46.

Grasmick, Harold G., John K. Cochran, Robert J. Bursik Jr., and M'Lou Kimpel. 1993. "Religion, Punitive Justice, and Support for the Death Penalty. In *Justice Quarterly*, Vol. 10, No. 2, pp. 289–314.

Grasmick, Harold G., and Anne L. McGill. 1994. "Religion, Attribution Style, and Punitiveness toward Juvenile Offenders." In *Criminology*, Vol. 32, No. 1, pp. 23–46.

Gregg v. Georgia, 428 U.S. 153 (1976).

Grzymała-Busse, Anna. 2015. *Nations under God: How Churches Use Moral Authority to Influence Policy*. Princeton, NJ: Princeton University Press.

Hagan, John, and Ronit Dinovitzer. 1999. "Collateral Consequences of Imprisonment for Children, Communities, and Prisoners." In *Crime and Justice: A Review of Research*, Vol. 26, pp. 121–162.

Hallett, Emma. 2014. "When Did the Length of Time Prisoners Serve in Jail Change?" BBC News. May 6. Available at http://www.bbc.com/news/uk-england-27021252 (accessed January 31, 2017).

Hallinan, Joseph T. 2001. *Going Up the River: Travels in a Prison Nation*. New York: Random House.

Haney, Craig. 2003. "The Psychological Impact of Incarceration: Implications for Postprison Adjustment." In *Prisoners Once Removed: The Impact of Incarceration and Re-entry on Children, Families, and Communities*, edited by Jeremy Travis and Michelle Waul. Washington, DC: Urban Institute Press.

Hans, Valerie P., and John H. Blume, Theodore Eisenberg, Amelia Courtney Hritz, Sheri Lynn Johnson, Caisa Elizabeth Royer, and Martin T. Wells. 2015. "The Death Penalty: Should the Judge or the Jury Decide Who Dies?" In *Journal of Empirical Legal Studies*, Vol. 12, No. 1, pp. 70–99.

Hartney, Christopher, and Caroline Glesmann. 2012. "Prison Bed Profiteers: How Corporations Are Reshaping Criminal Justice in the U.S." A National Council on Crime and Delinquency report. Available at http://nccdglobal.org/sites/default/files/publication_pdf/prison-bed-profiteers.pdf (accessed January 31, 2017).

Hartz, Louis. 1955. *The Liberal Tradition in America*. New York: Harcourt Brace.

Hawker v. New York, 170 U.S. 189 (1898).

Hebenton, Bill, and Terry Thomas. 1993. *Criminal Records: State, Citizen and the Politics of Protection.* Avebury, U.K.: Avebury.

Herzog-Evans, Martine. 2011. "Judicial Rehabilitation in France: Helping with the Desisting Process and Acknowledging Achieved Desistance." In *European Journal of Probation,* Vol. 3, No. 1, pp. 4–19.

Heumann, Milton. 1978. *Plea Bargaining: The Experiences of Prosecutors, Judges, and Defense Attorneys.* Chicago: University of Chicago Press.

Hirschfield, Paul. 2015. "Why American Cops Kill So Many Compared to European Cops." In *The Huffington Post.* Available at http://www.huffingtonpost.com/entry/american-cops-lethal_us_565cde59e4b079b2818b8870 (accessed January 31, 2017).

Hochschild Jennifer L., Vesla M. Weaver, and Traci Burch. 2012. *Creating a New Racial Order: How Immigration, Multiracialism, Genomics, and the Young Can Remake Race in America.* Princeton, NJ: Princeton University Press.

Hochschild Jennifer L., Vesla M. Weaver, and Traci Burch. 2011. "Destabilizing the American Racial Order." In *Daedalus,* Vol. 140, No. 2, pp. 151–165.

Hoffman, Peter B. 1997. "History of the Federal Parole System: Part 1." In *Federal Probation,* Vol. 61, No. 3, pp. 23–31.

Hohmann, James. 2016. "The Daily 202: Why Criminal Justice Reform May Actually Get Done This Year—If These Two Hurdles Can Be Overcome." In *The Washington Post.* May 9.

Holder, Eric. 2010. "Department Policy on Charging and Sentencing." Department of Justice. May 19. Available at http://sentencing.typepad.com/files/holder-charging-memo.pdf (accessed January 31, 2017).

Holzer, Harry. 1996. *What Employers Want: Job Prospects for Less-Educated Workers.* New York: Russell Sage.

Hörnle, Tatjana. 2013. "Moderate and Non-arbitrary Sentencing without Guidelines: The German Experience." In *Law and Contemporary Problems,* Vol. 76, No. 1, pp. 189–210.

Howard, John. 2004. "Waiting for Judgment Day." In *California Journal.* Center on Juvenile and Criminal Justice. May.

Howard, Marc Morjé. 2007. "American Civic Engagement in Comparative Perspective: Key Comparative Findings from the U.S. 'Citizenship, Involvement, Democracy' Survey." Georgetown University, Center for Democracy and Civil Society.

Howard, Marc Morjé. 2009. *The Politics of Citizenship in Europe.* New York: Cambridge University Press.

Howard, Marc M. 2011a. "Fear v. Facts," guest blog post on The Monkey Cage blog. May 25. Available at http://themonkeycage.org/blog/2011/05/25/fear-v-facts (accessed January 31, 2017).

Howard, Marc M. 2011b. "Lessons in Integrity with San Quentin State Prison's Tennis Team." June 16. Available at http://www.si.com/tennis/2011/06/16/san-quentinprison (accessed January 31, 2017).

Howard, Marc Morjé, James L. Gibson, and Dietlind Stolle. 2005. "The United States 'Citizenship, Involvement, Democracy' Survey." Georgetown University, Center for Democracy and Civil Society.

Huber, Gregory A., and Sanford C. Gordon. 2004. "Accountability and Coercion: Is Justice Blind When It Runs for Office?" In *American Journal of Political Science*, Vol. 48, No. 2, pp. 247–263.

Hudson v. McMillian, 503 U.S. 1 (1992).

Hughes, Kristen A. 2006. "Justice Expenditure and Employment in the United States, 2003." A Bureau of Justice Statistics Bulletin. Available at http://www.bjs.gov/content/pub/pdf/jeeus03.pdf (accessed January 31, 2017).

Hughes, Timothy A., Doris James Wilson, and Allen J. Beck. 2001. "Trends in State Parole, 1990–2000," a Bureau of Justice Statistics Special Report. Available at http://www.bjs.gov/content/pub/pdf/tsp00.pdf (accessed January 31, 2017).

Human Rights Watch. 1995. "Prison Conditions in Japan."

Human Rights Watch. 2004. "No Second Chance: People with Criminal Records Denied Access to Public Housing." Available at www.hrw.org/reports/2004/usa1104/usa1104.pdf (accessed January 31, 2017).

Human Rights Watch. 2009. "No Equal Justice: The Prison Litigation Reform Act in the United States." Available at https://www.hrw.org/report/2009/06/16/no-equal-justice/prison-litigation-reform-act-united-states (accessed January 31, 2017).

Human Rights Watch. 2012. "'The Root of Humiliation': Abusive Identity Checks in France." Available at https://www.hrw.org/news/2012/01/26/france-abusive-identity-checks-minority-youth (accessed January 31, 2017).

Hurst, Luke. 2015. "UK Only Western European Country to Ban Prisoners Voting." In *Newsweek*. February 10.

In the Public Interest. 2013. "Criminal: How Lockup Quotas and 'Low-Crime Taxes' Guarantee Profits for Private Prison Corporations." A publication of In the Public Interest. Available at http://www.inthepublicinterest.org/wp-content/uploads/Criminal-Lockup-Quota-Report.pdf (accessed January 31, 2017).

Institute for Criminal Policy Research. 2015. "World Female Imprisonment List," 3rd ed. University of London.

Institute for Criminal Policy Research. 2016. "World Prison Brief" (on Germany). Available at http://www.prisonstudies.org/country/germany (accessed January 31, 2017).

Institute for Criminal Policy Research. 2016. "World Prison Population List," 11th ed. University of London.

International Centre for Prison Studies. 2005. "World Prison Population List," 6th ed. Kings College London.

International Centre for Prison Studies. 2014. "World Pre-Trial/Remand Imprisonment List," 2nd ed. University of Essex.

Jacobs, James B. 2015. *The Eternal Criminal Record*. Cambridge, MA: Harvard University Press.

Jacobs, James B., and Elena Larrauri. 2012. "Are Criminal Convictions a Public Matter? The USA and Spain." In *Punishment & Society*, Vol. 14, No. 1, pp. 3–28.

Jefferson, Jelani, and John W. Head. 2008. "In Whose 'Best Interests'? – An International and Comparative Assessment of US Rules on Sentencing of Juveniles." In *Human Rights and Globalization Law Review*, Vol. 1, No. 1, pp. 89–146.

Johannès, Franck. 2014. "Cellule individuelle: la France menace de plaints." In *Le Monde*. December 2.

Johannès, Franck. 2012. " Les Baumettes, l'effroyable prison." In *Le Monde*. December 6.

Jones, Jeffrey M. 2010. "Americans See U.S. as Exceptional; 37% Doubt Obama Does." Gallop Poll Report. December 22. Available at http://www.gallup.com/poll/145358/Americans-Exceptional-Doubt-Obama.aspx (accessed January 31, 2017).

Jones, Trevor, and Tim Newburn. 2002. "Learning from Uncle Sam? Exploring U.S. Influences on British Crime Control Policy." In *Governance*, Vol. 15, No. 1, pp. 97–119.

Jones, Trevor, and Tim Newburn. 2006. "Three Strikes and You're Out: Exploring Symbol and Substance in American and British Crime Control Politics." In *British Journal of Criminology*, Vol. 46, No. 5, pp. 781–802.

Justice Policy Institute. 2011. "Gaming the System: How the Political Strategies of Private Prison Companies Promote Ineffective Incarceration Policies." Available at http://www.justicepolicy.org/uploads/justicepolicy/documents/gaming_the_system.pdf (accessed January 31, 2017).

Kaeble, Danielle, Laura M. Maruschak, and Thomas P. Bonczar. 2015. "Probation and Parole in the United States, 2014." Bureau of Justice Statistics Bulletin. Available at http://www.bjs.gov/content/pub/pdf/ppus14.pdf (accessed January 31, 2017).

Kaiser, Günther. 1984. *Prison Systems and Correctional Laws: Europe, the United States and Japan: A Comparative Analysis*. New York: Transnational.

Kalt, Brian C. 2003. "The Exclusion of Felons from Jury Service." In *American University Law Review*, Vol. 53, No. 1, pp. 65–189.

Kaplan, Thomas. 2014. "Cuomo Drops Plan to Use State Money to Pay for College Classes for Inmates." In *The New York Times*. April 2.

Karberg, Jennifer, and Doris J. James. 2002. "Substance Dependence, Abuse, and Treatment of Jail Inmates, 2002." A Bureau of Justice Statistics Special Report. Available at www.bjs.gov/content/pub/pdf/sdatji02.pdf (accessed January 31, 2017).

Katzenstein, Mary Fainsod, and Maureen R. Waller. 2015. "Taxing the Poor: Incarceration, Poverty Governance, and the Seizure of Family Resources." In *Perspectives on Politics*, Vol. 13, No. 3, pp. 638–656.

Katzenstein, Mary Fainsod, and Mitali Nagrecha. 2011. "A New Punishment Regime." In *Criminology & Public Policy*, Vol. 10, No. 3, pp. 555–568.

Katzenstein, Mary Fainsod, Leila Mohsen Ibrahim, and Katherine D. Rubin. 2010. "The Dark Side of American Liberalism and Felony Disenfranchisement." In *Perspectives on Politics*, Vol. 8, No. 4, pp. 1035–1054.

Keller, Bill. 2016. "Is Charles Koch a Closet Liberal?" The Marshall Project. Available at https://www.themarshallproject.org/2016/01/20/is-charles-koch-a-closet-liberal (accessed January 31, 2017).

Kleiman, Mark A. R. 2010. *When Brute Force Fails: How to Have Less Crime and Less Punishment*. Princeton, NJ: Princeton University Press.

Knafo, Saki. 2013. "California Prison Guards Union Pushes for Prison Expansion." In *Huffington Post*. September 9. Available at http://www.huffingtonpost.com/2013/09/09/california-prison-guards_n_3894490.html (accessed January 31, 2017).

Koch, Andrew M., and Paul H. Gates Jr. 2012. *Medieval America: Cultural Influences of Christianity in the Law and Public Policy*. Lanham, MD: Lexington Books.

Korte, Gregory. 2016. "Obama Promises More Pardons, but Can He Do It?" In *USA Today*. August 7.

Kukorowski, Drew, Peter Wagner, and Leah Sakala. 2013. "Please Deposit All of Your Money: Kickbacks, Rates, and Hidden Fees in the Jail Phone Industry." A Prison Policy Initiative report. Available at http://static.prisonpolicy.org/phones/please_deposit.pdf (accessed January 31, 2017).

Kupers, Terry A. 2001. "Rape and the Prison Code." In *Prison Masculinities*, edited by Don Sabo et al. Philadelphia: Temple University Press.

Kurki, Leena. 2001. "International Standards for Sentencing and Punishment." In *Sentencing and Sanctions in Western Countries*, edited by Michael Tonry and Richard S. Frase. New York: Oxford University Press.

Kuznia, Rob. 2016. "An Unprecedented Experiment in Mass Forgiveness." In *The Washington Post*. February 8.

Lacey, Nicola. 2008. *The Prisoners' Dilemma: Political Economy and Punishment in Contemporary Democracies*. Cambridge: Cambridge University Press.

Langan, Patrick A., and David J. Levin. 2002. "Recidivism of Prisoners Released in 1994." A Bureau of Justice Statistics Special Report. Available at http://bjs.ojp.usdoj.gov/content/pub/pdf/rpr94.pdf (accessed January 31, 2017).

Langbein, John H. 1979. "Land without Plea Bargaining: How the Germans Do It." *Michigan Law Review*, Vol. 78, No. 2, pp. 204–225.

Langbein, John H., and Lloyd L. Weinreb. 1978. "Continental Criminal Procedure: 'Myth' and Reality." In *Yale Law Journal*, Vol. 87, No. 8, pp. 1549–1569.

Lappi-Seppälä, Tapio, and Martti Lehti. 2014. "Cross-Comparative Perspectives on Global Homicide Trends." In *Why Crime Rates Fall and Why They Don't. Crime and Justice*. Vol. 43, edited by Michael Tonry. Chicago: University of Chicago Press.

Lartey, Jamiles. 2015. "By the Numbers: US Police Kill More in Days than Other Countries Do in Years." In *The Guardian*. June 9.

Le Monde. 2014. "La justice annule l'obligation de servir des repas halal en prison." July 23.

Lehmann, Vibeke. 2011. "Challenges and Accomplishments in U.S. Prison Libraries." In *Library Trends*, Vol. 59, No. 3, pp. 490–508.

Lerman, Amy E. 2013. *The Modern Prison Paradox: Politics, Punishment, and Social Community*. New York: Cambridge University Press.

Lerman, Amy E, and Vesla M. Weaver. 2014. *Arresting Citizenship: The Democratic Consequences of American Crime Control*. Chicago: University of Chicago Press.

Lewis v. Casey, 518 U.S. 343 (1996).

Lin, Ann Chih. 2000. *Reform in the Making: The Implementation of Social Policy in Prison*. Princeton, NJ: Princeton University Press.

Lipset, Seymour Martin, and Gary Marks. 2000. *It Didn't Happen Here: Why Socialism Failed in the United States*. New York: W. W. Norton.

Lipsey, Mark W. 1992. "Juvenile Delinquency Treatment: A Meta-analytic Inquiry into the Variability of Effects." In *Meta-analysis for Explanation: A Casebook*, edited by Thomas D. Cook, Harris Cooper, David S. Cordray, Heidi Hartmann, Larry V. Hedges, Richard J. Light, Thomas A. Lewis, and Frederick Mosteller. New York: Russell Sage Foundation.

Liptak, Adam. 2005. "To More Inmates, Life Term Means Dying behind Bars." In *The New York Times*. October 2.

Liptak, Adam. 2007. "Serving Life for Providing Car to Killers." In *The New York Times*. December 4, p. A1.

Liptak, Adam. 2008. "Inmate Count in U.S. Dwarfs Other Nations." In *The New York Times*. April 23.

Liptak, Adam. 2008. "U.S. Imprisons One in 100 Adults, Report Finds." In *The New York Times*. February 29, p. A14.

Liptak, Adam. 2008a. "Illegal Globally, Bail for Profit Remains in U.S." In *The New York Times*. January 29.

Liptak, Adam. 2008b. "Rendering Justice, With One Eye on Re-election." In *The New York Times*. May 25.

Liptak, Adam. 2015a. "Justices May Review Capital Cases in Which Judges Overrode Juries." In *The New York Times*. March 9, p. A11.

Liptak, Adam. 2015b. "Supreme Court Asked to Look Abroad for Guidance on Same-Sex Marriage." In *The New York Times*. April 6, p. A13.

Liptak, Adam. 2015c. "Supreme Court's Unsigned Rulings Show a Narrow View of Prisoners' Rights." In *The New York Times*. July 20, p. A18.

Lipton, Douglas, Robert Martinson, and Judith Wilks. 1975. *The Effectiveness of Correctional Treatment: A Survey of Treatment Evaluation Studies*. New York: Praeger.

Lomax, William, and Sonia Kumar. 2014. "Still Blocking the Exit." The Maryland Restorative Justice Initiative and the American Civil Liberties Union of Maryland. Available at http://www.abell.org/sites/default/files/publications/afr-stillblockingexit215.pdf (accessed January 31, 2017).

Loury, Glenn. 2007. "Why Are So Many Americans in Prison? Race and the Transformation of Criminal Justice." In *Boston Review*. July 1. Available at http://

bostonreview.net/loury-why-are-so-many-americans-in-prison (accessed January 31, 2017).

Lowenthal, Gary T. 1993. "Mandatory Sentencing Laws: Undermining the Effectiveness of Determinate Sentencing Reform." In *California Law Review*, Vol. 81, pp. 61–123.

Lynch, James P. 1995. "Crime in International Perspective." In *Crime*, edited by James Q. Wilson and Joan Petersilia (San Francisco: ICS Press).

Lynch, James P., Steven K. Smith, Helen A. Graziadei, and Tanutda Pittayathikhun. 1994. "Profile of Inmates in the United States and in England and Wales, 1991." U.S. Department of Justice, Office of Justice Programs, Bureau of Justice Statistics. Available at http://bjs.ojp.usdoj.gov/content/pub/pdf/Walesus.pdf (accessed January 31, 2017).

Lynch, Michael J. 1999. "Beating a Dead Horse: Is There Any Basic Empirical Evidence of the Deterrent Effect of Imprisonment." In *Crime, Law and Social Change*, Vol. 3, No. 4, pp. 347–362.

Lynch, Timothy. 2003. "The Case against Plea Bargaining." *Regulation*, Vol. 26, No. 3, pp. 24–27.

Ma, Yue. 2002. "Prosecutorial Discretion and Plea Bargaining in the United States, France, Germany, and Italy: A Comparative Perspective." *International Criminal Justice Review*, Vol. 12, pp. 22–52.

MacKenzie, D. L. 2006. *What Works in Corrections? Reducing the Criminal Activities of Offenders and Delinquents.* New York: Cambridge University Press.

Maguire, Mike, and Peter Raynor. 1997. "Revival of Throughcare: Rhetoric and Reality in Automatic Conditional Release." In *British Journal of Criminology*, Vol. 37, No. 1, pp. 1–14.

Mancini, Matthew J. 1996. *One Dies, Get Another: Convict Leasing in the American South, 1866–1928.* Columbia: University of South Carolina Press.

Manza, Jeff, and Christopher Uggen. 2006. *Locked Out: Felon Disenfranchisement and American Democracy.* New York: Oxford University Press.

Marcus, Martin. 1992. "Above the Fray or into the Breach: The Judge's Role in New York's Adversarial System of Criminal Justice." *Brooklyn Law Review*, Vol. 57, pp. 1193–1219.

Martinson, Robert. 1974. "What Works? Questions and Answers about Prison Reform." In *The Public Interest*, Vol. 35, pp. 22–54.

Martinson, Robert. 1979. "New Findings, New Views: A Note of Caution Regarding Sentencing Reform." In *Hofstra Law Review*, Vol. 7, No. 2, pp. 243–258.

Mason, Cody. 2012. "Dollars and Detainees: The Growth of For-Profit Detention." A Sentencing Project report. Available at http://www.sentencingproject.org/wp-content/uploads/2016/01/Dollars-and-Detainees.pdf (accessed January 31, 2017).

Mauer, Marc. 2000. "Felon Voting Disenfranchisement: A Growing Collateral Consequence of Mass Incarceration." In *Federal Sentencing Reporter*, Vol. 12, No. 5, pp. 248–251.

Mauer, Marc. 2001. "The Causes and Consequences of Prison Growth in the United States." In *Punishment and Society*, Vol. 3, pp. 9–20.

Mauer, Marc. 2004. "Felon Disenfranchisement: A Policy Whose Time Has Passed." In *Human Rights*, Vol. 31, No. 1, pp. 16–18.

Mauer, Marc. 2006. *Race to Incarcerate*, 2nd ed. New York: The New Press.

Mauer, Marc. 2015. "A Proposal to Reduce Time Served in Federal Prison." Testimony to Charles Colson Task Force on Federal Corrections. March 11. Available at http://www.sentencingproject.org/publications/a-proposal-to-reduce-time-served-in-federal-prison (accessed January 31, 2017).

Mauer, Marc, and Nazgol Ghandnoosh. 2013. "Can We Wait 88 Years to End Mass Incarceration?" In *The Huffington Post*. December 20. Available at http://www.huffingtonpost.com/marc-mauer/88-years-mass-incarceration_b_4474132.html (accessed January 31, 2017).

Mauer, Marc, and Virginia McCalmont. 2013. "A Lifetime of Punishment: The Impact of the Felony Drug Ban on Welfare Benefits." A Sentencing Project report. Available at http://sentencingproject.org/wp-content/uploads/2015/12/A-Lifetime-of-Punishment.pdf (accessed January 31, 2017).

Mauer, Marc, Ryan S. King, and Malcolm C. Young. 2004. "The Meaning of 'Life': Long Prison Sentences in Context. A Sentencing Project report. Available at http://www.sentencingproject.org/publications/the-meaning-of-life-long-prison-sentences-in-context/ (accessed January 31, 2017).

Mbodla, Ntusi. 2002. "Should Prisoners Have a Right to Vote?" In *Journal of African Law*, Vol. 46, No. 1, pp. 92–102.

McDonald, Douglas C. 1999. "Medical Care in Prisons." In *Crime and Justice*. Vol. 26, edited by Michael Tonry and Joan Petersilia. Chicago: University of Chicago Press.

Meares, Tracey L. 2014. "The Law and Social Science of Stop and Frisk." In *Annual Review of Law and Social Science*, Vol. 10, pp. 335–352.

Medwed, Daniel S. 2012. *Prosecution Complex: America's Race to Convict and Its Impact on the Innocent*. New York: New York University Press.

Mendelberg, Tali. 2001. *The Race Card: Campaign Strategy, Implicit Messages, and the Norm of Equality*. Princeton, NJ: Princeton University Press.

Merryman, John H. 1985. *The Civil Law Tradition*, 2nd ed. Stanford, CA: Stanford University Press.

Michel, Laurent, M. Patrizia Carrieri, and Alex Wodak. 2008. "Harm Reduction and Equity of Access to Care for French Prisoners: A Review." In *Harm Reduction Journal*, Vol. 5, No. 17, pp. 1–11.

Miethe, Terance D., and Hong Lu. 2005. *Punishment: A Comparative Historical Perspective*. Cambridge: Cambridge University Press.

Miller, Lisa L. 2008. *The Perils of Federalism: Race, Poverty, and the Politics of Crime Control*. New York: Oxford University Press.

Miller, Lisa L. 2016. *The Myth of Mob Rule*. New York: Oxford University Press.

Miller v. Alabama, 567 U.S. ____ (2012).

Minton, Todd D. 2013. "Jail Inmates at Midyear 2012 – Statistical Tables." A Bureau of Justice Statistics Special Report. Available at http://www.bjs.gov/content/pub/pdf/jim12st.pdf (accessed January 31, 2017).

Mitchell, David S. 2006. "Undermining Individual and Collective Citizenship: The Impact of the Exclusion Laws on the African-American Community." In *Fordham Urban Law Journal*, Vol. 34, No. 3, pp. 833–887.

Mondesire, J. Whyatt. 2001. "Felon Disenfranchisement: The Modern Day Poll Tax." In *Temple Political & Civil Rights Law Review*, Vol. 10, No. 2, pp. 435–442.

Moore, Molly. 2008. "In France, Prisons Filled with Muslims." In *The Washington Post*. April 29.

Morgenstern, Christine. 2011. "Judicial Rehabilitation in Germany: The Use of Criminal Records and the Removal of Recorded Convictions." In *European Journal of Probation*, Vol. 3, No. 1, pp. 20–35.

Morio, Joël. 2015. "Des prisons repaires de terroristes?" In *Le Monde*. June 3.

Mulch, Matthew. 2009. "Crime and Punishment in Private Prisons." In *National Lawyers Guild Review*, Vol. 66, No. 2, pp. 70–94.

Mumola, Christopher J., and Jennifer C. Karberg. 2006. "Drug Use and Dependence, State and Federal Prisoners, 2004." A Bureau of Justice Statistics Special Report. Available at www.bjs.gov/content/pub/pdf/dudsfp04.pdf (accessed January 31, 2017).

Munn, Nicholas. 2011. "Limits of Criminal Disenfranchisement." In *The Criminal Justice Ethics*, Vol. 30, No. 3, pp. 223–239.

Murphy, Daniel S. 2005. "Health Care in the Federal Bureau of Prisons: Fact or Fiction." In *California Journal of Health Promotion*, Vol. 3, No. 2, pp. 23–37.

Muffit, Eleanor. 2013. "The Old Debate: Punish Prisoners or Rehabilitate Them?" In *The Telegraph*. December 18. Available at http://www.telegraph.co.uk/news/uknews/crime/10514678/The-old-debate-punish-prisoners-or-rehabilitate-them.html (accessed January 31, 2017).

Mullainathan, Sendhil. 2016. "Ban the Box? An Effort to Stop Discrimination May Actually Increase It." In *The New York Times*. August 19.

Murakawa, Naomi. 2014. *The First Civil Right: How Liberals Built Prison America*. New York: Oxford University Press.

Musto, David F. 1999. *The American Disease: Origins of Narcotics Control*. New York: Oxford University Press.

National Association of Evangelicals. 2015. "New NAE Resolution Recognizes Different Views on Death Penalty." Available at http://nae.net/new-nae-resolution-recognizes-different-views-on-death-penalty (accessed January 31, 2017).

National Employment Law Project. 2015. "Ban the Box: U.S. Cities, Counties, and States Adopt Fair Hiring Policies to Reduce Unfair Barriers to Employment of People with Criminal Records." Available at http://www.nelp.org/page/-/SCLP/Ban-the-Box-Fair-Chance-State-and-Local-Guide.pdf (accessed January 31, 2017).

Nayeri, Rouhzna. 2014. "The Forever Scarlet Letter: The Need to Reform the Collateral Consequences of Criminal Convictions." In *Widener Journal of Law, Economics, and Race*, Vol. 5, No. 2, pp. 109–141.

Nellis, Ashley. 2013. "Life Goes On: The Historic Rise in Life Sentences in America." A Sentencing Project report. Available at http://sentencingproject.org/wp-content/uploads/2015/12/Life-Goes-On.pdf (accessed January 31, 2017).

New York Civil Liberties Union. 2015. "Stop-and-Frisk Data." Available at https://www.nyclu.org/en/stop-and-frisk-data (accessed January 31, 2017).

Newman, Jon O. 1996. "No More Myths about Prisoner Lawsuits." In *The New York Times*. January 3.

Nirappil, Fenit, and Jenna Portnoy. 2016. "VA High Court Invalidates McAuliffe's Order Restoring Felon Voting Rights." In *The Washington Post*. July 22.

O'Connor, Sandra Day. 2010. "Take Justice off the Ballot." In *The New York Times*. May 22.

O'Hear, Michael M. 2008. "Plea Bargaining Procedural Justice." *Georgia Law Review*, Vol. 42, No. 2, pp. 407–469.

O'Mahony, Paul Douglas. 2000. "The Criminal Justice System of Ireland." In *Comparative and International Criminal Justice Systems*, edited by Obi N. Ignatius Ebbe. Boston: Butterworth-Heinemann.

Open Society Institute. 2009. "Profiling Minorities: A Study of Stop-and-Search Practices in Paris." Available at https://www.opensocietyfoundations.org/reports/profiling-minorities-study-stop-and-search-practices-paris (accessed January 31, 2017).

Oppel Jr., Richard A., Sheryl Gay Stolberg, and Matt Apuzzo. 2016. "Justice Department to Release Blistering Report of Racial Bias by Baltimore Police." In *The New York Times*. August 9.

Oshinsky, David M. 1996. *Worse than Slavery: Parchman Farm and the Ordeal of Jim Crow Justice*. New York: Free Press.

Ouest-France. 2015. "Terrorisme. Les détenus radicalisés regroupés dans les prisons." February 3.

Overton v. Bazzetta, 539 U.S. 126 (2003).

Padfield, Nicola. 2010. "England and Wales." In *Release from Prison: European Policy and Practice*, edited by Nicola Padfield, Dirk van Zyl Smit, and Frieder Dünkel. Devon, U.K.: Willan, pp. 104–134.

Padfield, Nicola. 2011. "Judicial Rehabilitation? A View from England." In *European Journal of Probation*, Vol. 3, No. 1, pp. 36–49.

Pager, Devah. 2003. "The Mark of a Criminal Record." In *American Journal of Sociology*, Vol. 108, No. 5, pp. 937–975.

Pager, Devah, Bruce Western, and Bart Bonikowski. 2009. "Discrimination in a Low-Wage Labor Market: A Field Experiment." In *American Sociological Review*, Vol. 74, No. 5, pp. 777–799.

Pakes, Francis. 2004. *Comparative Criminal Justice*. Cullopton, U.K.: Willan.

Palmer, Ted. 1975. "Martinson Revisited." In *Journal of Research in Crime and Delinquency*, Vol. 12, No. 2, pp. 133–152.

Palmer, Ted. 1995. "Programmatic and Nonprogrammatic Aspects of Successful Intervention: New Directions for Research." In *Crime & Delinquency*, Vol. 41, No. 1, pp. 100–131.

Palmer, Vernon Valentine, and John Levendis. 2008. "The Louisiana Supreme Court in Question: An Empirical and Statistical Study of the Effects of Campaign Money on the Judicial Function." In *Tulane Law Review*, Vol. 82, pp. 1291–1314.

Pasteau, Benoist. 2014. "La prison de la Santé ferme ses portes. . . pour renovation." In *Europe 1*. July 21.

Peterka-Benton, Daniela, and Brian Paul Masciadrelli. 2013. "Legitimacy of Corrections as a Mental Health Care Provider: Perspectives from U.S. and European Systems." In *Journal of the Institute of Justice and International Studies*, Vol. 13, pp. 171–184.

Petersilia, Joan. 2003. *When Prisoners Come Home: Parole and Prisoner Reentry*. New York: Oxford University Press.

Petersilia, Joan, and Jimmy Threatt. 2017. "Release from Prison: The Evolution of Modern Parole and the Decline of Discretionary Release." In *The Encyclopedia of Corrections*, edited by Kent R. Kerley. Hoboken, NJ: Wiley-Blackwell.

Pew Charitable Trusts. 2015. "Imprisonment, Crime Rates Fell in 30 States over Five Years." Available at http://www.pewtrusts.org/en/multimedia/data-visualizations/2015/imprisonment-crime-rates-fell-in-30-states-over-five-years (accessed January 31, 2017).

Phillips, Kevin. 1969. *The Emerging Republican Majority*. New York: Arlington House.

Piel, Simon. 2014. "La mythique prison de la Santé vidée de ses détenus avant une large rénovation." In *Le Monde*. August 4.

Pinard, Michael. 2010. "Collateral Consequences of Criminal Convictions: Confronting Issues of Race and Dignity." In *New York University Law Review*, Vol. 85, pp. 457–534.

Pratt, John. 2008. "Scandinavian Exceptionalism in an Era of Penal Excess." In *British Journal of Criminology*, Vol. 48, No. 2, pp. 119–137.

Pratt, John, and Anna Eriksson. 2013. *Contrasts in Punishment: An Explanation of Anglophone Excess and Nordic Exceptionalism*. London: Routledge.

Prison Litigation Reform Act (PLRA). 1996. 18 U.S.C. § 3626(a)(1)(A).

Prison Radio Association. 2016. "Impact Snapshot: January 2016." Available at http://www.prisonradioassociation.org/wp-content/uploads/Prison-Radio-Association-IMPACT-SNAPSHOT-January-2016.pdf (accessed January 31, 2017).

Pruin, Ineke. 2012. "Recalling Conditionally Released Prisoners in Germany." In *European Journal of Probation*, Vol. 4, No. 1, pp. 63–72.

Rabuy, Bernadette, and Peter Wagner. 2015. "Screening out Family Time: The For-Profit Video Visitation Industry in Prisons and Jails." A Prison Policy Initiative report. Available at http://static.prisonpolicy.org/visitation/ScreeningOutFamilyTime_January2015.pdf (accessed January 31, 2017).

Radelet, Michael L. 2011. "Overriding Jury Sentencing Recommendations in Florida Capital Cases: An Update and Possible Half-Requiem." In *Michigan State Law Review*, Vol. 2011, pp. 792–822.

Radio France Internationale. 2015. "Cazeneuve et Taubira ensemble contre la radicalisation en prison." February 27.

Ramirez, Maria Emilia. 2008. "Barred from the Polls: Felony Disenfranchisement in the Bluegrass." In *Northern Kentucky Law Review*, Vol. 35, No. 4, pp. 371–392.

Rauxloh, Regina. 2011. "Formalization of Plea Bargaining in Germany: Will the New Legislation Be Able to Square the Circle?" In *Fordham International Law Journal*, Vol. 2, No. 2, pp. 296–331.

Reid, Stephen. 2012. *A Crowbar in the Buddhist Garden: Writing from Prison*. Saskatoon, SK: Thistledown Press.

Reilly, Ryan J. 2016. "Obama Just Granted Hundreds of Drug Offenders Freedom. Dozens Would Have Died behind Bars." In *The Huffington Post*. August 3. Available at http://www.huffingtonpost.com/entry/obama-clemency-drug-offenders_us_57a22c9ae4b04414d1f2fcff (accessed January 31, 2017).

Reitz, Kevin R. 2001. "The Disassembly and Reassembly of U.S. Sentencing Practices." In *Sentencing and Sanctions in Western Countries*, edited by Michael Tonry and Richard S. Frase. New York: Oxford University Press.

Reitz, Kevin R., and Curtis R. Reitz. 1993. "The American Bar Association's New Sentencing Standards." In *Federal Sentencing Reporter*, Vol. 6, pp. 169–173.

Reuflet, Kim. 2010. "France." In *Release from Prison: European Policy and Practice*, edited by Nicola Padfield, Dirk van Zyl Smit, and Frieder Dünkel. Devon, U.K.: Willan, pp. 169–184.

Rhodes v. Chapman, 452 U.S. 337 (1981).

Rhodes, Lorna. 2010. "Dreaming of Psychiatric Citizenship: A Case Study of Supermax Confinement." In *A Reader in Medical Anthropology: Theoretical Trajectories, Emergent Realities*, edited by Byron Good, Michael M.J. Fischer, Sarah S. Willen, and Mary-Jo DelVecchio Good. Hoboken, NJ: Wiley-Blackwell, pp. 181–198.

Richardson, Laura L. 2011. "Impact of Marsy's Law on Parole in California: An Empirical Study," unpublished paper available on SSRN at http://ssrn.com/abstract=1878594 (accessed January 31, 2017).

Richardson v. Ramirez, 418 U.S. 24 (1974).

Richer, Alanna Durkin, and Curt Anderson. 2016. "Trial or Deal? Some Driven to Plead Guilty, Later Exonerated." Associated Press. November 15, 2016. Available at https://apnews.com/24cfa961d3444be49901496fdcaa3fda/Trial-or-deal?-Some-driven-to-plead-guilty,-later-exonerated (accessed January 31, 2017).

Richert, John P. 1977. "Recent Changes in the Administration of Parole in France." In *Federal Probation*, Vol. 41, No. 3, pp. 19–22.

Ridgeway, James, and Jean Casella. 2013. "Solidarity and Solitary: When Unions Clash with Prison Reform." Solitary Watch. Available at http://solitarywatch.com/2013/

02/21/solidarity-and-solitary-when-unions-clash-with-prison-reform/ (accessed January 31, 2017).

Roberts, Julian V. 2013. "Sentencing Guidelines in England and Wales: Recent Developments and Emerging Issues." In *Law and Contemporary Problems*, Vol. 76, No. 1, pp. 1–25.

Robertson, Campbell, Shaila Dewan, and Matt Apuzzo. 2015. "Ferguson Became Symbol, but Bias Knows No Border." In *The New York Times*. March 7, p. A1.

Roché, Sebastian. 2007. "Criminal Justice Police in France: Illusions of Severity." In *Crime and Justice: A Review of Research*, Vol. 36, pp. 471–550.

Rodriguez, Michelle Natividad, and Beth Avery. 2016. "Ban the Box: U.S. Cities, Counties, and States Adopt Fair Hiring Policies." National Employment Law Project. Available at http://www.nelp.org/publication/ban-the-box-fair-chance-hiring-state-and-local-guide (accessed January 31, 2017).

Roeder, Oliver, Lauren-Brooke Eisen, and Julia Bowling. 2015. "What Caused the Crime Decline?" Brennan Center for Justice. Available at https://www.brennan-center.org/sites/default/files/analysis/What_Caused_The_Crime_Decline.pdf (accessed January 31, 2017).

Rosenberg, Tina. 2015. "Out of Debtors' Prison, With Law as the Key." In *The New York Times*. March 27. Available at opinionator.blogs.nytimes.com/2015/03/27/shutting-modern-debtors-prisons (accessed January 31, 2017).

Ross, Jacqueline E. 2008a. "Do Rules of Evidence Apply (Only) in the Courtroom? Deceptive Interrogation in the United States and Germany." In *Oxford Journal of Legal Studies*, Vol. 28, No. 3, pp. 443–474.

Ross, Jacqueline E. 2008b. "Undercover Policing and the Shifting Terms of Scholarly Debate: The United States and Europe in Counterpoint." In *Annual Review of Law and the Social Sciences*, Vol. 4, pp. 239–273.

Ross, Jacqueline E. 2007. "The Place of Covert Policing in Democratic Societies: A Comparative Study of the United States and Germany." In *American Journal of Comparative Law*, Vol. 55, pp. 493–579.

Roucaute, Delphine. 2014. "La cellule individuelle en prison, un droit encore repoussé." In *Le Monde*, December 4.

Rubin, Anat. 2015. "California's Jail-Building Boom." The Marshall Project. Available at https://www.themarshallproject.org/2015/07/02/california-s-jail-building-boom (accessed January 31, 2017).

Rummel v. Estelle, 445 U.S. 263 (1980).

Ruth, Henry, and Kevin R. Reitz. 2003. *The Challenge of Crime: Rethinking Our Response*. Cambridge, MA: Harvard University Press.

Sabol, William J., Heather C. West, and Matthew Cooper. 2009. "Prisoners in 2008," a Bureau of Justice Statistics Bulletin. Available at http://bjs.ojp.usdoj.gov/content/pub/pdf/p08.pdf (accessed January 31, 2017).

Samaha, Joel. 2009. *Criminal Law*, 10th ed. Belmont, CA: Wadsworth.

Santo, Alysia, and Lisa Iaboni. 2015. "What's in a Prison Meal?" The Marshall Project. Available at https://www.themarshallproject.org/2015/07/07/what-s-in-a-prison-meal (accessed January 31, 2017).

Santobello v. New York, 404 U.S. 260 (1971).

Savage, Charlie. 2016. "U.S. to Phase Out Use of Private Prisons for Federal Inmates." In *The New York Times.* August 18.

Schanzenbach, Max, and Emerson H. Tiller. 2007. "Strategic Judging under the United States Sentencing Guidelines: Positive Political Theory and Evidence." In *Journal of Law, Economics, and Organization*, Vol. 23, No. 1, pp. 24–56.

Schemmel, Alexander, Christian Corell, and Natalie Richter. 2014. "Plea Bargaining in Criminal Proceedings: Changes to Criminal Defense Counsel Practice as a Result of the German Constitutional Court Verdict of 19 March 2013." In *German Law Review*, Vol. 15, No. 1, pp. 43–64.

Schlanger, Margo. 2003. "Inmate Litigation." In *Harvard Law Review*, Vol. 116, No. 6, pp. 1555–1706.

Schlanger, Margo. 2006. "Civil Rights Injunctions over Time: A Case Study of Jail and Prison Court Orders." In *N.Y.U. Law Review*, Vol. 81, No. 2, pp. 550–630.

Schlanger, Margo. 2013. "*Plata v. Brown* and Realignment: Jails, Prisons, Courts, and Politics." In *Harvard Civil Rights-Civil Liberties Law Review*. Vol. 48, No. 1, pp. 165–215.

Schlanger, Margo. 2015. "Trends in Prisoner Litigation, as the PLRA Enters Adulthood." In *UC Irvine Law Review*, Vol. 5, No. 1, pp. 153–179.

Schlanger, Margo. 2015. "No Reason to Blame Liberals (Or, The Unbearable Lightness of Perversity Arguments)." The New Rambler. Available at http://newramblerreview.com/book-reviews/law/no-reason-to-blame-liberals-or-the-unbearable-lightness-of-perversity-arguments (accessed January 31, 2017).

Schlosser, Eric. 1998. "The Prison-Industrial Complex." In *The Atlantic Monthly*, Vol. 282, No. 6, pp. 51–77.

Schmitt, John, Kris Warner, and Sarika Gupta. 2010. "The High Budgetary Cost of Incarceration." Center for Economic and Policy Research. Available at http://www.cepr.net/documents/publications/incarceration-2010-06.pdf (accessed January 31, 2017).

Schneider, Cathy Lisa. 2014. *Police Power and Race Riots: Urban Unrest in Paris and New York*. Philadelphia: University of Pennsylvania Press.

Schulhofer, Stephen J. 1984. "Is Plea Bargaining Inevitable?" *Harvard Law Review*, Vol. 97, No. 5, pp. 1037–1107.

Schulhofer, Stephen J., Tom R. Tyler, and Aziz Z. Huq. 2011. "American Policing at a Crossroads: Unsustainable Policies and the Procedural Justice Alternatives." In *Journal of Criminal Law and Criminology*, Vol. 101, No. 2, pp. 335–374.

Schwartz, Ian. 2016. "Sen. Tom Cotton: America Has an 'Under-Incarceration Problem.'" Real Clear Politics. Available at http://www.realclearpolitics.com/

video/2016/05/20/sen_tom_cotton_america_has_an_under-incarceration_
problem.html (accessed January 31, 2017).

Schwartzapfel, Beth. 2015. "The FCC Looks into the Prison Telephone Racket."
The Marshall Project. Available at https://www.themarshallproject.org/2014/
12/04/the-fcc-looks-into-the-prison-telephone-racket (accessed January 31,
2017).

Schwartzapfel, Beth, and Bill Keller. 2015. "Willie Horton Revisited." The Marshall
Project. Available at https://www.themarshallproject.org/2015/05/13/willie-
horton-revisited (accessed January 31, 2017).

Selke, William L. 1993. *Prisons in Crisis*. Bloomington: Indiana University Press.

Sentencing Project. 2016. "Felony Disenfranchisement: A Primer." Available at http://
www.sentencingproject.org/publications/felony-disenfranchisement-a-primer/
(accessed January 31, 2017).

Sentencing Project. 2015a. "Fact Sheet: Trends in U.S. Corrections." Available at http://
sentencingproject.org/wp-content/uploads/2016/01/Trends-in-US-Corrections.
pdf (accessed January 31, 2017).

Sentencing Project. 2015b. "Fact Sheet: Incarcerated Women and Girls." Available at
http://www.sentencingproject.org/wp-content/uploads/2016/02/Incarcerated-
Women-and-Girls.pdf (accessed January 31, 2017).

Severson, Kim, and Robbie Brown. 2011. "Outlawed, Cellphones Are Thriving in
Prisons." In *The New York Times*. January 3, p. A12.

Sides, John, and Lynn Vavreck. 2013. *The Gamble: Choice and Chance in the 2012
Presidential Election*. Princeton, NJ: Princeton University Press.

Sieber, Ulrich. 2004. *The Punishment of Serious Crimes: A Comparative Analysis of
Sentencing Law and Practice*, 2 volumes. Freiburg, Germany: edition iuscrim.

Siegel, Robert. 2016. "From a Life Term to Life on the Outside: When Aging Felons
Are Freed." In National Public Radio, *All Things Considered*. February 18.

Silber, Rebecca, Ram Subramanian, and Maia Spotts. 2016. "Justice in Review: New
Trends in State Sentencing and Corrections 2014–2015." New York: Vera Institute
of Justice.

Silvestri, Arianna. 2013. "Prison Conditions in the United Kingdom." European Prison
Observatory. Rome: Antigone Edizioni.

Simon, Jonathan. 2007. *Governing through Crime: How the War on Crime Transformed
American Democracy and Created a Culture of Fear*. Oxford: Oxford University Press.

Simon, Jonathan. 2014. *Mass Incarceration on Trial: A Remarkable Court Decision and
the Future of Prisons in America*. New York: The New Press.

Simon, Roger. 1990. *Road Show: In America Anyone Can Become President. It's One of
the Risks We Take*. New York: Farrar Straus Giroux.

Snortum, John R., and Kåre Bødal. 1985. "Conditions of Confinement within Security
Prisons: Scandinavia and California." In *Crime & Delinquency*, Vol. 31, No. 4,
pp. 573–600.

Sombart, Werner. 1976 [1906]. *Why Is There No Socialism in the United States?* Translated by Patricia M. Hocking and C.T. Husbands. White Plains, NY: M.E. Sharpe.

Stanford Law School. 2013. "Progress Report: Three Strikes Reform (Proposition 36)." A Stanford Law School Three Strikes Project and NAACP Legal Defense and Education Fund report. Available at http://www.naacpldf.org/files/publications/ThreeStrikesReport_v6.pdf (accessed January 31, 2017).

Statistiches Bundesamt. 2011. "Justiz auf einen Blick." Available at https://www.destatis.de/DE/Publikationen/Thematisch/Rechtspflege/Querschnitt/BroschuereJustizBlick0100001099004.pdf?__blob=publicationFile (accessed January 31, 2017).

Steinacker, Andrea. 2003. "Prisoner's Campaign: Felony Disenfranchisement Laws and the Right to Hold Public Office." In *BYU Law Review*, Vol. 2003, No. 2, pp. 801–828.

Stemen, Don, Andres Rengifo, and James Wilson. 2006. *Of Fragmentation and Ferment: The Impact of State Sentencing Policies on Incarceration Rates, 1975–2002.* Washington, DC: U.S. Department of Justice. Available at http://www.ncjrs.gov/pdffiles1/nij/grants/213003.pdf (accessed January 31, 2017).

Stephan, James J. 1999. "State Prison Expenditures, 1996." A Bureau of Justice Statistics Bulletin. Available at http://www.bjs.gov/content/pub/pdf/spe96.pdf (accessed January 31, 2017).

Stevenson, Bryan. 2014. *Just Mercy: A Story of Justice and Redemption.* New York: Spiegel & Grau.

Stiber, Cecilia Zhang. 2006. "Discrimination Intent Requirement: The 'Separate but Equal' Doctrine of the Twenty-First Century?—A Critical Examination of Felon Disenfranchisement Laws and Related Government Practices in the United States." In *Gonzaga Law Review*, Vol. 41, No. 2, pp. 347–390.

Stith, Kate, and José A. Cabranes. 1998. *Fear of Judging: Sentencing Guidelines in the Federal Courts.* Chicago: University of Chicago Press.

Stuntz, William J. 2004. "Plea Bargaining and Criminal Law's Disappearing Shadow." In *Harvard Law Review*, Vol. 117, No. 8, pp. 2548–2569.

Stuntz, William J. 2005. "*Bordenkircher v. Hayes*: The Rise of Plea Bargaining and the Decline of the Rule of Law." Harvard Public Law Working Paper No. 120. Available at http://ssrn.com/abstract=854284 (accessed January 31, 2017).

Stuntz, William J. 2011. *The Collapse of American Criminal Justice.* Cambridge, MA: Harvard University Press.

Stute, Dennis. 2014. "Why German Police Officers Rarely Reach for Their Guns." In *Deutsche Welle*. August 27. Available at http://www.dw.com/en/why-german-police-officers-rarely-reach-for-their-guns/a-17884779 (accessed January 31, 2017).

Subramanian, Ram, and Alison Shames. 2013. "Sentencing and Prison Practices in Germany and the Netherlands: Implications for the United States." New York: Vera Institute of Justice.

Subramanian, Ram, Rebecka Moreno, and Sharyn Broomhead. 2014. "Recalibrating Justice: A Review of 2013 State Sentencing and Corrections Trends." New York: Vera Institute of Justice.

Sundt, Jody, Emily J. Salisbury, and Mark G. Harmon. 2016. "Is Downsizing Prisons Dangerous?" In *Criminology and Public Policy*, Vol. 15, No. 2, pp. 315–341.

Swarthout v Cooke, 562 U.S. ____ (2011).

Swavola, Elizabeth, Kristine Riley, and Ram Subramanian. 2016. "Overlooked: Women and Jails in an Era of Reform." New York: Vera Institute of Justice. Vera Institute of Justice and The Safety and Justice Challenge.

Tagliabue, John. 2003. "France Proposes Adoption of Plea Bargaining in Legal Overhaul." In *The New York Times*. April 10.

Tague, Peter. 2007. "Guilty Pleas and Barristers' Incentives: Lessons from England." *Georgetown Journal of Legal Ethics*, Vol. 20, No. 2, pp. 287–320.

Tallahassee Furniture Co. v. Harrison, 583 So. 2d 744 (Florida District Court of Appeals 1991).

Taylor, Jennifer Rae. 2012. "Constitutionally Unprotected: Prison Slavery, Felon Disenfranchisement, and the Criminal Exception to Citizenship." In *Gonzaga Law Review*, Vol. 47, No. 2, pp. 365–392.

Terrill, Richard J. 1997. *World Criminal Justice Systems: A Survey*. 3rd ed. Cincinnati, OH: Anderson.

The Guardian. 2015; 2016. "The Counted: People Killed by the Police in the US." Available at http://www.theguardian.com/us-news/ng-interactive/2015/jun/01/the-counted-police-killings-us-database (accessed January 31, 2017).

The New York Times Editorial Board. 2016. "States Lead the Way on Justice Reform." In *The New York Times,* May 30.

The Washington Post. 2015. "Investigation: People Shot and Killed by Police This Year." Available at https://www.washingtonpost.com/graphics/national/police-shootings (accessed January 31, 2017).

The Washington Post. 2016. "Fatal Force: A *Washington Post* Investigation of People Shot and Killed by Police in 2016." Available at https://www.washingtonpost.com/graphics/national/police-shootings-2016 (accessed January 31, 2017).

The Young Review. 2014. "Improving Outcomes for Young Black and/or Muslim Men in the Criminal Justice System." Available at http://www.youngreview.org/sites/default/files/clinks_young-review_report_dec2014.pdf (accessed January 31, 2017).

Thornburgh v. Abbott, 490 U.S. 401 (1989).

Thorpe, Rebecca U. 2015. "Perverse Politics: The Persistence of Mass Imprisonment in the Twenty-first Century." In *Perspectives on Politics*, Vol. 13, No. 3, pp. 618–637.

Tocqueville, Alexis de. 1966 [1835]. *Democracy in America*. Translated by George Lawrence, edited by J.P. Mayer. New York: Harper & Row.

Tonry, Michael. 1996. *Sentencing Matters.* New York: Oxford University Press.

Tonry, Michael. 2001. "Punishment Policies and Patterns in Western Countries." In *Sentencing and Sanctions in Western Countries*, edited by Michael Tonry and Richard S. Frase. New York: Oxford University Press.

Tonry, Michael. 2007. "Determinants of Penal Policies." In *Crime, Punishment, and Politics in Comparative Perspective*, edited by Michael Tonry. Chicago: University of Chicago Press.

Tonry, Michael. 2009. "Explanations of American Punishment Policies: A National History." In *Punishment and Society*, Vol. 11, No. 3, pp. 377–394.

Tonry, Michael. 2014. "Why Crime Rates Are Falling throughout the Western World." In *Why Crime Rates Fall and Why They Don't. Crime and Justice*. Vol. 43, edited by Michael Tonry. Chicago: University of Chicago Press.

Tonry, Michael, and David P. Farrington. 2005. "Punishment and Crime across Space and Time." In *Crime and Punishment in Western Countries, 1980–1999*, edited by Michael Tonry and David P. Farrington. Chicago: University of Chicago Press.

Tonry, Michael, and Richard S. Frase, eds. 2001. *Sentencing and Sanctions in Western Countries*. New York: Oxford University Press.

Travis, Jeremy, Amy L. Solomon, and Michelle Waul. 2001. "From Prison to Home: The Dimensions and Consequences of Prisoner Reentry." An Urban Institute report. Available at http://www.urban.org/UploadedPDF/from_prison_to_home.pdf (accessed January 31, 2017).

Travis, Jeremy, and Sarah Lawrence. 2002. "Beyond the Prison Gates: The State of Parole in America." Research Report for the Urban Institute. Available at http://www.urban.org/research/publication/beyond-prison-gates (accessed January 31, 2017).

Turner v. Safley, 482 U. S. 78 (1987).

Uggen, Christopher, and Jeff Manza. 2002. "Democratic Contraction? Political Consequences of Felon Disenfranchisement in the United States." In *American Sociological Review*, Vol. 67, No. 6, pp. 777–803.

Uggen, Christopher, Ryan Larson, and Sarah Shannon. 2016. "6 Million Lost Voters: State-Level Estimates of Felony Disenfranchisement, 2016." A Sentencing Project report. Available at http://www.sentencingproject.org/publications/6-million-lost-voters-state-level-estimates-felony-disenfranchisement-2016/ (accessed January 31, 2017).

U.K. Ministry of Justice. 2012. "IPP Fact Sheet." Available at https://www.justice.gov.uk/downloads/legislation/bills-acts/legal-aid-sentencing/ipp-factsheet.pdf (accessed January 31, 2017).

U.K. Ministry of Justice. 2015. "Offender Management Statistics Bulletin, England and Wales." Available at https://www.gov.uk/government/uploads/system/uploads/attachment_data/file/449528/offender-management-statistics-bulletin-jan-mar-2015.pdf (accessed January 31, 2017).

Ulmer, Jeffery T., Christopher Bader, and Martha Gault. 2008. "Do Moral Communities Play a Role in Criminal Sentencing? Evidence from Pennsylvania." In *The Sociological Quarterly*, Vol. 49, No. 4, pp. 737–768.

United Nations. 1989. "Convention on the Rights of the Child." Available at http://
    www.ohchr.org/en/professionalinterest/pages/crc.aspx (accessed January 31, 2017).

United States Constitution, Article II, Section 2, Clause 3.

United States Constitution, Sixth Amendment.

United States v. Booker, 543 U.S. 220 (2005).

United States v. Jackson, 390 U.S. 570 (1968).

U.S. Census Bureau. 2017. "Population and Housing Unit Estimates." Available at
    http://www.census.gov/programs-surveys/popest/data/data-sets.2016.html
    (accessed January 31, 2017).

U.S. Department of Justice. 2003. "History of the Federal Parole System." Available at
    http://www.justice.gov/uspc/history.pdf (accessed January 31, 2017).

U.S. Department of Justice. 2006. "Report of the United States Parole Commission."
    Available at http://www.justice.gov/uspc/commission_reports/annual-report-
    100105-093006.pdf (accessed January 31, 2017).

U.S. Department of Justice. 2013. "Smart on Crime: Reforming the Criminal Justice
    System for the 21st Century." Available at http://www.justice.gov/ag/smart-on-
    crime.pdf (accessed January 31, 2017).

U.S. Department of Justice. 2014. "Progress Report on the Department of Justice's
    Implementation of the Prison Rape Elimination Act." October. Available at https://
    oig.justice.gov/reports/2014/e151.pdf (accessed January 31, 2017).

U.S. Department of Justice. 2015. "Investigation of the Ferguson Police Department."
    Civil Rights Division. March 4. Available at http://www.justice.gov/sites/default/
    files/opa/press-releases/attachments/2015/03/04/ferguson_police_department_
    report_1.pdf (accessed January 31, 2017).

U.S. Department of Justice. 2016. "Report and Recommendations concerning the Use
    of Restrictive Housing." Available at https://www.justice.gov/dag/file/815551/
    download (accessed January 31, 2017).

U.S. Sentencing Commission. No date. "The Sentencing Reform Act of 1984: Principal
    Features." Available at http://www.ussc.gov/research-and-publications/working-
    group-reports/simplification/simplification-draft-paper-2 (accessed January
    31, 2017).

Unnever, James D., and Francis T. Cullen. 2006. "Christian Fundamentalism and
    Support for Capital Punishment." In *Journal of Research in Crime and Delinquency,*
    Vol. 43, No. 2, pp. 169–197.

Unnever, James D., Francis T. Cullen, and Brandon K. Applegate. 2005. "Turning the
    Other Cheek: Reassessing the Impact of Religion on Punitive Ideology." In *Justice
    Quarterly,* Vol. 22, No. 3, pp. 304–339.

Vallas, Rebecca, and Sharon Dietrich. 2014. "One Strike and You're Out: How We Can
    Eliminate Barriers to Economic Security and Mobility for People with Criminal
    Records." A Center for American Progress report. Available at https://cdn.ameri-
    canprogress.org/wp-content/uploads/2014/12/VallasCriminalRecordsReport.pdf
    (accessed January 31, 2017).

Varsho, Kelly J. 2007. "In the Global Market for Justice: Who Is Paying the Highest Price for Judicial Independence?" In *Northern Illinois University Law Review*, Vol. 27, No. 3, pp. 445–518.

van Zyl Smit, Dirk. 2002. *Taking Life Imprisonment Seriously in National and International Law*. The Hague: Kluwer Law International.

van Zyl Smit, Dirk, and Sonja Snacken. 2011. *Principles of European Prison Law and Policy: Penology and Human Rights*. Oxford: Oxford University Press.

Vasseur, Véronique. 2000. *Medicin-chef à la prison de la Santé*. Paris: Le Cherche-Midi.

Vasseur, Véronique, et Gabriel Mouesca. 2011. *"La prison doit changer, la prison va changer" avait-il dit*. Paris: Flammarion.

Vavreck, Lynn. 2009. *The Message Matters: The Economy and Presidential Campaigns*. Princeton, NJ: Princeton University Press.

Vera Institute of Justice. 2015. "Segregation Reduction Project." Available at http://archive.vera.org/project/segregation-reduction-project (accessed January 31, 2017).

Waby, Michael. 2005. "Comparative Aspects of Plea Bargaining in England and Canada: A Practitioner's Perspective." In *Criminal Law Quarterly*, Vol. 50, No. 1–2, pp. 148–164.

Wacquant, Loïc. 1999. *Les Prisons de la Misère*. Paris: Raisons d'agir.

Wacquant, Loïc. 2000. "The New 'Peculiar Institution': On the Prison as a Surrogate Ghetto." *Theoretical Criminology*, Vol. 4, No. 3, pp. 377–389.

Wagner, Peter. 2003. *The Prison Index: Taking the Pulse of the Crime Control Industry*. Prison Policy Initiative and Western Prison Project.

Wagner, Peter. "Uncovering Securus' Profits." Prison Policy Initiative. Available at http://www.prisonpolicy.org/blog/2015/06/19/securus-profits (accessed January 31, 2017).

Wagner, Peter, and Bernadette Rabuy. 2016. "Mass Incarceration: The Whole Pie 2016." A Prison Policy Initiative report. Available at http://www.prisonpolicy.org/reports/pie2016.html (accessed January 31, 2017).

Wagner, Peter, and Alison Walsh. 2016. "States of Incarceration: The Global Context 2016." A Prison Policy Initiative report. Available at http://www.prisonpolicy.org/global/2016.html (accessed January 31, 2017).

Ward, Katie, Amy J. Longaker, Jessica Williams, Amber Naylor, Chad A. Rose, and Cynthia G. Simpson. 2013. "Incarceration within American and Nordic Prisons: Comparison of National and International Policies." In *Engage: The International Journal of Research and Practice on Student Engagement*. Vol, 1, No. 1, pp. 1–6.

Weaver, Vesla. 2007. "Frontlash: Race and the Development of Punitive Crime Policy." In *Studies in American Political Development*, Vol. 21, No. 2, pp. 230–265.

Weigend, Thomas, and Jenia Iontcheva Turner. 2014. "The Constitutionality of Negotiated Criminal Judgments in Germany." In *German Law Review*, Vol. 15, No. 1, pp. 81–105.

Weisberg, Robert, Debbie A. Mukamal, and Jordan D. Segall. 2011. "Life in Limbo: An Examination of Parole Release for Prisoners Serving Life Sentences with the Possibility of Parole in California." Stanford Law School, Stanford Criminal Justice Center.

Weschler, Joanna, and Alejandro Garro. 1992. "Prison Conditions in Spain." A Helsinki Watch Report.

Western, Bruce. 2006. *Punishment and Inequality in America*. New York: Russell Sage Foundation.

Western, Bruce, Becky Pettit, and Josh Guetzkow. 2002. "Black Economic Progress in the Era of Mass Imprisonment." In *Invisible Punishment: The Collateral Consequences of Mass Imprisonment*, edited by Marc Mauer and Meda Chesney-Lind. New York: The New Press.

Whitley v. Albers, 475 U.S. 312 (1986).

Whitman, James Q. 2003. *Harsh Justice: Criminal Punishment and the Widening Divide between America and Europe*. New York: Oxford University Press.

Whitman, James Q. 2005. "The Comparative Study of Criminal Punishment." In *Annual Review of Law and Social Science*, Vol. 1, pp. 17–34.

Whitman, James Q. 2016. "Presumption of Innocence or Presumption of Mercy? Weighing Two Western Modes of Justice." In *Texas Law Review*, Vol. 94, No. 5, pp. 933-993

Wilkinson, Katherine and Joanna Davidson. 2010. "An Evaluation of the Prison Radio Association's Activity. Year 3: The Way Forward." A Sheffield Hallam University Report. Available at http://shura.shu.ac.uk/7052/1/Wilkinson_evaluation_prison_radio_year3.pdf (accessed January 31, 2017).

Williams, Timothy. 2015. "The High Cost of Calling the Imprisoned." In *The New York Times*. March 30.

Wilson, James Q. 1975. *Thinking about Crime*. New York: Basic Books.

Wilson, James Q. 1980. " 'What Works?' Revisited: New Findings on Criminal Rehabilitation." In *The Public Interest*, No. 61, pp. 3–17.

Wilson v. Seiter, 501 U.S. 294 (1991).

Wines, Michael. 2016. "Virginia's Governor Restores Voting Rights for 13,000 Ex-Felons." In *The New York Times*. August 22.

Witherspoon, Floyd D. 2007. "Mass Incarceration of African-American Males: A Return to Institutionalized Slavery, Oppression, and Disenfranchisement of Constitutional Rights." In *Texas Wesleyan Law Review*, Vol. 13, No. 2, pp. 599–618.

Witte, Griff. 2015. "Do Britain's Gunless Bobbies Provide Answers for America's Police?" In *The Washington Post*. June 11.

Woodward v. Alabama, 571 U. S. _____ (2013).

Wright, Ronald F. 2009. "How Prosecutor Elections Fail Us." In *Ohio State Journal of Criminal Law*, Vol. 6, pp. 581–610.

Yale Law School Liman Program, and Association of State Correctional Administrators. 2015. "Time-In-Cell: The ASCA-Liman 2014 National Survey of Administrative

Segregation in Prison." Available at https://www.law.yale.edu/system/files/area/center/liman/document/asca-liman_administrativesegregationreport.pdf (accessed January 31, 2017).

Yant, Martin. 1991. *Presumed Guilty: When Innocent People Are Wrongly Convicted.* Buffalo, NY: Prometheus Books.

Young, Robert L. 2000. "Punishment at All Costs: On Religion, Convicting the Innocent, and Supporting the Death Penalty." In *William & Mary Bill of Rights Journal*, Vol. 9, No. 1, pp. 237–246.

Zak, Dan. 2016. "In this Class, Prisoners and Georgetown Students Grapple with Difficult Lessons.". In *The Washington Post Magazine*. September 11.

Zimring, Franklin E., and Gordon Hawkins. 1995. *Incapacitation: Penal Confinement and the Restraint of Crime.* New York: Oxford University Press.

Zimring, Franklin E., and Gordon Hawkins. 1997. *Crime Is Not the Problem: Lethal Violence in America.* New York: Oxford University Press.

Zimring, Franklin E. Gordon Hawkins, and Sam Kamin. 2001. *Punishment and Democracy: Three Strikes and You're Out in California.* New York: Oxford University Press.

Index